THE LONG DARK NIGHT OF THE SOUL

Sandy Vogelgesang

THE LONG DARK NIGHT OF THE SOUL

*The American Intellectual Left
and the Vietnam War*

HARPER & ROW, PUBLISHERS
New York, Evanston, San Francisco, London

To my parents—for their loyalty and kind wisdom during all the dark nights

FIRST EDITION

Designed by C. Linda Dingler

Library of Congress Cataloging in Publication Data

Vogelgesang, Sandy.
  The long dark night of the soul.

  Bibliography: p.
  1. Vietnamese Conflict, 1961-   —Public opinion—
United States. 2. Intellectuals—United States.
I. Title.
DS557.A68V64   1974   320.9′73′0924   74-1866
ISBN 0-06-014512-9

Contents

Prologue

If I could turn you on, if I could drive you out of your wretched mind, if I could tell you, I would let you know.

R. D. Laing
The Politics of Experience, 1967

Drawing by David Levine. Reprinted with permission from *The New York Review of Books.* Copyright © 1966 The New York Review.

"Turn on" the American people?! If anything, the nation's Intellectual Left seemed to turn off the public in the 1960s and tune out. It has sulked on the political periphery ever since the end of

1

the Johnson era—embittered, divided, and largely ineffectual.

Much of this despair began—or became explicit—with the shift to antiwar "resistance" in the mid-1960s and the successive shocks of the 1968 Democratic convention in Chicago, the advent of the Nixon Administration, and record bombing in Indochina. When and how it will end is less clear. For many leftist intellectuals in the United States, the Vietnam experience already compares with the Spanish civil war as a long dark night of the soul.[1]*

The gloom persists. So do the questions that American leftist intellectuals raised throughout the 1960s. Yet obituaries on the Left of that decade proliferate. What went wrong and why does it matter?

A preliminary autopsy of intellectual commentary from that time reveals that those questions are, in fact, related. It suggests further that the response of one group—the American Intellectual Left—to one policy—Lyndon Johnson's intervention in Vietnam—could and did reflect some of the most important issues of that decade and this. What of the conflict in Southeast Asia? Was it, as charged, immoral? Did the government which waged and rationalized that war betray its political legitimacy? Could the country survive the inner division wrought by the war? If so, at what price?

The turmoil of the 1960s indicated that the United States might never be the same. How different it has or can become is another question. It is not yet certain that this nation possesses the political maturity to hear and heed dissent. None can guarantee that we have learned enough, for example, to avoid another Vietnam. Most official debate on that conflict was an in-house quarrel over management of the American empire, rather than a challenge to the empire itself or its assumptions.

In 1972, four Americans in ten felt alienated from their government.[2] The "protest" vote was touted as pivotal in the Presi-

---

* Notes begin on page 181.

dential race. Yet, the protest candidate—for reasons both within and beyond his control—won only Massachusetts and the District of Columbia. "Law and order" was a central campaign theme. Yet, few asked, in Dostoevsky's words, "Whose law?" Madison Avenue appropriated the "New Politics" and its rhetoric with jingles on "pucker power" and bids to "Join the Dodge Rebellion." "Peace at hand" replaced "the light at the end of the tunnel" just weeks before Richard Nixon resumed massive bombing of North Vietnam and repeated the rationale of Lyndon Johnson. World opinion rebuked the United States and recalled Thomas Jefferson's observation: "I tremble for my country when I reflect that God is just."

As if in poetic irony, the Vietnam cease-fire was announced the day Johnson was brought to lie in state at the Capitol. The nation was relieved by what seemed peace but saddened by the passing of the President whom peace might have most pleased. America was moving out of Vietnam. When could or would the Vietnam experience of the Johnson years move out of the American mind?

As the citizens try to sort out what has become of themselves and their country, there is special interest in what the nation's naysayers have been saying for the past decade and why they seem to have been ignored. No matter what added historical detachment the passage of time brings, there is value now in studying whatever record already exists.

ALL IN THE RECORD

The U.S. Intellectual Left has long accommodated the curious with its almost compulsive candor. The Johnson era was no exception. In the parlance of the times, the leftist intellectuals let it all hang out. The verbal fallout was prodigious. Essays, editorials, and correspondence sections in journals ranging from *The New Republic* to *The New York Review of Books*; published accounts of their teach-ins, read-ins, and Sunday salons; their political cartoons; their confessional literature (*The Armies of the Night, Styles of Radical Will, In a Time of Torment*)—the printed record of the 1960s is there. With an eye to the enduring historical value of the intellectuals' stated position on the war at the time, this book stresses what the leftist intellectuals themselves wrote, *not* what others said about them.

Their own writing defines, in large measure, who the intellectuals were. The "little magazine" has long been one of the key indices to elite expression in the United States. An identifiable list of about twenty-five journals certifies and connects the most influential American intellectuals.[3] Though one can and should define intellectuals in terms of their historic role and utopian mission—as one chapter will—the simple test of who writes where produces a comparable list of contemporary U.S. intellectual leaders.

That same list confirms the traditionally leftist political orientation of the country's intellectual vanguard. The political scientist Seymour Martin Lipset,[4] the historical sociologist Christopher Lasch,[5] and the historian Richard Hofstadter[6] have affirmed that characterization. Since the American intelligentsia and the U.S. Intellectual Left have been generally interchangeable since about 1890, they will be considered as such unless otherwise noted.

Few would contest that, for the 1960s, *National Review* paled in significance before the phalanx of the Left led by *The New York Review of Books*. Therefore, while drawing on a variety of materials, this book relies on an in-depth analysis of four publications of the leftist intelligentsia: *The New Republic, Partisan Review, Studies on the Left*, and *The New York Review* itself. While the U.S. intelligentsia is no monolith, it does draw on a surprisingly small oligarchy of journals. Three of the above four ranked among the most influential in the 1960s, according to a survey made of American intellectuals.[7] The tone and content of these "control" journals, together with recurring reference to such writers as Noam Chomsky, Irving Howe, Dwight Macdonald, Mary McCarthy, Norman Mailer, Susan Sontag, Paul Goodman, and Norman Podhoretz, provide a range of commentary from which to generalize about the American Intellectual Left.[8]

This record reflects a sequence of attitudinal change among most leftist intellectuals from the Kennedy to the Nixon eras. It was a transformation that proceeded gradually at several levels of consciousness and effect.

CHANGE OF FOCUS

At the most obvious level, they shifted their perception of the Vietnam War. Daniel Ellsberg was to put the sequence thus: "I have seen it first as a problem; then as a stalemate; then as a crime."[9] The quantum leap from *The New Republic*'s pleas for negotiations in 1964 to the teach-ins of 1965 to *The New York Review*'s "Call to Resist Illegitimate Authority" in 1967 documented the direction and intensification of intellectual opinions. Because of that shift over time, the intellectuals' metamorphosis is most simply—and perhaps most aptly—put chronologically. Most of them moved more or less together through three stages in their perception of the Indochina conflict. They saw it progressively as:

1. A Lapse in Judgment: Early 1960s to January, 1965
2. An Exercise in Immorality: February, 1965 through December, 1966
3. A Reflection of Political Illegitimacy: January, 1967 through December, 1968

RETURN TO RADICALISM

Though all three views of the war existed during the Johnson period, the intellectuals adjusted their focus because the changing war changed them. Their preoccupation with their normative

5

role as critics grew in direct relation to their frustration with the escalating involvement in Southeast Asia. Movement from critique of diplomatic error to condemnation of systemic legitimacy prompted the repoliticization and reradicalization of many leftist intellectuals. Arthur Waskow, for example, recalled "running riot" through the 1960s. His internal journey took him from being a "stubborn but narrow liberal who praised non-violent protest" toward becoming "an angry, more subtle, and more flexible radical who wants the people to take control of their own schools and factories, and learn to run them democratically—against the government."[10]

The impetus for such a leftward odyssey had existed for some time. Even in the quiescent 1950s, important changes had begun to emerge in international affairs. Monolithic Communism was giving way to polycentrism. As the revisionist historiography of the changing times would have it, there was a need for new interpretations of U.S. foreign policy. By 1965, a symposium in *Partisan Review* could claim that the "new radicalism" sprang from revulsion against mindless anti-Communism and the Cold War.

Domestic developments were no less important in this process of repoliticization. Witness the intellectual preamble to the 1960s penned by the "Beat Generation" and the activation of university youth spurred by the civil rights movement, the Cuban Revolution, and the alleged dehumanization of "growing up absurd." The backdrop had been set and but lacked E. M. Forster's injunction: "Only connect."

Thence, Vietnam. Commentary from the 1960s suggests that the war synthesized for the Intellectual Left the contradictions of the American system and coalesced previously fragmented dissent. For writers like Susan Sontag, it became an "ideal Other," offering the "key to a systematic criticism of America."[11] It catalyzed the change for many—like Waskow—from liberal (one on the Left who works for reform within the system) to radical (one who seeks a fundamental upheaval of society's institutions). It prompted, finally, one writer for *The New York Times Magazine*—hardly a freaked-out forum—to ask, "Are We in the Middle of a Revolution?" and to answer "Yes."[12]

CAUGHT IN CONTRADICTION

If so, so what? The point, as Waskow saw it, was the *process*. The *problem* was where the trip left you. Events so far suggest that the repoliticization and reradicalization of the leftist intellectuals caused by Johnson's Vietnam policy left them in an apparent dead end.

Three related concerns have traditionally characterized Western intellectuals: their espousal of moral conscience, their obsession with their own identity as intellectuals, and their relationship to power. All three preoccupations have dominated the U.S. intelligentsia since its emergence as a definable social group late in the nineteenth century.

More to the point, all three concerns lay behind much of the intellectuals' response to the Vietnam War in the 1960s. The growing moral basis of the leftist intellectuals' antiwar critique reflected their exercise of moral conscience. Their insistence on protesting as intellectuals reaffirmed their obsession with their own identity and group responsibility. Their challenge to the Johnson Administration—"truth to power," in Hans Morgenthau's phrase—revealed their concern with the relation to authority.[13]

Yet the intellectuals' confrontation with the war in those terms revived what may have been and may still be an irresolvable dilemma for the American Intellectual Left. To what extent are truth and power compatible? If not at all, what are the consequences for American intellectuals in a society prone to moralizing its mission at home and abroad?

Much writing from the last decade showed the U.S. Intellectual Left at once fascinated by power as a means to effect its moral ideal and to consummate its group identity and repelled by the potentially amoral implications of association with power. Was it accidental that some on the Intellectual Left tried to discredit politics by linking it to power, that "enemy of life"?[14] What of the war between the intellectual purists and the "new mandarins"? Did the critic of power cease being an intellectual when he became an agent of power? Did moral advocacy taken to its extreme—the absolute dissociation of politics and morality —only accentuate the real powerlessness of the Intellectual Left?

Antipolitics did come to characterize many intellectuals' reaction to Johnson's Vietnam policy, just as it had often before shaped their relation to power and political leaders. How could the man on the street or in the White House know when or whether to take the intellectuals literally? How could either assume that their words were meant, as some claimed, mainly as metaphors to "break the 'objective' view" intellectuals had of themselves?[15]

THE LONG AND SHORT OF INTELLECTUAL PROTEST

The task of the naysayer may lie in treading or expressing the fine line between the self-serving existentialist and the constructive philosopher. To miss that balance may risk political irresponsibility and perhaps jeopardize the espoused cause. Still, to judge the intellectual's performance as a political actor suggests a tale of two time frames. The intellectual just may be doomed to short-run political impotence for the sake of long-range moral recompense.

Most American leftist intellectuals did assemble a sorry record in the immediate context of the 1960s. No matter how commendable their intentions, few then resolved for themselves how they could or should respond effectively to the Vietnam War. Few answered the question posed by one of their own: "Is what's intended a moral gesture only or a determined attempt to transform the American power structure?" Their repoliticization often lapsed into the moralism they condemned in others. It prompted, in turn, their own depoliticization or dwindling capacity to relate effectively to the political process. Hence their recurrent and perhaps inevitable exile on the periphery.

However, long-term vindication may reward that frustration. Although U.S. leftist intellectuals agonized before the apparent impasse between politics and morality and erred in their approach to power in the short run, they affirmed, by the very nature of their opposition to the Vietnam War, their continuing claim as the nation's conscience. The fact that George McGovern became Presidential nominee for the Democratic Party just four years after "Chicago" attested to the longer-term effect of the intellectuals' protest, even if the Nixon landslide belied the depth of that impact.

Norman Mailer concluded *The Armies of the Night*: "Brood on that country who expresses our will. She is America. . . ." Mailer's preoccupation with the national destiny reflected a recurrent theme of the 1960s: most leftist intellectuals' quest after their meaning as Americans and their reassertion of the American Dream. Stripped of "radical chic," that may prove to have been the very unfashionable core of leftist intellectual response to the Indochina struggle.

It was a lonely and disheartening mission, as is any cause before its time has come. Hence the gloomy interim of the Johnson years for the country's internal exiles. It suggested what F. Scott Fitzgerald called the long "dark night of the soul when it is always three o'clock in the morning."[16] The title of this book is suggested by that phrase because it best characterizes the mood of the U.S. Intellectual Left during the Johnson period. More than coincidence made such contrasting figures as Daniel Berrigan and Norman Mailer choose that image to characterize their opposition to the Vietnam War. Father Berrigan compared his antiwar

9

experience to the original line from St. John of the Cross in *The Dark Night of Resistance*. Mailer borrowed the phrase for his coverage of the March on the Pentagon in 1967.

It was an apt appropriation. Mailer emerged as the Nick Carraway of that event. He became, furthermore, the decade's narrator-cum-arbiter obsessed by "identity with this country." He understood that America prides itself on a Dream. He grasped the fragility of that Dream in a country where vast power cohabits with myth. Sensitive to that national anomaly, he, like most leftist intellectuals, saw the Vietnam War as a threat to the Dream.[17]

Most Americans in the 1960s did not. The Intellectual Left's view of morality clashed with the alleged moralism of the public and the government. To what avail? That is the question with which this book begins and ends. It is why the reaction of the U.S. Intellectual Left to the Vietnam War still begs its own response.

Part One

WHO THEY WERE

A Short Sketch on Intellectuals—American and
Other—and Four Chronicles They Kept. . . .

The great mission of the Utopia is to make room for the possible as opposed to a passive acquiescence in the present actual state of affairs. It is symbolic thought which overcomes the mutual inertia of man and endows him with a new ability constantly to reshape his human universe.

Ernst Cassirer
An Essay on Man, 1944

Drawing by David Levine. Reprinted with permission from *The New York Review of Books.* Copyright © 1967 The New York Review.

Contrary to some contentions, the response of the American Intellectual Left to the Vietnam War was more than an isolated instance of guerrilla histrionics. That reaction emerged, instead,

13

from both a general tradition of the modern, secular intelligentsia and a specific experience of intellectuals within the United States. It lacks meaning without reference to that background. Hence this brief introduction to the main purpose at hand: a recapitulation and critique of leftist intellectual protest against Johnson's Vietnam policy.

CLASH OF SYMBOLS

Writing on intellectuals has been voluminous. If they have been the most maligned of mortals, they have also been among the most scrupulously dissected. Yet no definitive sociology or history of the intellectual has come to the fore.[1]

What does stand out from the literature is the conception of intellectuals as symbolic legitimists. They are the men and women of ideas who explore and challenge the underlying values of society. Theirs is a normative function: to prescribe what ought to be.

In that way, "legitimacy" has assumed a dual character for the intellectual. It is at once conventional and symbolic. It refers both to support for what Cassirer called the "actual state of affairs" and to the quest after a utopian society. Only rarely do the two converge. Therein lies the challenge to the intellectuals.

"Symbol" is a term often bandied by contemporary American intellectuals. To their way of thinking and that of analysts ranging from Edward Shils to Talcott Parsons, "symbol" refers generally to the words or ideals which reveal the values of a society. Not surprisingly, the intelligentsia and the public have usually disagreed over the choice and intent of their symbols. The moral basis of a symbolic code entails a subjective judgment about what is "right." It is bound to vary over time or with different groups.

The U.S. Intellectual Left's opposition to Lyndon Johnson's Vietnam policy illustrated this inevitable clash of interpretation.

14

Both the government and the intelligentsia justified their stands on the war according to what each believed right or moral. Each invoked symbolic rhetoric to rationalize its position. Each often used the same phrases—"right of self-determination" or "peace with honor." However, because each meant something different by what it said, the two diverged actually, if not symbolically, in their judgment of the war and the authority responsible for it. Hence the dichotomy during the Johnson era between the intellectuals' symbolic legitimacy and the government's (and the public's) conventional legitimacy. The Vietnam War so repelled most intellectuals that they tried to delegitimate conventional legitimacy by superimposing their own transcendent symbolic legitimacy.

Significantly and coincidentally, symbolism of a most explicit sort was central to that effort. It loomed conspicuously in the antiwar movement. It recurred, for example, in the place where demonstrations were held—the Pentagon or Independence Hall; the timing—Thanksgiving or the Fourth of July; or the act itself —burning draft cards or the flag. As intellectual activists thus assaulted conventional feelings of national identity to make their point of peace, they considered *themselves* the true exponents of the symbols and the American Dream. Hence the confusion, moral motivation, and larger significance behind the intellectuals' "resistance" in the 1960s, the continuing confrontation between the Establishment and the "adversary culture," and the perennial tension between immediate and ultimate political responsibility.

A utopian drive has always gone far toward defining who the intellectuals think they are. Their identity springs from needs that are both internal and social. Shils and Karl Deutsch have explained how intellectuals feel an "interior need to penetrate beyond the screen of immediate concrete experience," to use symbols to transcend the time and space of everyday life.[2] This compulsion to "live for and off symbols" forces upon the intellectuals the role of society's moral conscience. According to William

Kornhauser, the intellectuals are "least able to suffer a vacuum in the symbolic sphere."[3] Their standards are high. Society must do more than operate efficiently to retain their allegiance. Its institutions must possess what Charles Frankel called symbolic legitimacy.[4]

Two intellectuals have spoken to this point with special feeling. The poet Denise Levertov and her husband, Mitchell Goodman, explained their opposition to the Vietnam War in the 1960s thus: "The task of the poet [intellectual] is to make clear to himself, and thereby to others, the temporal and eternal questions." They felt an obligation as "verbal people" to be "spokesmen for humanity."[5] By their felt need and social performance, they demonstrated how modern secular intellectuals have replaced the clergy as what Arthur Koestler called the "introspective organs of the social body."[6]

That function has traditionally provided the main political significance for intellectuals. The intelligentsia can dispute the viability of a particular policy or herald the more general disintegration of the political system. American leftist intellectuals moved from condemning the disproportion between means and ends in Johnson's Vietnam policy to discredit the legitimacy of the liberal consensus. They helped transform a conflict of interests into a conflict of values. No society easily sustains such a challenge, particularly when the challenge remains unresolved.

If society agonizes before such onslaughts, the intelligentsia copes no less easily. As noted in the Prologue, three interconnected preoccupations have characterized Western intellectuals since they emerged as a social group during the Enlightenment: the exercise of moral conscience, obsession with their identity as intellectuals, and their relationship to power. In each case, the intellectuals have felt torn. They have served their society by being at once part of and apart from the body politic.

16

The Long Dark Night of the Soul

The intellectuals' relation to power has been a source of particular anguish in this respect. Henry Kissinger, intellectual-cum-policymaker in the Nixon Administration, anticipated his own dilemma and confirmed that of intellectuals in general when he wrote in 1959: ". . . the intellectual . . . must steer between the Scylla of letting the bureaucracy prescribe what is relevant or useful and the Charybdis of defining these criteria too abstractly."[7] On the one hand, the intellectual risks becoming "a promoter of technical remedies"; on the other, of "confusing dogmatism with morality and of courting martyrdom."

The quandary is not new. Intellectuals have traditionally fostered a cult of contempt for power at the same time they have pined after its perquisites. The humanists of Renaissance Florence asserted individualism at the same time they served the centralization of power under the Medici family. The *philosophes* of the French Enlightenment espoused liberty while they sought power to realize their vision of a rational order and fawned at the feet of that century's "enlightened" despots.

The dilemma came to bear on American intellectuals in the 1960s. One of their own, Professor Hans Morgenthau, set it forth in terms that were more than coincidentally suggestive. In an essay for *The New Republic* and a later book, Morgenthau spoke of the two different worlds of the intellectual and the politician.[8] He considered those realms *separate* because they are oriented toward different ultimate values: "the intellectual seeks truth; the politician, power"—but *intertwined*: "truth has a message that is relevant to power, and the very existence of power has a bearing upon the expression and recognition of truth"—and *mutually antagonistic*: "truth threatens power and power threatens truth."

It is little wonder, given the ambiguity of the "existential estrangement and potential interconnectedness between truth and power," that American intellectuals of the 1960s scattered in

17

their choice of worlds. Some retreated into an academic ivory tower, some offered their expertise to the government, some challenged the government in prophetic confrontation, and some simply surrendered. The complexity of decision-making for a technologically advanced nation of over 200 million had already institutionalized an intellectual technocracy within the Federal government.

John Kennedy simply embellished a *fait accompli* with status. However, though he gilded bureaucratic fact with glamour, he could not conceal the political fact that inevitably betrayed the intellectuals' growing self-regard. First, there were the contradictions between apparent and actual participation in power. Second, there were the consequences of that association for the leftist intellectual critics with whom this book is primarily concerned, as opposed to the in-house liberals and technocrats they condemned.

The Kennedy era disappointed many intellectuals with both its brevity and its achievements. Most principal members of the Kennedy Administration continued to work for Lyndon Johnson. With the escalation of the Vietnam War, the ascendance to authority by the Camelot on the Charles redounded to the dishonor and division of all leftist intellectuals. Vietnam was formulated and rationalized by those closest to "their own kind," with apparent priority for military considerations over political and moral consequences.

For many antiwar intellectuals, it was the ultimate sacrilege that the chairmen of the Departments of Political Science and Government of the two great universities in Cambridge, Massachusetts, both "liberal intellectuals" in good standing, had respectively been Pentagon adviser and director of the South East Asia task force for the State Department.[9] Noam Chomsky, one of the most insistent critics of intellectual "mandarins" during the Johnson era, wrote:

. . . Recent American history suggests that one should look forward with alarm to the society in which intellectuals . . . eagerly take on the role of service to power. We can anticipate further corruption of national policy as well as a tendency to abandon intellectual and moral values.[10]

Referring to the defense intellectuals allegedly responsible for the Vietnam policy, Ronald Steel asked: "If war is too serious to be left to the generals, is strategy safe in the hands of the strategists?"[11]

It was a betrayal of intellectual aspirations by and for power which turned many intellectuals against power just as it seemed within the grasp of some. The sense of general disillusionment engendered by some intellectuals' participation in Vietnam decision-making led many intellectuals *outside* government to condemn the intellectual consorts of power within government and to reject power itself as an absolute evil. Growing numbers of radical intellectuals denied the complementarity of functions advocated by the historian Richard Hofstadter:

What is important for society as a whole is that the intellectual community should not become hopelessly polarized into two parts, one part of technicians concerned only with power and accepting implicitly the terms power puts to them, and the other of willfully alienated intellectuals more concerned with maintaining their sense of their own purity than with making their ideas effective.[12]

By the end of the Johnson era, an intellectual mandarinate persisted within the government. However, the Bundys, Rostows, and Sorensens had been delegitimated for the symbolic legitimists by their complicity with Vietnam. Chomsky and Marcuse personified the contemporary American counterpart to Julien Benda, by turning skepticism toward power into dogma.[13] For his part, Arthur Schlesinger, Jr., wondered whether Chomsky and Marcuse represented an even greater example of the *trahison des clercs* than those who had "committed the occasional sin of association with power."[14] Perhaps, future historians can identify the real traitors. In the interim, it appears that too many U.S. intellectuals served their nation ill by renouncing power out of hand, rather than taking it in hand with a substantive critique and a broad-based appeal to the American public.

Much in the American setting has only exacerbated the kinds of tensions peculiar to all Western intellectuals, whether in the expression of symbolic legitimacy or in the clash between truth and power. Such problems began to emerge most clearly on this side of the Atlantic at about the turn of the century.

WATERSHED OF 1890

With the 1890s, the United States began to emerge as an urbanized and industrialized society with severe problems at home and a fledgling empire abroad. The crisis of the cities, the excesses of "Big Business," and the closing of the frontier first inspired the intelligentsia as a group to protest against the political direction of American society. Just as Michael Harrington's *The Other America* (1962) roused contemporary American intellectuals from the torpor of the Eisenhower era, so, too, had Jacob Riis's *How the Other Half Lives* (1890) jolted their predecessors from the genteel idealism of the nineteenth century. Hofstadter wrote that after 1890 "it became possible for the first time to speak of intellectuals as a class."[15] Christopher Lasch dated his survey of the "intellectual as a social type" from the same point. He asserted that "modern radicalism or liberalism can best be understood as a phase of the social history of the intellectuals."[16]

The irony of the turn-of-the-century transformation was that American intellectuals tried to defend "the people" against special interests at the same time they were diverging more than ever from the sensibilities of the general public. Whether pursuing populist, progressive, Marxist, or neo-Marxist causes all the way from the 1890s to the 1970s, the American intellectual has had to confront the tension between the elite character of his class and his democratic aspiration. Marcuse's justification of leftist intellectual prerogatives in a society disarmed by repressive tolerance reflected one aspect of that conflict for American intellectuals during the 1960s.

Because the 1890s also brought America's first taste of empire, the intellectuals rallied against the nation's nascent "imperialism." Schlesinger observed: "For most intellectuals, power had too long bred resentment and timidity, and, with the *fin-de-siècle* imperialism of the Spanish-American War, it began to breed guilt."[17] That early outcry was more than a critique of U.S. foreign policy. The anti-imperialists of 1898 were always most concerned with the morality of American diplomacy:

The Spanish-American War provoked a major crisis of belief and attitude that caused men not only to wrestle with the problems directly raised by the war, but also to inquire into more general questions about the makeup of American society, the future of American democratic institutions, and the nation's future role in international affairs.[18]

The Philippine Insurrection also raised the question of the right to dissent and made Mark Twain quip:

. . . When there is no question that the nation is any way in danger, but only some little war away off, then it may be that on the question of politics the nation is divided, half-patriot and half-traitors, and no man can tell which from which.[19]

Since that time, most American intellectuals have been sensitive to the expansion of American power abroad and to discrepancies between official justification and political reality. Significantly, those opposed to "Johnson's war" used many of the arguments and invoked the same moral outrage as did their predecessors against William McKinley's "splendid little war."

WHO ARE WE?

Both before and after 1890, the newness of the American idea and the heterogeneity of the population have fostered a national propensity for introspection. Being American constitutes more a process than a condition. Hofstadter wrote that Americans, for all their outward braggadocio, are "the most anxiously self-conscious people in the world." He claimed that "this very uncertainty has given their intellectuals a critical function of special interest."[20] Norman Mailer referred in 1965 to that same national incertitude when he spoke of the minority-group psychology that sits upon every American.[21]

This tendency toward national self-consciousness, combined with the intelligentsia's own introspective bent, has inspired many American intellectuals to address political and social concerns beyond their immediate realms of creativity and knowledge. It has accounted for the prevalent soul-searching in their journals. *Partisan Review*'s symposia "Our Country and Our Culture" (1952) and "What's Happening to America?" (1967) reflected the interplay between national and group identities. The "anti-Americanism" of *The New York Review* expressed a major, if paradoxical, trend in the national self-awareness of the intellectuals during the 1960s.

AT ODDS WITH EQUALITY

Freedom and egalitarianism have been mixed blessings for American intellectuals. Although those qualities have facilitated free expression, as early as the 1830s Alexis de Tocqueville foresaw the isolation democracy could bring:

. . . Not only does democracy make every man forget his ancestors, but it hides his descendants and separates his contemporaries from him; it throws him back forever upon himself alone, and threatens in the end to confine him entirely within the solitude of his own heart.[22]

Unlike his European confrere, who has operated as part of a clearly defined social group within a hierarchically ordered society, the American intellectual has floundered without status or sponsorship. Many writers have attributed the American intellectuals' self-depreciation and even their leftist political orientation to their gloried conception of the status of the European intellectuals. Seymour Martin Lipset wrote that "what the American intellectual fails to see is that he is really objecting to the egalitarianism of the United States, rather than to a lower evaluation of his occupation by its citizens."[23]

The American intellectual's uncertainty about his role explains much of his attraction to the millennial ideology or movement. There he has often hoped to find meaning and a sense of belonging. However, as the dismal record of twentieth-century radicalism suggests, that tactic has failed and, most often, burned the U.S. intellectual badly. The American intelligentsia's reaction against the "end of ideology" and his hot pursuit of a new proletariat among students and blacks in the 1960s were just further reflections of the old egalitarian dilemma.

THE MIND DOESN'T MATTER

The life of the mind has received notoriously short shrift in the United States. Although the scholarly achievements of many of the Founding Fathers indicated admiration for intellectual leadership, Americans have more typically assessed intellect in terms of its practical worth. Hofstadter argued that "anti-intellectualism," defined as "a resentment and suspicion of the life of the mind and of those who are considered to represent it and a disposition constantly to minimize the value of that life," has dominated the United States.[24]

With the intellectuals' emergence as a social group in the 1890s, a burgeoning anti-intellectualism paradoxically confirmed the new prominence of the nation's naysayers. Thereafter, the intellectuals' ambiguity about U.S. entry into World War I; their postwar disillusionment, concern over the Sacco–Vanzetti case, and exile on the Left Bank during the 1920s; their Marxism of the 1930s; and their vulnerability during the McCarthy era all accentuated the cyclical recurrence of American anti-intellectualism. Schlesinger remarked after Eisenhower's Presidential victory in 1952, "Anti-intellectualism has long been the anti-Semitism of the businessman."[25]

This environment has complicated the American intellectual's preoccupation with his identity, his role as moral conscience, and his relationship to power, and it has intensified his group defensiveness. It has left intellectuals ill prepared to balance the functions of critic and associate of power. It has tempted them to vacillate between the extremes of absorption by and withdrawal from society. By the middle of the twentieth century, American intellectuals shifted between despair over their alienation from authority and the public and fear of their acceptance. It was one thing, as Emily Dickinson observed, to write letters to a world which never wrote back. It was quite another to be courted by *Time*. More to the point for the 1960s, it was one thing to have the Johnson Administration condone the intellectuals' anti-Vietnam protest and another for it to ignore the substance of their dissent.

FROM THE GENERAL TO THE SPECIFIC

Most of that dissent came from the "little magazines," "at once the public birthplace, the homestead, the prison, and sometimes the rescue mission of many contemporary intellectuals."[26] Because such journals have best reflected the vacillating fortunes of the American Intellectual Left, this chapter concludes with analyses of this book's four "control" periodicals. Together, these profiles make specific the more general preceding discussion and introduce some of the personalities and themes which persisted in the 1960s. Of all the most influential journals,[27] they provide a spectrum of political experience stretching over five generations. Their perspectives encompass progressive liberalism to

24

revolutionary radicalism, young New Left militants to famous figures of the Old Left, New York-based writers to Washington-oriented political analysts to campus-entrenched theoreticians.

ADVOCATE FOR PROGRESSIVE LIBERALISM

Sheer longevity and ideological consistency help qualify *The New Republic* (*TNR*) for its rank in this roster. Herbert Croly, author of *The Promise of American Life*, founded *TNR* in 1914 with the hope that it would be "radical without being social-istic" and "pragmatic rather than doctrinaire."[28] That line still characterized the journal under Gilbert A. Harrison, its editor in chief during the 1960s.[29]

The triumvirate of Croly, Walter Lippmann, and Walter Weyl believed in the possibilities of social control and the planned society. Progressivism was, after all, at its peak in the United States. Tragically, World War I broke out the day *TNR* opened its offices and dashed many of the journal's original expectations.

The New Republic encountered challenges in that conflict and postwar bouts with Babbitts which molded each succeeding gen-eration of the American Intellectual Left. It was inconsistent in its approach toward the war, first condemning Wilson and then supporting his policy of intervention. At the same time, it dis-missed the antiwar objections of Randolph Bourne, one of the journal's frequent contributors. Unlike other critics who con-demned munitions makers, bankers, or imperialists for causing the war, Bourne stressed the moral consequences for his fellow intellectuals. He cautioned colleagues who were tempted to idealize the war to resist "herd-instinct become herd-intellect."[30] He blamed the conflict between the desire for peace and the quest after an American role in world affairs for the betrayal of the intellectuals' ideals. He wrote in 1917:

Mental conflicts end either in a new and higher synthesis or adjust-ment, or else in a reversion to more primitive ideas. . . . The American intellectual class, having failed to make the higher synthesis, regresses to ideas that can issue in quick, simplified *action*. Simple, unquestioning action has superseded the knots of thought. The thinker dances with reality.[31]

Bourne's prophecies did come to pass. The "gay debauch" of the war did create "its own anti-toxin of ruin and disillusionment." The specter of that early disappointment lingered to haunt leftist intellectuals. Revulsion against the moralism of Johnson's Vietnam policy derived, in part, from previous disillusionment with Wilsonian idealism.

Once so close to men of power, the *TNR* found itself part of an isolated intellectual minority in the 1920s. The Wall Street crash of 1929 undermined the complacency of businessmen and exceeded even the progressives' forecasts of social strain. With Croly's death in 1930, the magazine turned to younger men like Edmund Wilson and John Dos Passos and reflected their new impatience and growing radicalism. Politics dominated *The New Republic* in the 1930s. Early skepticism toward the New Deal gave way to grudging and eventually enthusiastic support for President Franklin Roosevelt. Foreign events reinforced the journal's growing loyalty to Roosevelt and his New Deal. Despite a great debate between isolationism and intervention among *TNR* writers, the magazine "surrendered its perfectionism to its sense of international responsibility."[32]

The New Republic underwent a period of traumatic readjustment after World War II with Henry Wallace as editor. The Hiss trial put an entire generation of leftist intellectuals into the dock. Not until Adlai Stevenson's campaign in 1952 did *TNR* regain its progressive morale, only to have Stevenson lose and *TNR* regress to an isolation comparable to that of the 1920s. Like most of the American intellectual journals in the 1950s, *TNR* contented itself with, in Croly's earlier words, "raising insurrections in men's minds" and marking time. With both Kennedy and the early Johnson Administration, *TNR* moved closer to the journal's dreams of progressive enlightenment than had been true for almost half a century.

Its high hopes foundered on the Vietnam question. The regular column by TRB,[33] the weekly editorials, and political commentaries on Asia—especially those by Bernard Fall on Vietnam and Edgar Snow on China—moved only gradually from gentlemanly reproach to harsh reproof of Johnson's Vietnam policy. Even *TNR*'s cartoonists, Bill Mauldin and Robert Osborn, lacked the cutting line of *The New York Review*'s David Levine or *The Village Voice*'s Jules Feiffer.

However, when it became clear that military priorities were supplanting domestic needs, *TNR* spoke out. Recalling the social reform advocated by Croly and Lippmann, its editors admired Johnson's Great Society. They were sad and frustrated when the President isolated himself from divergent opinion and undercut domestic legislation with what they considered a "mistaken" foreign policy. Schlesinger had argued that *TNR*'s evolution could be interpreted in terms of the fluctuating status of Eastern metropolitan progressivism. Vietnam was just the latest deflator of progressive fortunes to which *TNR* responded with its characteristic mix of critique and reformism. Though it welcomed Tom Hayden and Stokely Carmichael in its "Young Radicals" series and moved leftward, it remained true to the liberal tradition of change from within the system.

EXPONENT OF LITERARY ANTI-STALINISM

Partisan Review (*PR*) serves as a primary source of intellectual reaction to the Vietnam War because of its unique place in the history of American literary radicalism, the continuity of its development under editors William Phillips and Philip Rahv, and its base in New York City. It first appeared in 1934, proclaiming itself "a bi-monthly of revolutionary literature published by the John Reed Club of New York."

The Long Dark Night of the Soul

The young editors looked to proletarian literature to overcome one of the problems that have dominated twentieth-century American writing, the estrangement of the intellectual from society and middle-class life. However, disillusioned by political expediency in literature and disappointed by Soviet Communism in the Spanish civil war and the Moscow trials, Rahv and Phillips suspended PR in October, 1936, and broke with the Communist Party in June, 1937. PR thus distinguished itself by anticipating the subsequent trend of American intellectual defection from Communism. Rahv and Phillips revived the intellectual, rather than the worker, as their main concern. By considering the intellectual as the radical man of their times, they arrived at a position comparable to that of Randolph Bourne twenty years before and prophetic of C. Wright Mills twenty years later.

When PR reappeared in December, 1937, it declared its "unequivocal independence" and disclaimed "obligation to any organized political expression." It exuded an aura of aesthetic revolt that continued to characterize the journal into the 1960s. Its style became synonymous for many with the quality of intellectuality itself. Dwight Macdonald and Mary McCarthy, early adherents of Trotskyism, joined Rahv and Phillips and others on the new PR staff. Together they constituted part of what Norman Podhoretz has called the "first generation" of the New York literary Establishment.[34] That generation of the 1930s, in turn, connected with the "fourth generation" of the 1960s to form a leftist intellectual bloc against the Vietnam War. PR emerged and thus remained one of the main "family" magazines for the "New York intellectuals."[35]

The editors' concern with the role of the intelligentsia in the United States and what they considered its greatest digression, the brief affair with Stalinism, established the distinctive pattern of thought in PR. The journal's anti-Stalinism persisted into the 1960s and accounted for part of the tension between the Old and New Left in the intellectuals' opposition to the Vietnam War.

28

The Long Dark Night of the Soul

The debate over the intellectual as alienated man or political activist pitted Rahv and Phillips against Dwight Macdonald and Fred Dupee. The two original editors inclined toward the view that the intellectual had to be alienated to be true to himself and history. When Rahv and Phillips shifted after Pearl Harbor to support the American struggle against fascism, they left Macdonald virtually alone with his concentration on political activism, his journal *Politics* (started in 1944), and his opposition to U.S. involvement in World War II. Macdonald invoked Bourne to warn that war would precipitate the merger between liberalism and imperialism in American culture.[36] Radical critics of the Vietnam War were subsequently to confirm Macdonald's caveat by condemning Johnson's Southeast Asian policy as the culmination of that merger.

World War II swept away radical expectations of the 1930s. *Partisan Review* writers responded to Arthur Koestler's call in *Darkness at Noon* for an "active fraternity of pessimists." They embraced him as the ideologue of the "homeless radical" in the 1940s. He prefigured the conception of the intellectual as neurotic iconoclast that underlay the American intelligentsia's sense of alienation in the 1950s and 1960s.[37]

Their break with Communism notwithstanding, the *PR* editors continued after World War II to seek a political world where choices were clear and uncompromising. They interpreted the Soviet Union and the Communist Party as the greatest dangers in the immediate postwar era. *PR* and *Commentary*, the main "second generation" journals of the Intellectual Left for that period, led the "family's" support for U.S. foreign policy in the Cold War and denounced "the liberal fifth column" which had once favored accommodation with the Russians. Irving Howe later charged that *PR*, like *Commentary* under Elliot Cohen, "failed to take the lead on the issue of freedom which might once again have imbued the intellectuals with fighting spirit."[38] A *PR* symposium, entitled "The Future of Socialism" (1947), rejected socialism as a practical alternative for the United States and accepted capitalism as a temporary ally. *PR*'s disdain for liberalism was part of that philosophy's continuing cyclical disfavor with the American Intellectual Left. Liberalism was once disliked because it was nonrevolutionary, then disparaged because it became nationalistic before World War II, later rejected because it smacked of pro-Stalinism, and finally condemned in the 1960s because it seemed responsible for the Vietnam War.

Coincident with these developments within *Partisan Review*, Dwight Macdonald was becoming more disillusioned during the postwar period. The assassinations of his heroes Trotsky and Gandhi made him believe that history consumed its most remarkable offspring. He was to recall that suspicion in a *New York Review* symposium after the death of John F. Kennedy. His faith in radicalism eroded, he stopped publishing *Politics* in 1949. In a debate with Norman Mailer in 1951, Macdonald stunned American intellectuals with his confession "I choose the West."

Pacifism, socialism, and anarchism had all failed. What had begun as revolutionary isolation ended as simple isolation. According to James Gilbert: "Macdonald's choice of the West entailed, for him, an end to politics, just as he had once argued that the *PR*'s implicit alliance with America early in the Cold War would lead to an end of politics."[39] More important, Macdonald's choice reflected the larger trend of political apathy among intellectuals during the Eisenhower era, just as his opposition to the Vietnam War signaled the repoliticization of the leftist intelligentsia in the Johnson period.

Partisan Review's symposium "Our Country and Our Culture" underscored the extent of the *embourgeoisement* of the American intellectuals in the early 1950s. It concluded: "For better or worse, most writers no longer accept alienation as the artist's fate in America; on the contrary, they want very much to be part of American life."[40] Rahv wrote that one must give up the struggle to change the nation. Although supporting the United States against the Soviet Union, the *PR* intellectuals did not embrace America without reservations. Their accommodation with their nation in the 1950s simply concealed the questions about "being on the side of America" that erupted in the 1960s. Irving Howe started *Dissent* in 1954 to shake the family's "conformity." To his credit, he anticipated the issues which *PR* suppressed in its obsession with literary criticism during the Eisenhower years. By the early 1960s, *PR* fell victim to the general drift of the American Intellectual Left, the long power struggle between Rahv and Phillips, the acculturation of its children, and the triumph of its own ideas.

Not until the emergence of the Vietnam crisis in 1965 did *PR* begin to shift focus from "taste" to politics. A three-part symposium in 1965, "Is There a New Radicalism?," suggested a range of political questions and aspirations avoided by the journal since World War II. However, most respondents to *PR*'s "Statement on Vietnam and the Dominican Republic" in 1965 condemned the authors for their "milk of magnesia" compromise and anachronistic policing of the American Left. *Partisan Review*'s anti-Stalinism died hard. With the claim that Vietnam had brought out the latent madness of the land, the 1967 symposium on "What's Happening to America?" illustrated how far *PR* had come from the confident exhilaration of 1952. Prodded by the Vietnam War, *PR* seemed to vindicate its tradition of intellectual naysaying and helped define the increasingly radical intellectual mood of the 1960s.

CHAMPION OF RADICAL SCHOLARSHIP

Studies on the Left lost little time laying the intellectual foundation for the radicalization of U.S. universities. From a modest start as "a journal of research, social theory and review" at the University of Wisconsin, it quickly became an influential voice for a new generation of graduate students far to the left of most professors. Its founders, mostly young socialists and disciples of the revisionist historian William Appleman Williams, set out to disavow the Old Left and define the New.[41]

The extent to which they succeeded told as much about the entire Intellectual Left as about *Studies*. Even in its short life (1959–67), it suffered the growing pains—the tensions between movement theoreticians and activists, the pressures for reform versus revolution—which plagued most of the intellectual community. The stages in its demise anticipated or paralleled those elsewhere.

For the first few years, *Studies*'s editors concentrated on defining "the function of socialist intellectuals in the American political climate" and developing a new analysis of U.S. society. The key pillars in their perceptual framework were "No" to academic "objectivity" as an illusory aim in an area of "counter-revolutionary subordination"; "No" to their elders' celebration of American achievements; "No" to liberal corporate capitalism; "Yes" to C. Wright Mills and his critique of "power elites"; "Yes" to the utopian moralism of Marx and Engels for a society they considered "institutionalized madness."

The Cuban Revolution was to help provide the "radical humanist" underpinnings of "participatory democracy" in the United States. *Studies*'s editors sensed that connection. After their visit to Cuba in 1960, they presented the revolution there as proof of the deterioration of Cold War ideology and America's reactionary isolation from a changing world. The 1962 editorial "The Ultra-Right and Cold War Liberalism" was a seminal piece in New Left literature because of its plea to intellectuals to break the shackles of liberal rhetoric and "recognize that, at heart, the leaders of the United States are committed to the warfare state as the last defense of the large-scale corporate system."

In 1963, *Studies* shifted its location and role. The move to New York and a new emphasis on the student "movement" and community organizing unleashed a furore among the staff. Should

Studies commit itself to an explicitly socialist politics? What of the relationship between theory and action? Like *New Left Notes, New Politics,* and *Liberation,* the journal vacillated between quasi-populism and academic analysis, between "arguments about the instrumentalities of social action" and "examination of the nature of the transformation we seek."[42] In the spring of 1966, three editors—Norm Fruchter, Tom Hayden, and Staughton Lynd—resigned. They left the journal to those committed to "conceptualization" as the special responsibility of radical intellectuals and with *Studies* as the presumed vehicle of expression. Without a theoretical framework for the new society, the remaining editors feared that radical activists would continue to feel frustrated or, worse, be absorbed by the "more sophisticated molders of the liberal consensus."

Black Power and the growing antiwar movement seemed to support that choice. A comprehensive critique of American corporate capitalism appeared in order. James Weinstein and David Eakins moved to ally *Studies* more closely with the peace movement. They considered the Students for a Democratic Society's March on Washington (April 17, 1965) the decisive event establishing a "new" peace movement that "did not rely on moral appeals within the Cold War frame of mind, but that could fit into a view of the United States as the leading imperialist power in the world."[43]

Only belatedly did *Studies*'s editors perceive the trap in making the antiwar movement a substitute for a new revolutionary party. The peace movement focused necessarily on ending the Vietnam War and educated thousands of Americans about U.S. "imperialism." Yet it failed to establish a theoretically coherent movement for revolutionary change. Disagreement on the editorial board grew between those who looked to the peace movement for a spontaneous development of a new socialist politics and those who, though realizing the historic significance of the peace movement, believed that only a self-consciously socialist party could achieve the theoretical and programmatic coherence necessary for a revolutionary movement. The latter position called for the formation of a preliminary organization consisting mostly of intellectuals to define the problems of revolution. The *Studies* board split in half on that issue and stopped publication. Frustration with Johnson's escalation of the Vietnam War accelerated the radicalization of American intellectuals. It thus contributed, as much as financial pressure and editorial division, to *Studies*'s collapse. The era leapfrogged that journal's loyalty to theory and mercurial faith in dissent. In that sense, *Studies* was a microcosm of the factionalism and confusion which the Vietnam experience caused for most leftist intellectuals.

PURVEYOR OF POLITICAL CHIC

Future historians may well consider *The New York Review of Books* (*NYR*) the most important single index to the political and literary temperament of the U.S. intelligentsia during the Johnson period. After less than a decade in existence, it became the journal most read by the American educated elite.[44] In view of the dispersion of the nation's intelligentsia on the campuses, *NYR*'s prestige in the 1960s was all the more remarkable testimony to the continuing hegemony of the New York literary family and the city itself. Seventy percent of the editorial offices of the top twenty intellectual journals were still within ten miles of Times Square and more than half of the intellectuals themselves were within easy commuting distance.

The New York Review first appeared during the city's newspaper strike in February, 1963. It drew most of its early contributors from the New York family, including the founding editors of *PR* and *Dissent* and several former editors of *Commentary*. Robert Silvers and Barbara Epstein, editors, continued to rely on a nucleus of about a dozen established and middle-aged contributors. The journal depended on book reviews converted into showcase essays. Its writers strutted with self-conscious bravura and soared from the nominal subject to larger moral and political considerations. Their articles epitomized the "honest testimony" and "exhibitionism" noted by Norman Podhoretz and Irving Howe, respectively, as characteristic of American intellectuals' writing in the 1960s.

The New York Review's initial aim was to convey a critical style and sophisticated liberalism to a larger audience than that reached by its more specialized competitors. However, with its symposium on the reaction of leading intellectuals to the death of John Kennedy, *NYR* shifted gears early to political journalism. A sequence of subsequent political events seemed to overwhelm the nation. *NYR* decided that politics was where the rhetorical action was and published accordingly.

Vietnam dominated the *NYR's* political commentaries and, indeed, the tone of the journal throughout the decade. By attacking the American involvement in Southeast Asia through reports on Vietnam by Bernard Fall and Jean Lacouture and on policy formation by Hans Morgenthau, Joseph Kraft, and Theodore Draper, the *NYR* helped mobilize intellectuals against the war. The *NYR* played a key role in disrupting the White House Festival of the Arts in June, 1965, and turning that event into a collective slap by the intelligentsia against President Johnson. Thereafter, the *NYR* urged the Intellectual Left to protest against the war through petitions, demonstrations, and campaigns of civil disobedience. The "Call to Resist Illegitimate Authority," printed in the issue of October 12, 1967, emulated the example of the "Manifesto of 121" against French policy in Algeria. It became a central document in the intellectuals' campaign against Lyndon Johnson.

Vietnam put not just the Johnson Administration but the whole concept of democratic political action into question for writers and readers of the *NYR*. Dennis Wrong has speculated that this development had a "remissive" psychological impact on many intellectuals.[45] They felt reborn politically and revitalized by their radical renaissance. Susan Sontag's *Styles of Radical Will* and Norman Mailer's *The Armies of the Night* illustrated this psychopolitical phenomenon and the youth-centered ethos of the age. The war's effect on the reradicalization of the Intellectual Left was comparable to the reaction against Stalinism in the 1930s and 1940s. Many intellectuals, first born politically through Marxism and reborn through anti-Stalinism, were "thrice-born" with their opposition to the Vietnam War. Each experience delegitimated the intelligentsia's previous political position and provided new political and spiritual vistas. For that reason, many *NYR* writers made anti-Stalinism, often equated with liberalism, the scapegoat for the Vietnam War. The *NYR* of the Johnson period repeated the cycle by which American intellectuals let one era's excesses produce the next's overcompensation.

The New York Review's turn to anti-Americanism, its approval of the New Left, its antiliberalism, and its growing radicalism stemmed primarily from its writers' reaction to the Vietnam War. By 1966, the reports of Noam Chomsky, Mary McCarthy, and I. F. Stone set a tone of emotionalized anti-Americanism comparable to the anti-Communism of the 1950s. Indeed, anti-Americanism—drawing at will from conservative, neo-Marxist, anarchist, and populist inspiration—pervaded the *NYR* during the Johnson period. Norman Podhoretz wrote that the *NYR* "outflanked *Commentary* on the Left in the mid-1960s with a stance of opposition to the Vietnam War which . . . was mainly serving the objective of proving how dreadful the United States was."[46]

The year 1966 also marked the *NYR*'s turn toward the New Left and away from traditional liberalism. It was a shift indicated by Stokely Carmichael's attack on "white liberals" (September 22, 1966), Christopher Lasch's critique of liberal anti-Communist views of the 1930s (October 6, 1966), Stone's three-part series on Senator J. William Fulbright (December, 1966, and January, 1967), and Chomsky's landmark piece, "The

Responsibility of Intellectuals" (February 23, 1967). Irving Howe took the lead in condemning the *NYR*'s contempt for liberal values and the intellectual respectability its writers gave the New Left. In his estimation, publishing the writing of Andrew Kopkind, Tom Hayden, Edgar Friedenberg, and Jason Epstein fostered a self-defeating verbal radicalism.

Epstein's "The CIA and the Intellectuals" (April 20, 1967) represented a turning point in the development of the *NYR* and its relationship to the American intellectual environment.[47] His political point was to extol the radical faction supplanting the anti-Stalinist, Cold War fellow travelers on the Intellectual Left. It was part of the growing tendency among intellectuals to speak of a unified anti-Communism, in much the same way that the Administration referred just as inaccurately to a "Communist monolith." Epstein's article helped inspire *Commentary*'s lengthy symposium on "Liberal Anti-Communism Revisited" in September, 1967.

The *NYR*'s issue of August 24, 1967, climaxed its radicalism during the Johnson era with its cover showing how to make a Molotov cocktail and with articles by Andrew Kopkind and Tom Hayden on "Violence and the Negro." Kopkind redefined the responsibility of the intellectual as "the same as that of the street organizer, the draft resister, the Digger." He declared: "Morality, like politics, starts at the barrel of a gun."

The New York Review's treatment of the student revolt at Columbia University in the spring of 1968 deepened the division between the so-called New and Old Left precipitated by Vietnam. The *NYR* sided with the New Left and often glossed over the more violent elements of the student movement. Writers like Lewis Coser, Nathan Glazer, and Midge Decter, who criticized the New Left or *NYR*'s political position, stopped appearing in the magazine. Except for one statement in behalf of Eugene McCarthy, Irving Howe's writing was dropped from the journal after a confrontation with Philip Rahv.[48] However, such admitted sympathizers of the "movement" as Eugene Genovese, Paul Goodman, Christopher Lasch, and Barrington Moore, Jr., did write critically about contemporary radicalism in their pieces for the *NYR*.

Vietnam brought the magazine a long way in five years from its original dedication to high culture and liberal humanism. Mary McCarthy's *Hanoi* and *Vietnam* and Noam Chomsky's *American Power and the New Mandarins*, both of which first appeared in the *NYR*, displayed more moral absolutism than hard political analysis. Their position harked back to that of the Abolitionists—"the nearest thing to a resistance movement the Republic has had," according to Miss McCarthy. Invoking the Abolitionists to help justify opposition to the Vietnam War revealed the moral fervor and potential depoliticization toward which the *NYR* nudged the Intellectual Left in the Johnson period. Although a powerful vehicle for intellectual expression in the 1960s, the *NYR* sometimes moved so far to the Left that its writers verged on becoming guerrillas with tenure.

IN SUM

Although all four of the foregoing journals began publication with a variety of objectives, philosophies, and formats, the Vietnam War brought each to a logical culmination of its own politics, forced each to express new political concerns, and pushed each further to the left. *The New Republic* had to confront its New Deal-progressivism; *Partisan Review*, its persistent anti-Communism; *Studies on the Left*, its devotion to radical theory; and *The New York Review*, its neoliberal cultural orientation. The impact varied. Issues forced by the war killed *Studies*, revitalized *TNR* and *PR*, and propelled the *NYR* to the pinnacle of intellectual preeminence and/or notoriety in the United States. Most important, Vietnam evoked the "symbolic legitimist" from each journal since each eventually concentrated on the issues of morality and governmental authority raised by the war.

Reactions in these intellectual journals command interest not only for their intrinsic significance but also for their reflection of consistent themes in twentieth-century American intellectual history: preoccupation with the role of the intellectual, division over American participation in war, the cyclical disrepute of liberalism, frustration for native radicalism, and concern about political legitimacy. Henry David Thoreau and Randolph Bourne loom as prototypes cited regularly by the U.S. intelligentsia to justify their moral objections to the government's foreign policy. Thoreau refused to pay his private taxes as a protest against the Mexican War of 1846–48 and defended that action in his "Essay on the Duty of Civil Disobedience." He thus anticipated campaigns for withholding income tax and the "Call to Resist Illegitimate Authority" publicized by *The New York Review*. Bourne's essays were republished in the 1960s and the Bourne legend resurfaced in Noam Chomsky's *American Power and the New Mandarins*.[49]

Both the general backgrounds of these four representative journals and the responses evoked by the Vietnam War suggest that the American leftist intelligentsia has tended to choose moral purity at the expense of political pragmatism—or at least confront the question, whether in the liberalism of *The New Republic*, the anti-Stalinism of *Partisan Review*, or the antiliberalism and anti-anti-Stalinism of *Studies on the Left* and *The New York Review*. This state of affairs seemed to arise from a problem inherent in the role of Western intellectuals in general and their American counterparts in particular. Did the nation's leftist intellectuals of the 1960s impale themselves on the horns of their own dilemma, caught by the contradiction between the "ethic of ultimate ends" and the "ethic of responsibility"?[50] Having set forth *Who They Were*, we turn for the answer in *What They Wrote* about "Johnson's war."

Part Two

WHAT THEY WROTE

A Longer, Chronological Account and Critique of the
U.S. Intellectual Left Jousting with Johnson

First Stage: The Vietnam War
Seen as a Lapse in Judgment
—*From the Early 1960s to February, 1965*

The men who create power make an indispensable
contribution to the Nation's greatness, but the men who
question power make a contribution just as indispensable
. . . for they determine whether we use power or power
uses us.

John F. Kennedy

Drawing by David Levine. Reprinted with permission from *The New York Review of Books.* Copyright © 1969 The New York Review.

What ended in a whimper began with a whisper. There was little criticism in the early 1960s to foretell the eventual howl of leftist protest against Lyndon Johnson's Vietnam policy. What little was heard centered on U.S. involvement in Southeast Asia as a lapse in judgment—variously described as an unfortunate digression from the national interest or an inadvertent error. Daniel Patrick Moynihan, onetime Kennedy liberal and sometime Nixon tory, admitted belatedly that "the great mass of American liberal opinion was uncritical, indeed, approving, until the war began to go badly."[1]

ALL QUIET IN CAMELOT

"The best and the brightest" of Cambridge, Massachusetts, descended on the Kennedy White House with the belief that problems persisted primarily because the right people had not yet tackled them. Arthur Schlesinger, Jr., proclaimed: "We are Sons of Liberty once again!"

Although not all leftist intellectuals reveled in the "new Augustan age" heralded by Robert Frost and many had reservations about John Kennedy, few focused at the time on American policy toward Indochina. Few dwelt on the potential consequences of initiatives launched then, even though McGeorge Bundy stated later that Vietnam posed "the most divisive issue in the Kennedy Administration." Few listened to those challenges within the Kennedy retinue.[2] Few heeded the warning of American journalists, many of whom diverged early from the policy of "sink or swim with Ngo Dinh Diem."[3] Fewer still protested President Kennedy's attempt to throttle David Halberstam's critical reporting from Vietnam.

Most were silent even though the germ of every major argument that critics were to use later against Johnson existed during the Kennedy years. Peking complained in 1962 that America's "undeclared war" in South Vietnam threatened Chinese security and thus raised the specter of Chinese intervention which subsequently haunted intellectual doves. From the beginning, the Diem regime did not fulfill the "needed reforms" stipulated as a

44

condition for continuing U.S. support by President Eisenhower. Although intellectuals later justified American withdrawal on the basis of corruption in Saigon, they said little about Diem's dictatorial regime from 1961 to 1963. They did not challenge the Kennedy Administration when it changed the character of American involvement in Vietnam, both in terms of the number of men and the nature of the mission in late 1961. Only belatedly did most intellectuals question the anti-Communism behind U.S. policy, even though Kennedy clearly and repeatedly said that we were there to save Saigon from Communism.

Most were later to ignore the fact that no one could have predicted Johnson's policy reversal on the basis of what he said up to and even after November, 1963. The Presidential campaign of 1968 was to tempt both Robert Kennedy, who had offered to serve as Johnson's ambassador to Saigon in 1964, and many New Frontier intellectuals to dissociate themselves from the Kennedy record in Vietnam without proclaiming open disloyalty to it. It was a transparent *volte-face*, with writers like Schlesinger attacking Secretary of State Dean Rusk as if he did not know whose appointee Rusk had been. Midge Decter, an outspoken writer and wife of *Commentary* editor Norman Podhoretz, mused belatedly:

Perhaps America is indeed settling into the spiritual condition of a great conservative imperial power. If so, the lesson of the 1960's and of the Kennedys is that it has taken no bloody-minded or profit-greedy class of imperialists to lead her into that condition.[4]

In fact, it was not until the Buddhist uprising against Diem in May, 1963, that the leftist intelligentsia began to bestir itself about U.S. policy in Vietnam. Why?

Part of the reason lay in Kennedy himself. Vietnam remained on the periphery of Washington's concerns from 1961 to 1963 and never attracted the President's full attention. Furthermore, the Kennedy Administration either believed that its policy in Vietnam was succeeding or managed to delude most potential critics with a calculated optimism.[5] It did so despite the military and political problems already apparent in the Maxwell Taylor–Walt Rostow program by late 1962. Kennedy summed up the prevailing mood in his State of the Union message of 1963: "The spearpoint of aggression has been blunted in South Vietnam."

The more fundamental basis for the intellectuals' *sang-froid* on the Vietnam issue lay in the backdrop of the 1950s, the persistence of Cold War attitudes, and the intellectuals' perennial vulnerability before power.

Most leftist intellectuals had accorded Dwight Eisenhower's piety on the Potomac an apolitical ho-hum. Only a few writers like Jack Kerouac had tried to express the latent state of the Union. The President played golf, the people tended backyard barbecues, and the intellectuals rediscovered Henry James. *Commentary*, for example, dwelt on liberalism as a "strategy for adapting to the *status quo.*" *Partisan Review* flaunted its accommodation to the times with a sycophantic symposium, "Our Country and Our Culture."

FLEDGLING CHALLENGE TO POSTWAR DIPLOMACY

The postwar dry spell of liberal bipartisanship had left a shrunken pool of competent critics of U.S. foreign policy. Most antiwar protest was to come from a surprisingly small corps of commentators. Revisionist historiography had yet to challenge the "consensus school" of a George Kennan in the Kennedy years. William Appleman Williams had published his *The Tragedy of American Diplomacy* in 1959. His critique of U.S. foreign policy since the 1890's was to do as much as any other work to spur the subsequently fashionable re-evaluation of the Cold War and American diplomacy. Yet his views had not won recognition or wide respect within the United States Intellectual Left and were not to do so until the teach-in movement of the mid-1960s in which he was so active.

The Long Dark Night of the Soul

That is not to argue that leftist intellectuals were wholly enamored of U.S. foreign policy in the early 1960s. They were not. Many were beginning to consider the Administration and the public to which it catered to be out of step with new alignments of world power. The Truman Doctrine had set the pattern for the postwar period with its statement of American willingness to help free people withstand aggression for the sake of international peace and U.S. security. The subsequent universalization of the Truman Doctrine suggested a growing equation between world order and American security and an identification between national purpose and security which more and more leftist intellectuals were finding inappropriate. Allen Ginsburg was to write in *Wichita Vortex Sutra* in 1966, "Communism is a 9 letter word used by inferior magicians."

For the intellectuals, rejecting anti-Communism as the fulcrum of U.S. foreign policy meant a painful disengagement from the national consensus. They moved gingerly to detach themselves. Their first instinct, as evident in the 1960–64 period, was to invoke the pragmatic criterion of national interest. With that argument, they condemned what liberal commentators like Walter Lippmann called the "overexpansion" of American power since the Truman Doctrine. Only later did the Intellectual Left advance other lines of criticism, warning against the moralistic pretense of American diplomacy or challenging its ideological base.

Many in the Intellectual Left were slow to make that kind of transition in diplomatic critique because it forced them to face their own responsibility for Cold War anti-Communism. Some have argued that the leftist intellectuals' relationship with Stalinism in the 1930s paved the way for the subsequent orgy of apology and the disavowal of anything left of light pink. Christopher Lasch, for example, wrote:

When they began to compete with the Right in their unremitting anti-Communism, giving "containment" of Communism priority over everything else, American liberals deprived themselves of any effective

47

grounds on which to resist the absurdities to which that policy so easily led. In effect, they appropriated the major demands of the Right and then caviled at the outcome.[6]

Perhaps even more important to the intellectuals' muted protest against Vietnam was their relationship to Kennedy and what he represented to them. By the time Kennedy became President, the government and the intelligentsia had already consummated a striking symbiotic relationship. Intellectuals *got* research contracts, governmental appointments, consultantships, and foreign travel. They *gave* an intellectual gloss to the Administration in power or an aura of objectivity to a partisan position. The process simply seemed to accelerate with JFK. The intellectual migration to Washington during the Kennedy era was a marriage of convenience after the fact.

Not until Vietnam emerged full blown in the mid-1960s did that liaison lose its allure for many leftist intellectuals and betray its real ties and complexities. Thereafter, many intellectuals were to agonize over their vulnerability to power, to condemn those in their midst who had succumbed most conspicuously to its blandishments, or to spurn power itself. The so-called "raping of the intellectuals"[7] by John Kennedy and the surprisingly long honeymoon with Lyndon Johnson anticipated many intellectuals' subsequent revulsion against both the man from Camelot and the President from the Pedernales. Such experiences only bore testimony to the peculiar vacillations of the U.S. Intellectual Left before power noted in Part One.

The relative silence of the Intellectual Left during the Kennedy period and the later rationalization for acquiescence did not reflect well on many liberal intellectuals' capacity to serve as checks on power. The point was not lost on either "Kennedy intellectuals" or their critical colleagues.

For that reason, many liberal intellectuals were to become more interesting out of power than when in Washington. Miss Decter seized on Theodore Sorensen's mode of dealing with U.S. involvement in Vietnam during the Kennedy era as typical: "Namely, I was right to begin with, and when I changed my mind, or had it changed for me, I was right still."[8] Although Sorensen stated that "all" of Kennedy's principal advisers on Vietnam favored the commitment of American combat troops[9] and Schlesinger admitted that Kennedy's decision by late 1961 "was to place the main emphasis on the military effort,"[10] both asserted that past American policy gave the President no choice. To that defense of Kennedy, Theodore Draper—a frequent contributor to *Commentary*—retorted: "There is nothing so devastating about our entire Vietnam policy as the sense of fatality, and this is the best argument that Kennedy's friends have been able to muster in his behalf."[11]

STATE OF THE UNION—LATE 1963

Although free-lance naysayers within the Intellectual Left can and must be distinguished from liberals working within the government, their record was little better at the time than that of the "mandarins" they subsequently pilloried. The commemorative issue of *The New York Review* after Kennedy's death was more instructive for what most intellectuals did *not* say than for what they did.[12]

Most neither glorified Kennedy nor denounced Johnson. Although intended in part as a political projection, there was no reference to Vietnam. Dwight Macdonald was among the majority stressing the continuity of policy from the Kennedy to the Johnson Administration. Hans Morgenthau remarked: "In the field of foreign policy, it is difficult to see what initiatives a Johnson Administration would take that Kennedy's did not take." The issue marked *The New York Review*'s first important departure from cultural affairs. It was a political debut most notable for its political naïveté.

Irving Howe's contribution to that landmark issue was an exception to the "pieties of 'national reconciliation'" prevailing among his colleagues. Howe had been inveighing against the political torpor of the Intellectual Left since the mid-1950s. He believed that the mentality of the Fifties lingered and that intellectual concerns remained "privatized." David Bazelon and David Riesman were among the few to grasp what Howe meant by the "sickness of culture" and to anticipate the grounds for subsequent antiwar reaction. Bazelon was struck by the unfulfillment of Kennedy, "which America suddenly recognized as its own unfulfillment." Potentiality had been martyred. Riesman counseled that "among our own tasks, as intellectuals, would seem to be the discovery of the visions which we have not yet dreamed and the plans not yet planned. . . ." He believed that Johnson was inheriting a "situation of polarization in America between some of the best tendencies of men and some of the meanest." He referred specifically to the growing estrangement of the young, who were already shunning politics. SDS, after all, had issued its plea for "participatory democracy" in 1962. Howe claimed that Kennedy had not understood "the necessity or value of trying to arouse the masses of people to a strongly felt political involvement and participation." If they did not appreciate the significance of Vietnam then, Riesman and Howe at least sensed the malaise which preceded the Johnson era and helped explain the virulent reaction to the Asian war.

HONEYMOON FOR LBJ

There is a tacit agreement in American politics that a President enjoys the benefit of the doubt for his first months in office. Lyndon Johnson gained from this political tradition even more because of the nation's desire for continuity after the shock of

Dallas. The intellectual community acceded to that tradition out of respect for national sentiments, alarm over Barry Goldwater, and admiration for Johnson's domestic record. TRB of *The New Republic* wrote: "LBJ isn't JFK. So what?"[13]

Despite the eventual disintegration of relations between the President and the intellectuals, Johnson began his tenure with conspicuous efforts to woo the intellectual community. Following Kennedy's precedent with the appointment of Arthur Schlesinger, Jr., Johnson named the historian Eric Goldman as his "intellectual-in-residence" early in 1964. Goldman was to be responsible for facilitating communication between the President and the intelligentsia. Furthermore, the President recruited eminent academicians for important positions, included intellectuals in White House social functions, dispatched task forces to canvas college campuses for new ideas, dedicated speeches to intellectuals, and quoted Macaulay, MacLeish, and Leonardo da Vinci.

Whether responding to LBJ's courting or not, the leftist intellectuals' first objections to the new President's Vietnam policy were polite. They stressed U.S. involvement in Indochina as a mistaken divergence from national interest. For example, early in 1964 the editors of *The New Republic* foresaw a "perpetuated war" despite the assurance of Defense Secretary Robert McNamara that American troops could be withdrawn by 1965.[14] They urged the Administration to review its policy after General Nguyen Khanh's coup in January, 1964, since the frequent governmental shuffles in Saigon bespoke a thin popular base and raised questions about the American investment. Where, they wondered, was the "payoff" for the three billion dollars poured into Vietnam in the last decade? They found no direction to U.S. policy, only "more of the same." Moving north would violate the very principle of nonaggression the United States claimed to be defending.[15] Besides, Secretary Rusk stated in early 1964 that it would not be necessary to attack North Vietnam since the problem was in South Vietnam.

The Long Dark Night of the Soul

Bernard Fall stressed during the early stages of U.S. involvement in Vietnam the discrepancy between facts he observed there firsthand and what he called "official mythology." He referred, for example, to Washington's "steady silence about the enemy's forces" when the European and Saigon press was detailing serious setbacks to the strategic hamlet program.[16] Fall's incisive style—combined with in-depth reporting, field experience in Indochina rare in the early 1960s, and his frequent contributions to *The New Republic* and *The New York Review*—gave him extraordinary influence over the change in the intellectuals' attitudes on Vietnam. He underscored increasingly the issue of credibility, a precursor to the larger question of legitimacy. Appropriately enough, *The New York Review*'s "Call to Resist Illegitimate Authority" was to emerge from doubts sown by Fall and from his specific suggestion.

From May through July, 1964, journals like *The Nation* and *The New Republic* dwelt on the danger of Chinese intervention, should the United States expand the Vietnam conflict. In fact, the fear that the Administration might blunder into a war with China preoccupied such liberal sources throughout the Johnson period. Furthermore, contradictions in the U.S. position puzzled them even at that relatively early juncture. The editors of *The New Republic* noted, "We say that we are in Southeast Asia to save it from Communism and yet South Vietnam and Laos are politically unstable to a degree that Communist military presence or proximity does not wholly account for." They observed that the United States had at least 14,000 troops in South Vietnam, "though according to the Geneva Agreement, whose spirit we invoke but which the U.S. never signed, there ought to be only a few hundred."[17] Even so, they believed that there was "room for skillful maneuver and diplomacy" to settle the "civil" wars in Southeast Asia.

The Long Dark Night of the Soul

We must convince the living that the dead cannot sing.

LeRoi Jones
A Guerrilla Handbook, 1964

In this atmosphere of mixed hope and ambiguity, news of the events in the Gulf of Tonkin on August 2–4, 1964, stunned the leftist intellectual community. On August 2, North Vietnamese torpedo boats attacked the U.S. destroyer *Maddox* in international waters off the coast of North Vietnam. Although the United States protested immediately, North Vietnamese PT boats were reported to have attacked the *Maddox* and another destroyer, the *C. Turner Joy*, two days later. President Johnson retaliated with American air strikes against North Vietnamese gunboats and certain supporting facilities in North Vietnam itself.

It was the first turning point in American involvement in Vietnam during the Johnson period. As such, it evoked instant scorn from the intellectual community. Writers for *The New Republic* considered the American response an unwarranted and unexpected reversal of policy.[18] When Johnson defended U.S. reprisals with rhetoric that recalled Munich ("The world remembers—the world must never forget—that aggression unchallenged is aggression unleashed"), Murray Kempton scoffed:

Mr. Johnson is talking about an aggression launched from the coast of the aggressor against an American vessel as far away from our shores as it could get without being on its way back. It is an incident of great complexity; but there is a kind of assumption of divine right in choosing language to describe it which might, with greater geographical precision, have been used by Ho Chi Minh.[19]

DELAYED REACTION TO TONKIN GULF

Disturbing as events in the Tonkin Gulf were then, their full notoriety for the Intellectual Left emerged only over time. In part, there was a delayed reaction because the record of the Senate hearings on those events was not released for more than two years after being held in August, 1964. I. F. Stone contended in 1968 that prompt publication of official testimony would have alerted the public and Congress to the Administration's plans to expand the war and would have "ruined Johnson's image as a peace candidate" in the 1964 Presidential election.[20] Citing the "steps taken to widen the war *before* the Tonkin Gulf incidents provided the public excuse for them," Stone charged the Johnson Administration with "conspiracy":

All this goes back to the question not just of decision-making in a crisis *but of crisis-making to support a secretly pre-arranged decision.* Here the war-making power of Congress was clearly usurped by a private cabal in the executive department, which was soon to confront Congress and the country with a *fait accompli,* and to do so within a few months after Johnson was re-elected on the pledge not to do what this inner circle had already decided he could do.[21]

That kind of military "provocation" reminded Stone of the Mukden incident of 1931, in which Japanese officers had blown up their own troop and supply trains as a pretext for war on China. The Intellectual Left's subsequent acceptance of Tonkin as a latter-day Mukden was in marked contrast to its original interpretation.

The Presidential campaign explained much of the initial reticence of both Lyndon Johnson and the intelligentsia about the implications of Tonkin Gulf. Johnson played the "awkward role of contortionist" with Vietnam throughout the year.[22] He tried to deter Hanoi while he assured the American electorate and propped up Saigon. Johnson had little interest or experience in international affairs. Nevertheless, the North Vietnamese PT attacks aroused what few primordial instincts he did have in foreign policy: the determination to meet "aggression" and avoid miscalculation of American will and the eagerness to prove himself internationally before becoming President in his own right. Only Senators Wayne Morse and Ernest Gruening dared try to deny Johnson his blank check for action in Vietnam when he justified his request in terms of unified national resolve during a Presidential campaign. The Tonkin Gulf resolution passed 416 to 0 in the House and 88 to 2 in the Senate, with J. William Fulbright blocking an amendment to restrict expansion of the war.

Johnson wanted to keep Vietnam quiet since he did not have time during the campaign to give the war his full attention. Hence the medley of hawk-squawks and dove-coos in 1964. For voters, he spoke with calculated moderation to contrast with Goldwater's nuclear bluster. His refrain against escalation at Manchester, New Hampshire, on September 28, 1964, was typical of campaign statements which intellectuals subsequently quoted with cynical relish:

As far as I am concerned, I want to be very cautious and careful, and use it [escalation] only as a last resort, when I start dropping bombs around that are likely to involve American boys in a war in Asia with seven hundred million Chinese. So just for the moment, I have not thought that we were ready for American boys to do the fighting for Asian boys.[23]

Saigon was the weakest link in Johnson's holding operation on the war. The remaining "Kennedy brain trust" on Southeast Asia within the Johnson Administration was advocating quick and large counterinsurgency measures to reverse the political disaster in Saigon and military deterioration in the countryside. Yet Johnson believed then that South Vietnam could not sustain the strain of expanded American involvement or the North Vietnamese reaction that such expansion might bring. Just two days before the American Presidential election, the Vietcong destroyed the Bien Hoa base, the symbol of U.S. air power in Vietnam. Ambassador Maxwell Taylor requested retaliation against North Vietnam, lest the point of American resolve made at Tonkin Gulf be lost. Presumably because of South Vietnamese vulnerability and because it was Election Eve and Johnson still dreamed of sweeping all fifty states, the Chief Executive did nothing.

Johnson's contortionist act flopped on all counts. His procrastination, conciliatory campaign line, and inaction at Bien Hoa violated his own instinct to make American will clear, contradicted his stand in August, and misled Hanoi. Peace pledges at home backfired when later escalation raised charges of political duplicity.

The rapidity of events, together with Johnson's plea for national unity and concern about the unpredictability of Goldwater, had combined to mute the intellectuals' protest against Tonkin Gulf at the time. The Senator from Arizona lost the battle of images. Most intellectuals preferred Johnson-style brinksmanship when the only alternative was President Goldwater's finger on the nuclear trigger.

The Senator's alleged bellicosity was not the only reason for the intellectuals' almost unanimous opposition to him. They flocked to Johnson because Goldwater seemed to threaten the very foundations of the American intellectual community. *Partisan Review*'s symposium "Some Comments on Senator Goldwater" demonstrated the range and depth of the intellectuals' fears. Goldwater exposed the raw nerve of their alienation and made them feel more vulnerable to the "neanderthalism lurking in the so-called average man." William Phillips admitted that "the experience of fascism shell-shocked my generation into a fear of everything on the Right."[24] Most believed that Goldwater appealed to a public suffering from a "backlog of irritability" and susceptible to moralistic postures on foreign policy. Intellectuals saw Goldwater using the people's frustrations to his own advantage and thus pre-empting the "radical" appeal they themselves might have tried. In your heart, you knew he was right. Yet, though the intellectuals identified the basis for the later attraction of George Wallace and Spiro Agnew, they seemed unable to do anything but opt for the "lesser evil" in 1964. It was part of the recurring political dilemma of the American Intellectual Left—as 1968 was to prove even more conclusively.

NEGOTIATIONS, PLEASE

During the 1964 Presidential campaign, intellectuals urged Johnson to avert disaster in Vietnam with negotiations before it was too late.[25] Johnson opposed negotiations for the same reason that the intellectuals recommended them: the weakness of South Vietnam. He believed that the war in that nation was going too badly for the United States to get an acceptable settlement. Furthermore, the President reacted to the Vietnam situation according to the principles of domestic politics to which he was most attuned. Given the Communists' strength in 1964, why, Johnson asked an aide, should the enemy accept anything but surrender—any more than he himself should negotiate with Goldwater?

The intellectuals' pursuit of negotiations in late 1964 and early 1965 was to become a *cause célèbre* in their estrangement from the President. Subsequent reports in 1965 disclosed a peace initiative begun by U Thant, Secretary-General of the United Nations, just two days after the Tonkin Gulf occurrence, which the Johnson Administration allegedly blocked. Whether it could be blamed for the failure of the Thant mission was debatable, though not among most leftist intellectuals. They were in no mood for official explanations when the story finally broke in the fall of 1965.

The fracas over negotiations revealed, *ex post facto*, how the intelligentsia and the Johnson Administration diverged early over specific points (the desirability or possibility of negotiations) and larger issues (the basic assumptions of American foreign policy). Many intellectuals believed that there could be no negotiations without an evaluation of U.S. objectives. What intellectuals ex-

57

cused in 1964 as inadvertence they were to condemn later as conscious distortion of national priorities.

The stubbornly individualistic journalist I. F. Stone was among the few on the Intellectual Left not taken in by Johnson's initial courting of the intellectuals. He warned against the "personality cult chorus" surrounding Johnson in 1964 and the President's need for a new liberal look: "The trouble with disguising this crafty moderate conservative as a liberal and taking the liberals into camp is that this deprives his program of the push that an opposition to the left would give it."[26]

Stone thus anticipated the consequences of the lemminglike surge of the Left to the Democratic Party in November, 1964. It was a lapse from criticism for the sake of political expediency which the expanding Vietnam War helped to expose. During the 1964 Presidential election, the intellectuals overlooked much in Johnson to support the "peace President." When he later reversed his campaign pledges on Vietnam, the leftist intellectuals felt doubly deceived. They never forgave Johnson for not debating the grounds for U.S. involvement in Vietnam before events forced a qualitative change in the American mission there. Subsequently, the Intellectual Left was to oppose the Vietnam War with such bitterness and to turn its critique into a personalized vendetta against Johnson in part because of that betrayal and its own role in the stampede to the Texan.

QUICK ANNULMENT

By Election Day, the intellectuals' honeymoon with Lyndon Johnson verged on annulment. Murray Kempton disparaged Johnson as a latter-day Warren G. Harding, appealing "because he so contents."[27] Although the traditionally more conciliatory *New Republic* editors commended the President's "many qualities of greatness," they admitted that the election campaign was "wasted" since the "Present debated the Past."[28] Paul Goodman

58

blamed liberals for their united front against Goldwater which had allowed Johnson and Humphrey to be elected without explaining how they would achieve peace abroad and social progress at home. He bewailed "the amazing spectacle of Professors, Scientists, and Engineers, and Fellows of the Institute for Policy Studies hailing the 'lesser evil' as if he were Gandhi, Talleyrand, and Lorenzo de' Medici rolled into one."[29] By singling out liberals for censure and branding liberalism "Tokenism," Goodman expressed the radicals' rejection of liberals which increasingly dominated the intellectual character of the 1960s.

Many intellectuals balked at the trend of Johnson's Vietnam policy even before he was inaugurated. When U.S. forces assumed responsibility for peripheral security of American installations after the Bien Hoa debacle, *The New Republic* editors observed: ". . . Without any new policy ever having been consciously formulated, the U.S. edges away from an 'advisory' role in Vietnam toward unambiguous military involvement. . . ."[30] When General Taylor urged the same extension of the war for which Johnson had condemned Goldwater, intellectual critics chanted the litany of Johnson campaign promises. They wondered how the Administration thought bombing Laotian jungle trails or North Vietnamese ports would stop the rot in Saigon, undermine the will of the Vietcong, or transform the soldiers of the South into effective fighters.

With the beginning of 1965, many leftist intellectuals flailed about in a quandary, lest U.S. policy *drift* to its doom in Vietnam. They blamed the President for a close-to-the-chest strategy in communications which most considered effective in the Senate cloakroom but disastrous in public diplomacy. Johnson alienated the media and the intelligentsia by claiming that the war in South Vietnam was being "lost" by the American press.[31] He missed the opportunity afforded by his State of the Union message on January 4, 1965, to assert the lead requested by intellectuals. *The New Republic* editors felt that his treatment of Vietnam resembled the known facts no more than a heraldic lion did the creature in the zoo. Yet they comforted themselves with the hope that Johnson was aiming his "story" abroad and that he would actually seize the first opportunity to get out of Southeast Asia:

There is no justification for assuming that the State of the Union message has nailed our flag to the mast of Vietnam. All it did was reiterate United States determination not to retreat in disorder.[32]

Less than one month later, the United States bombarded North Vietnam and foreclosed all foreseeable chances for retreat.

Second Stage: The Vietnam War
Seen as an Exercise in Immorality
—From February, 1965 through December, 1966

At the first step you are free, at the second you are a slave.

Mephistopheles to Faust

Drawing by David Levine. Reprinted with permission from *The New York Review of Books*. Copyright © 1967 The New York Review.

Military escalation of the Vietnam War in early 1965 jolted American leftist intellectuals into a new perception of that conflict. In the ensuing two years, they were in turn angered by new

U.S. bombing, galvanized by campus teach-ins, antagonized by White House overtures, divided by their own disagreements, and, finally, embittered enough to embrace *Schadenfreude* à la *MacBird!*

RESPONSE TO PLEIKU

If Tonkin Gulf was the first turning point for U.S. involvement in Vietnam during the Johnson Administration, Pleiku was the second. On February 7, 1965, Communist guerrillas attacked American and South Vietnamese military installations, the most important of which was the American compound in Pleiku. That same day U.S. planes reciprocated with bombardment of North Vietnam. The reprisals for Pleiku initiated regular U.S. air warfare against the North and led to the introduction of American combat troops within two months.

Some accounts have suggested that Pleiku only provided the pretext for escalation which Johnson had been planning for some time. It is more likely, however, that the Administration turned to bombing as a last resort to prevent the imminent collapse of South Vietnam. Officials reversed their objections to an enlarged U.S. role and argued that attacking North Vietnam might bolster the Saigon regime and help the United States in negotiations. Kremlinologists interpreted Soviet Premier Alexei Kosygin's projected trip to Hanoi on February 6 as a sign of lost American credibility with the Communists. By late January, the Administration had decided to expand the war and "the rest of the problem was timing, and method, and appearance."[1]

Few observers at the time realized that the Johnson Administration, behind the smoke screen of official explanations, had shifted from spot reprisals to systematic bombing. The President struggled to make air strikes acceptable at home and abroad. He feared that a sudden proclamation of war or call for American troops would shock Congress and public opinion. Just beginning the process of enlargement seemed politically safer. The strategy accorded with Johnson's preference for saying and doing the minimum at a difficult juncture. His understated public diplomacy succeeded in most quarters during 1965. Neither China nor the Soviet Union retaliated by greatly increasing aid to North Vietnam. Gallup polls at the time revealed that most Americans applauded the President's "decisiveness" at Pleiku.

Yet, by shifting from his campaign contention that most of South Vietnamese insurgency was internal to the argument that everything would be all right if North Vietnam left its neighbor alone, Johnson redefined the American mission in terms of total victory over aggression. The majority of American citizens could and did support that position as long as success seemed possible. But with protracted frustration, the Pleiku watershed became the President's Waterloo. His support in the polls was to plummet from 79 percent, when he became President, to 29 percent, just before his renunciation of future office in March, 1968. Even assuming that Johnson wanted to hasten peace through a fiercer war, his secrecy came to be seen as secretiveness. Bill Moyers, his Special Assistant from 1963 to 1967, admitted as much later on.[2] One irony of the President's Vietnam policy was that politics itself undid the politician.

The leftist intellectuals reacted quickly and critically to the Administration's about-face at Pleiku. Thereafter they held the Chief Executive personally accountable for the war.

The New Republic was among the first journals to mount the attack. Its editors blamed the Johnson Administration for both the substance and the presentation of its action at Pleiku. Attacking the North skirted the real problem in the South and threatened to stiffen the Northern resolve it was meant to break. Captured American weapons, not North Vietnamese supplies, equipped the Vietcong. Visiting U.S. policymakers seemed to know as much about Vietnam as Americans led around by Intourist knew about the Soviet Union. The Administration failed to answer questions or else contradicted itself. Government statistics fed skepticism. *The New Republic* editors quipped that the " 'hardest' figures are derived from 'double-confirmed' sources, which usually means two unreliable prisoners instead of one." The Administration's explanations for the retaliatory bombing seemed unrealistic: "No one should expect official explanations of military adventure to coincide with reality." Even worse in their eyes, Pleiku showed that Johnson was not only handing out misinformation but also acting on it.[3]

Once fallen from the grace of credibility with the intellectuals, the Johnson government never recovered their confidence. Thenceforth, even *The New Republic* colored its references to the Administration: Government officials no longer spoke but "rationalized," and foreign policy became synonymous with "the cliché of the day." Most leftist intellectuals rejected the argument that Johnson was seeking a "position of strength" for negotiation, just as Kennedy did during the Cuban missile crisis. They could not accept the comparison, no matter how it was presented.

In fact, the discrepancy in historical analogies cited by the intellectuals and officials to justify their positions on Vietnam demonstrated the serious gap between their perspectives. In referring to the 1930s, President Johnson and Secretary Rusk defended a strong American stand by invoking the lesson of Munich. Intellectuals believed that Vietnam was being reduced to a military proving ground like Spain during its civil war. And for every official who recalled the Greek insurrection and cutoff of support from Yugoslavia following World War II, there was a critic to challenge the comparability between Greece and Vietnam. Intellectuals stressed what they considered the farsighted statesmanship of French withdrawal from Algeria. They drew parallels between intellectual opposition within France and the United States, caused by Algeria and Vietnam respectively.

If the State Department's White Paper of February 27, 1965, was meant to meet criticism of U.S. action at Pleiku with its seventy-one-page exposé of North Vietnamese infiltration, it only fired the wrath of intellectual opponents. *The New Republic* editors stated:

The best that can be said about the State Department's White Paper on Vietnam is that it is entirely unconvincing. The worst is that it is contradictory, illogical and misleading. It has a desperate purpose: to prepare the moral platform for widening the war.[4]

For them, the White Paper failed to prove that there was a militarily crucial input of men or matériel from Hanoi. It destroyed credibility by citing only those findings which supported its case. Vietnam seemed more a civil war than a case of foreign aggression, as argued by the Johnson Administration.

Stone ranked the White Paper of 1965 with the Blue Book of 1961 as an effort to manipulate the public and an instance of official self-delusion.[5] Morgenthau rejected it as a rationalization for a futile policy which showed how American diplomacy had become the victim of its own successes in containing Communism. He stressed the right and duty to dissent from that curse on U.S. foreign policy.[6] With that sentiment growing on the Intellectual Left, the stage was set for the teach-ins of 1965.

That movement of mass open sessions with lectures and discussions on the Vietnam War began at the University of Michigan, March 24–25, 1965. Teach-ins spread to hundreds of U.S. campuses that spring, and culminated in the National Teach-in in Washington, D.C., on May 15. The organizers of that event considered it "the most significant political gathering of American intellectuals since the Constitutional Convention."[7]

The extraordinary mobilization of intellectuals against Goldwater in 1964 provided the backdrop for the reaction against Johnson's acting like Goldwater at Pleiku. That, in turn, spurred the first "T-Day" at Ann Arbor.[8] The teach-ins were intended as a "counterforce to the engineering of consent," a counterforum to redress the imbalance of information and opinion provided by the Johnson Administration and the national press and media.[9] The teach-ins tried to compensate for the Congress's previous forfeiture of criticism of foreign policy. They thereby helped bring about the Vietnam hearings by the Senate Foreign Relations Committee in February, 1966.[10]

IMPACT OF YOUTH

A new generation of radicals has been spawned from the chrome womb of affluent America.

Jack Newfield
A Prophetic Minority, 1966

The teach-ins in particular and college activists in general deserve special consideration in any review of the leftist intellectuals' response to Johnson's Vietnam policy. More than any other single phenomenon, the teach-in brought together the American Intellectual Left and dissident U.S. youth. It served to revive many an intellectual's political consciousness. It helped many come to see the Vietnam War as an exercise in immorality. If, as Norman Podhoretz put it, the New Left was "midwived by the Negroes in the South,"[11] U.S. student activism helped make possible the political renaissance of the American Intellectual Left. The figurative midwife: Vietnam.

To document that argument, one must drop back momentarily to chart the coming of age of the nation's "prophetic minority." While the U.S. Intellectual Left was occupying itself with familial squabbling over "the end of ideology" and nursing regrets for Adlai Stevenson, American youth had begun to surface politically by 1960. The Student Nonviolent Coordinating Committee (SNCC) and Students for a Democratic Society (SDS) emerged that year under John Kennedy's "friendly umbrella for the New Left."[12] Two events stand out from that period for their influence on the style and substance of subsequent antiwar protest: at home, the civil rights movement; abroad, the Cuban Revolution.

The Long Dark Night of the Soul

Youth's initiative in behalf of civil rights for Southern blacks broke the cynical belief of the 1950s that ordinary people could not and would not act against injustice. If the Supreme Court decision on school desegregation in 1954 was the movement's legal turning point, the student sit-in at a lunch counter in Greensboro, North Carolina, in 1960 was the psychological breakthrough for Southern race relations and for the general political involvement of American youth. Though unreported the next day by *The New York Times,* Greensboro was the critical "improvised act of will."[13] It precipitated a spate of sit-ins and marches and anticipated the mode of nonviolent moral witness which dominated political activism in the 1960s.

That effect was not immediately apparent. Since few New York writers or their colleagues elsewhere spent their summers registering Mississippi blacks to vote, the movement's impact was indirect and gradual. But it was deceptively important. Through those few young people who did go to the South and who later applied their experience to the anti-Vietnam movement, intellectuals absorbed the ethos of the Freedom Riders.

Tom Hayden was typical of those initiated politically by redneck beatings. He and Staughton Lynd were to explain after their trip to North Vietnam in 1965 that they had met and developed their sensitivity to U.S. policy in Southeast Asia because of their participation in the American civil rights campaign.[14] Hayden drafted the "Port Huron Statement" on participatory democracy for SDS and helped launch the teach-ins and mass demonstrations which were to engage the intellectuals' commitment to the peace movement.

The nonviolent direct action of the civil rights campaign particularly impressed intellectuals. Its aura of decentralized spontaneity helped them to overcome their sense of separation between an elite and the masses. It made them feel closer to their romanticized image of "the people" and the millennial movement. The merger of theory and practice in the "improvised act of will" corresponded to many intellectuals' quest for identity and moral authenticity defined in action. The spirit of Greensboro compelled a rediscovery of self through confrontation. That process was repeated in the "readiness to take moral leaps" that Norman Mailer admired in young draft resisters and in his own "rite of passage" during the March on the Pentagon in October, 1967.[15]

Furthermore, the direct action of young civil rights workers (or, later, of peace demonstrators) appealed to the intelligentsia for being *symbolically* demonstrative if not always politically effective. The symbolic value has always been critical for intellectuals—if only, as noted earlier—because they are least able to suffer a vacuum in that sphere.

¡VIVA CUBA!

Khrushchev's "De-Stalinization" speech of 1956, the worldwide movement against atomic testing, the birth of a new literary Left in Europe—all such events abroad meshed with happenings at home and contributed to the politicization of young American students. Yet, in this context, the Cuban Revolution still stands pre-eminent.

Although writers like James Baldwin and Norman Mailer did challenge U.S. policy toward the Castro regime and C. Wright Mills published *Listen, Yankee: The Revolution in Cuba* in 1960, students took the initiative. Many founded chapters of the Fair Play for Cuba Committee, visited the island, or protested official decisions in the early 1960s.

Cuba was crucial to many young American activists for what it contributed to their own emerging political ideology and mythology and what it revealed about U.S. foreign policy. Like the civil rights movement, the Cuban Revolution colored the cast of repoliticization and reradicalization in the United States during the

1960s. It was important for its stress on youth, moral versus material incentives, a sense of community, and the creation of a political consciousness; the belief that action per se creates organization and a revolutionary situation; and emphasis on intense anti-Americanism, especially with regard to U.S. "imperialism" as the embodiment of corrupt bourgeois society.[16]

As with civil rights, the American youth movement provided the transferal filter through which the Cuban experience influenced leftist intellectuals and thereby their response to the Vietnam War. For example, student reaction against Kennedy's handling of Cuba helped unmask the myth of a special relationship between the intelligentsia and the Administration. President Kennedy, as pointed out earlier, had glamorized power. He had made it seem attractive and redeeming, accessible to youth, and exercised with reason and virtue. When students charged that "Kennedy liberals" themselves abjured liberal values during the invasion of the Bay of Pigs, older leftist intellectuals were prompted to conclude that *raisons d'état* had outweighed reason. Would that always be the case? The fact that many leftist intellectuals began to think so simply exacerbated their perennially ambiguous relationship with power.

On a less obvious level, student glorification of Fidel Castro provided the leftist intellectuals with one of their cultural heroes of the decade. Castro was political, a self-proclaimed "radical humanist,"[17] and—crucial to the subsequent polarization on the Intellectual Left!—the opposite of the liberal hero. Radical intellectuals, especially, were to invoke Castro to resolve the existential dilemma inherent in their preoccupation with power and identity. For example, Mailer wrote of the American leftist intellectuals' attempt to assuage their inadequacy through the guerrilla martyr:

You were aiding us, you were giving us psychic ammunition, you were aiding us in that desperate silent struggle we have been fighting with sick dead hearts against the cold insidious cancer of the power that governs us.[18]

The image of the guerrilla martyr was to recur throughout the 1960s. It helped explain why many radical intellectuals were to feel an identity with Vietcong revolutionaries, student demonstrators, or black militants. By the middle of the decade, the intellectuals were to make the Negro a symbolic American-Mod Castro in blackface.

CONVERGENCE AT MID-DECADE

Accordingly, 1965 provided a unique convergence of provocative event with residual disaffection. The integrationist phase of the civil rights movement was drying up. Stokely Carmichael became president of SNCC. The Black Panther Party emerged with the proposition that whites could serve thenceforth only as technicians in the black movement.

That transmutation of the civil rights movement left whites—students and leftist intellectuals alike—aroused without a cause. President Johnson expanded the Vietnam War just when their mounting concerns and sensibilities most needed an outlet. Largely in that way, the first teach-in at Ann Arbor acquired the same significance for the peace movement that the first sit-in at Greensboro had for the civil rights campaign. The times were ripe for a political gesture, a symbolic confrontation.

LINKAGE ON THE LEFT

They were also ready for a coalition of student and intellectual energies against the Vietnam War. Hence the vital function and lingering significance of the 1965 teach-ins. Besides drawing on the heritage of the civil rights and Cuban experiences, they underscored other important grounds for cooperation between young activists and older leftist intellectuals.

First and most obviously, the teach-ins took place on the country's university campuses. It was altogether fitting that many

The Long Dark Night of the Soul

U.S. intellectuals should make their political debut of the 1960s there. By that time, the university was the national institution harboring the largest concentration of leftist intellectuals. The absorption of the intelligentsia by the academy put that group into the midst of a college population of unprecedented size, affluence, and political awareness.

The teach-ins proved to be a uniquely effective means of attracting national attention to the views of this new constituency. Richard Flacks wrote at the time: "The teach-ins suggest that a substantial segment of the academic community has become a self-conscious public, both willing and able to hold the decision-makers to account."[19] There was the growing belief "that as students and intellectuals their basic source of power was in the examples they set, in their ability to articulate dissent and cause the Government embarrassment and discomfort."[20]

Related to that development was the fact that many leftist intellectuals tended to see students as part of a new proletariat. Students were to replace the class that had failed, labor.[21] It seemed a logical liaison of alienated soul mates. It accorded with Mills's advocacy of the educated as the "radical agency of change." Many American leftist intellectuals were to extrapolate later from the magnitude of the French uprising in 1968 the chance for a revolution based on university youth since that was the major group not integrated into society. Most understood only *after* the Democratic convention in Chicago that year why and how the French revolt had been "swallowed whole by bourgeois democracy—just as Marcuse had feared."[22]

Student activists of the 1960s made a point of disparaging anyone over the age of thirty. Yet they drew most from writing begun before many of them could read. Such figures of the "Freudian Left" as Wilhelm Reich, Erich Fromm, Herbert Marcuse, and Paul Goodman dominated the theoretical input for the New Left. Even so, it was young people who brought to prominence many writers previously ignored or reviled by the

71

older intelligentsia. Youth was the intermediary—at once beholden to its elders and bringing them to new awareness. For example, *Studies's* publication of Mills's "Letter to the New Left," Che Guevara's "We Are Practical Revolutionaries," and Jean-Paul Sartre's "Ideology and Revolution" reflected the young radicals' debt to older or international sources. Those, in turn, helped set the intellectual tone of the decade. By espousing the views of William Appleman Williams, long shunned in respectable intellectual circles, *Studies* anticipated the turn toward revisionist historiography which underlay much of the intellectuals' case against the Vietnam War.

Once attracted to the teach-ins, many intellectuals did not leave the peace movement for the duration of the Johnson era. For example, although the first teach-in was an "in-house" event at the University of Michigan, its leading spokesmen—Anatol Rapoport, Kenneth Boulding, and Arnold Kaufman—remained to influence the intellectual direction of the entire peace drive. The roster for the Berkeley teach-in reads like a "who's who" of the nascent peace movement.[23]

Many intellectuals came to use teach-ins among themselves to express dissent from Johnson's Vietnam policy. For instance, the Committee of the Professions organized a series of "Read-ins for Peace in Vietnam" in which they read from works conveying their sentiments on the war. Susan Sontag's "We Are Choking with Shame and Anger" was typical of such statements. In addressing her colleagues in the Town Hall (New York City, February 20, 1966), she said:

We meet here tonight to bear witness to our sorrow and anxiety and revulsion at the American war on Vietnam, . . . to feel and to help each other to go on feeling strongly, to go on protesting, to have the courage to go on being afraid—though, clearly, our feelings, already known to our rulers and written off in advance by them, can hardly halt this crime or count much in the forestalling of even greater ones.[24]

The Long Dark Night of the Soul

Despite her pessimism, Miss Sontag stressed the responsibility of intellectuals to speak out because of their "vocational connection with the life of truth" and the special "integrity of our voices." She urged her fellow intellectuals "to invent and sustain appropriate responses" and to shun protest for the sake of "emotional recreation" or "conscious virtue." She focused, finally, on a theme which predominated throughout intellectual gatherings and writings in the 1960s and showed the depth of their disaffection from the Johnsonian consensus: the need to reject "the myth of a special American virtue."

America has become a criminal, sinister country—swollen with priggishness, numbed by affluence, bemused by the monstrous conceit that it has the mandate to dispose of the destiny of the world, *of life itself,* in terms of its own interests and jargon.[25]

Because Vietnam was an *American* war, it was necessary for intellectuals to "confront the bloodstained face of America."

TEACH-IN THEMES

The teach-ins of the spring of 1965 marshaled the specific arguments which intellectuals employed thereafter, with little change, against the Vietnam War. They put that conflict into the context of Cold War policies which the teach-in organizers believed needed reappraisal. They forced intellectuals to reconsider what it had meant for Dwight Macdonald to "choose the West." Isaac Deutscher, a renowned Marxist and biographer of Leon Trotsky, received a standing ovation from an audience of twelve thousand at the Berkeley teach-in when he declared that the "West is sick with the myths and distortions of the Cold War."[26]

Although the teach-ins started with the issue of Vietnam and foreign policy, discussions soon ranged afield because of the dissidents' stress on the relationship between domestic and foreign affairs. Critics believed that Johnson's Vietnam policy distorted national priorities. Most teach-in speakers claimed that the Vietnam War drained funds from urban and racial crises into a futile military quagmire. For example, Professor Seymour Melman stated: "The war on poverty has been transformed into war and poverty."[27] On those grounds, war critics opposed the domination of "experts" in government and related the division between humanists and technicians to the peace movement:

. . . To restrict public discussion to "experts" leads to a dangerous elitism because, in the end, decisions on foreign policy are based on value judgments, not just on a simple recording of facts. The issues on Vietnam are too important to be settled by Cold War gamesmanship or academic hairsplitting. . . . The problem of Vietnam is the problem of the *soul of America.* . . . [Italics added.] One of the purposes of Vietnam Day is to transfer the discussion from the RAND Corporation to the streets.[28]

Reference to the "soul of America" struck to the motivational core of the teach-ins. Above all, critics emphasized the moral dilemma raised by the Vietnam War. Leaders of the Vietnam Day Committee at Berkeley invoked the Nuremberg ethic: "When the state acts immorally, it is the duty of the individuals to refuse to participate in its immorality."[29] Professor Williams stressed concern with "the moral crisis involved in justifying American action by reference to the actions of others, instead of by reference to our own moral heritage and tradition and in blatantly invoking a double standard."[30] The stress on such considerations—the morality of U.S. policy, the moral imperative to protest or the immorality of silence and inaction—proved paramount in attracting leftist intellectuals to the peace movement.

IMPASSE FOR THE INTELLIGENTSIA

Moral mission or not, it was one thing for the teach-ins to reach the campus and intellectual peers, and quite another to convert the rest of the country. The air war, which precipitated the teach-in movement, struck most Americans as bold Presidential action that cut through the "Vietnam mess." Two out of three poll respondents approved Johnson's reply to the attack on Pleiku. Gallup opinion data for the 1964–69 period indicate that the average U.S. citizen judged Johnson's Vietnam policy according to two criteria: whether the President seemed "decisive" and whether he was curbing Communism. The man in the street did not ask: Is Johnson's policy militarily viable or morally right? or, Is "containment" appropriate to Southeast Asia? Nor was he

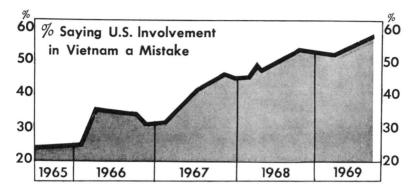

From: The Gallup Opinion Index, Report No. 52, October, 1969.

likely to do so. His Cold War mentality rested on over twenty years of unquestioned assumptions. Predictably, the Internal Security Subcommittee of the Senate Judiciary Committee discounted the teach-ins as a Communist front:

Whatever the intent of those who originated the teach-in movement, the fact is clear beyond challenge that the Communist propaganda apparatus has been able to expand and exploit the teach-in movement and the anti-Vietnam agitation in general to advance the cause of Red imperialism.

No wonder, then, that Johnson—the politician par excellence —felt not only disposed but constrained to expand U.S. involvement in Indochina. There was little the Intellectual Left could or did do to stop the Administration at that point. The number of U.S. troops in Vietnam was to grow from 25,000 when the peace movement began to more than 400,000 by the end of 1966.

That was no trend to cheer the hearts of antiwar dissidents. The historian Christopher Lasch was so discouraged by the apparent futility of countering Johnson's Vietnam policy that he advocated force:

Until the political complexion of the country is radically changed, the political liabilities of liquidating the Cold War will continue to outweigh its advantages. . . . The Administration cannot be persuaded; it has to be forced to change the direction of American policy. The real question, which critics ought to be considering, is what kind of force promises the earliest success.[31]

Professor Rapoport asserted that attacking official dogma, such as the "menace of Communism," meant invoking concepts foreign to the Administration. It might entail discussion which Presidential Assistant McGeorge Bundy, according to his correspondence with Rapoport, would not find "intellectually responsible dialogue." Even so, Rapoport reflected the argument espoused by *Studies on the Left*: Intellectuals must challenge the relevance of conventional frameworks in political science, economics, and military strategy. That meant confronting the Administration with issues of morality. It meant making clear that intellectuals did not impugn the humanity of decision-makers as people but rather the irrelevance of their humanity to the conduct of the Vietnam War. Rapoport stated:

The supreme tragedy of our time is the circumstance that it is no longer necessary to be evil in order to do evil. This is what military technology has brought about. A man has to be indeed evil . . . to kill a human being with a knife. . . . *Anyone* can sit in a comfortable control room and move levers in response to flashing lights.[32]

The Long Dark Night of the Soul

That view indicated how far the Administration and the leftist intelligentsia were diverging by mid-decade in their interpretation of evil and moral action. Moreover, it suggested how, if the intellectuals were to reach the American public, they might wreak psychic havoc within a nation previously detached from the "evil" of a depersonalized war. Some speculated that most Americans had constructed defense mechanisms against the common humanity of war victims and themselves. In Martin Buber's terms, they had converted the Vietnam they saw on television from Thou to It.[33]

Although the Johnson Administration could not completely ignore such criticism from the intellectual community, it responded with little tact or sensitivity for the intellectuals' point of view. Secretary Rusk fired the opening salvo against the teach-ins: "I sometimes wonder at the gullibility of educated men and the stubborn disregard of plain facts by men who are supposed to be helping our young to learn—especially to learn how to think."[34]

That kind of approach merely confirmed the intellectuals' fears about the insularity of an Administration itself in need of "plain facts." A statement by the Greater Boston Faculty Committee on Vietnam, signed by more than 750 faculty members and published by *The New York Times* on May 9, 1965, was representative of dissident response. State Department "truth teams" visited selected universities. The President himself remained aloof from the first phase of protests. McGeorge Bundy, instead, assumed the brunt of attack by his notorious nonappearance at the National Teach-in and his television confrontation with Professor Morgenthau on June 21, 1965.

For many intellectuals, the Administration's response to the teach-ins reeked of repressive tolerance. Joan Wallach Scott wrote of Bundy's last-minute withdrawal from the National Teach-in to cover a crisis in the Dominican Republic: "The inherent implication was a complete denial of political meaning for the teach-in—for, while the critics were talking, the Administration was not listening, but continuing its actions."[35] Carl Oglesby concluded that the teach-ins enabled "totalitarian liberals" to praise the United States as a free country permitting dissent without making clear that it ignored the substance of that radical critique.[36]

Thus, while the teach-ins mobilized many leftist intellectuals against the Vietnam War, they were frustrating experiences in the short run. As if in mock vindication of Marcuse, American society apparently absorbed the teach-ins with manageable systemic indigestion. Paraphrasing Trotsky, Irving Howe suggested that, after the initial outrage on which their titillation depended, the bourgeoisie relished the new radicals' assaults: "Oh, baby, *épater* me again. . . ."[37] It was symptomatic of the era that many radical intellectuals were to become entertainers. The revolution turned pop guerrilla theater, whether in the existential gesturings of Norman Mailer or the Yippie happenings of Abbie Hoffman. Mailer playing himself in *Esquire* came to personify the futility of a revolution betrayed in the discrepancy between rhetoric and reality.

CONFLICT BETWEEN SOUL MATES

If that fact rankled within the Intellectual Left, so did the growing perception of differences between some leftist intellectuals and their student counterparts in the peace movement. The teach-ins no sooner brought them together in shared concerns than tensions emerged. Such disparities did not prevail throughout the entire Intellectual Left. Many of its older members were more youthful than the young in their political fervor or were dupes of a romanticized juveniphilia. Still, there was a generational cleavage and it was to grow in the 1965–68 period.

Central to that conflict were the different conditions in which different generations matured politically. Jack Newfield called the thrust of youthful protest "one generation's revolt against the last one's definitions of reality."[38] More to the point, the "new radicalism" was more than a simple extension of older radical traditions in the United States. It did not draw from the discontents of the Old Left, such as the Depression or the threat of fascism or McCarthyite repression. It was derived instead from a newer desperation with the trappings of technocratic society—its amorality, its purposelessness, and lack of power for the individual.

While most older leftist intellectuals empathized with those concerns, many were hampered by the political traumas of the 1930s and the 1950s. In referring to "the odor of decayed radicalism" of Irving Howe and Sidney Hook, Hal Draper wrote:

The new radicals . . . first found Communism to be the bogey, not only of the reactionaries but also of the Establishment liberals, and finally found anti-Communism to be an overshadowing preoccupation also of a whole generation of decayed radicals, "old Leftists" of a certain type.[39]

Most young New Leftists came of political age after the 1956 watershed in the Cold War. They could not accept the vestigial anti-Stalinism in *Partisan Review*, *Commentary*, and *Dissent*.

Of even more immediate relevance, the majority of the older leftist intellectuals had not shared youth's involvement in the civil rights movement—at least beyond perfunctory praise or financing from the sidelines. As noted before, that movement's effect, though important, was indirect. There was a big difference between belated or vicarious involvement and being on the receiving end of a KKK cattle prod.

Elizabeth Hardwick, author and *New York Review* advisory editor, admitted that "the intellectual life in New York and the radical life of the Thirties" were "the worst possible preparation" for her generation's participation in the civil rights movement. She felt "intellectual pride . . . out of place" in an action-oriented, outdoor battleground that demanded "a certain youthful athleticism that would . . . rip the veins of the old Stalinists and Trotskyites."[40] The shift from previous intellectual disregard for blacks to the crowds of witnesses and confrontations between good and evil stunned her:

Looking back, it is curious to remember how small a part the Negro's existence played in the left-wing movements. The concentration on labor problems, the Soviet Union, and the Nazis left the Negro as only a footnote to be acknowledged sometime by the unions or a welfare state. That it could have come to this was unthinkable. . . .[41]

THE ROLE OF IDEOLOGY

The "unsharable experiences" of the civil rights movement—as important to young activists of the 1960s as the Spanish civil war had been for many of their predecessors in the 1930s—along with the linkage generation lost to the Eisenhower era (the "Silent Generation" of the 1950s), contributed to yet another kind of struggle. Ideology—do we need it and, if so, what kind?—was both a cause of and index for more tension between leftist intellectuals and campus radicals.

Since most of the debate over ideology revolved around questions raised by Daniel Bell at the beginning of the 1960s, both sociological justice and general utility are served by using his definition. Bell wrote of ideology: "An all-inclusive system of comprehensive reality, it is a set of beliefs, infused with passion and seeks to transform the whole of a way of life."[42] For him, ideology involved the "conversion of ideas into social levers," transforming both ideas and people and demanding a commitment to action. Passion and action infused ideology with force and meaning:

For the ideologue, truth arises in action, and meaning is given to experience by the "transforming moment." He comes alive not in contemplation, but in "the deed."[43]

Although Bell drew radical fire for proclaiming "the end of ideology,"[44] he in fact anticipated the existential orientation for the radical intellectuals' politics in the 1960s with his definition of the ideologue. Furthermore, the fact that writers from *Studies* to *The New York Review* returned repeatedly to the subject belied the "end of ideology." Ideology was, indeed, central to the very identity of that decade's re-emergent Intellectual Left.

Even so, it became the intellectual fashion of the 1960s to debate what Hal Draper called the "nonideological hang-up" of the "new radicals."[45] That was a limiting characterization of the New Left. It overlooked the movement's development over time (1962–68) and the dynamic connection between theory and practice. Although the Port Huron Statement declared, "We have no sure formulas, no closed theories," it did invoke "values," as Bell prescribed, "to transform the whole of a way of life." Action defined the theoretical construct of participatory democracy. The editors of *Studies* bore witness to the new radicals' commitment to theory and constructive ideology. To them, "the end of ideology" meant the rejection of discredited *liberal* formulas for change or rationalizations for the status quo—but not the repudiation of ideology itself.

Through the Vietnam experience, new radicals made clear to increasing numbers of intellectuals the hollowness of liberal rhetoric and the need to define truth in action. Much of the radical (as opposed to liberal) intellectuals' response to the war revolved around their effort to reclaim personal and political authenticity through a redefinition of symbolic legitimacy for the United States—in effect, a new ideology. That attempt fostered division between the young and some older intellectuals and among members of the same older generation of the Intellectual Left. Dissension flared over the following issues: the nature of the Vietnam War, the appropriate strategy for the peace movement, the desirability for Communist participation in the movement, and the meaning of pacifism and totalitarianism.

Ideological division often corresponded to or explained the different reasons for intellectual opposition to the Vietnam War. Liberal theoreticians opposed American involvement in Southeast Asia as an unfortunate miscalculation of national interest, but not one which merited scrapping the entire political system. Nathan Glazer spoke for those intellectuals who believed that "the Vietnam War must be understood as the result of a series of monumental errors." He believed that "America would not have had to be very different . . . for some President to have gotten us out of Vietnam. . . ."[46] Like most of his liberal colleagues, he rejected the "anti-institutional bias" of the radicals because he could imagine no substitute for institutions in advanced society.

Herbert Marcuse was one of the most influential spokesmen for radical intellectuals. He put their opposition to the Vietnam War into the larger context of a sweeping political critique. To him and his largely youthful brood, that conflict represented the exhaustion of American political culture. It required, therefore, a direct confrontation with the delegitimated institutions of the Johnson Administration.

The ideologically derived disagreement between Glazer and Marcuse over the nature of the Vietnam conflict divided the young and the leftist intellectuals on the *strategy* of the antiwar movement. They split over how much change was necessary to liquidate American involvement in Vietnam and whether that change could be achieved inside the political system. Liberal critics favored normal channels of dissent. Other responses ranged from those of the guerrilla warrior LeRoi Jones (now Imamu Amiri Baraka) to those of the Old Left coalitionist Irving Howe. For his counsel against "desperate" tactics and Vietcong sympathizers that might consign social reform and peace to a political cul-de-sac, Howe became the *bête noire* of the advocates of a *Realpolitik*. In fact, he stood between the radical and liberal sectors of the Intellectual Left, disowned by and disavowing both.[47] Like every intellectual of the period, he was not subject to flip classification.

"Communism" brought the ideological past of the Intellectual Left to bear on the tactical turn of peace strategy in the mid-1960s. Many intellectuals, scarred by Stalinism or impressed by the early years of the Cold War, retained an anti-Communist fastidiousness toward the peace movement. Herbert Gans typified those who felt that coalition with Communist organizations and expression of pro-Vietcong sympathy could only hurt the peace movement.[48] Most younger radicals lacked such qualms. Hence the conflict between "exclusionists" (those who wanted to keep out the Communists) and "nonexclusionists" in the SDS March on Washington in April, 1965, and in many later antiwar demonstrations.

Yet another reflection of ideological tension was the changing nature of pacifism, a kaleidoscopic philosophy of many colors in the peace movement. There was a widening gap between absolute and relative pacifists. The principle itself underwent a subtle inversion of meaning. Self-proclaimed pacifists like Staughton Lynd said that violence was necessary to change American foreign policy and achieve peace. In effect, that sector of the Intellectual Left personified by the Quaker historian disengaged itself from pacifism with respect to Vietnam.[49] Reinhold Niebuhr's "Case Against Pacifism" had anticipated the change.[50]

Interpretations of totalitarianism began to change, too—for the same reasons and with comparable consequences. Whereas the Old Left associated totalitarianism with secret police and thought control, the New Left equated it with "power"—the "power elite" of the corporations, the universities, or the "system." Because they condoned power applied with "social benevolence," new radicals could and did condemn Berkeley as totalitarian while they praised Cuba as democratic.[51] In like manner, they reflected the existentialism of Gandhi and Albert Camus by seeking peace, not just for the sake of survival but because the war machine was a *machine*. Youth and the intelligentsia found each other in the 1960s largely because of a sense of shared powerlessness. By the end of the Johnson era, it was not to be clear that they meant the same thing by power.

Despite such division within the peace movement and the seeming failure of the teach-ins, the Johnson Administration was not entirely deaf to the antiwar protests of 1965. The President was political enough to want to cover all flanks. In his speech at Johns Hopkins University on April 7, the President hoped to blunt criticism from the Intellectual Left by offering to negotiate with Hanoi and to launch a billion-dollar aid program for Southeast Asia.

The Intellectual Left was not appeased. It seized on the alleged contradictions between Presidential word and deed. George Kahin, director of the Southeast Asia Program at Cornell University, reminded Johnson: "Our [U.S.] cavalier dismissal of the UN Secretary-General's efforts hardly constituted an example of serious American interest in negotiations."[52] Morgenthau, just returned from Moscow, wrote that in Soviet eyes the constructive elements of the President's statement were "obliterated by the massive air raids on North Vietnam, following the President's speech by less than twenty-four hours."[53]

To reach its war critics, the Johnson Administration was taking steps in addition to the Johns Hopkins address. James C. Thomson, Jr., in the White House and State Department from 1961 to 1966, has related how doubters within the Administration received such regular callers as A. J. Muste and Norman Thomas. They thereby spared nondoubting policymakers such encounters and left them free to pursue policy as usual. Johnson himself invited Walter Lippmann for an advance reading of his Johns Hopkins "peace" speech. That gesture impressed many critics until they learned that the President had accepted the venerable journalist's plaudits while posing for a sculptor.

INSURRECTION IN SANTO DOMINGO

In the midst of the rising furor over Vietnam, a revolt erupted in the Dominican Republic on April 24, 1965. To American intellectuals, Johnson's explanations of U.S. involvement in that Caribbean nation seemed irrelevant; his reconstruction of events debatable; and his reversal of motives, unforgivable. In short, Johnson's policy in the Dominican Republic compounded the credibility crisis being raised by Vietnam.

Suddenly, Marines seemed to be landing everywhere. Johnson's dispatch of troops confirmed the intellectuals' original estimate of the President as impetuous, prone to military solutions, and hostile to all potentially Communist revolutionary movements. Johnson appalled intellectuals when he rationalized the landing of Marines in terms of the need to protect American lives but reserved the option to use American forces against a possible Communist take-over. Johnson wanted to avoid "another Cuba." Rusk related events in the Dominican Republic to a global Communist conspiracy which could affect the American position everywhere, but especially in Vietnam. Therefore the Administration shifted its argument for U.S. intervention to stress countering the threat of a Communist coup d'état.

That change, combined with the circumvention of the Organization of American States and the fresh memory of Johnson's escalation in Vietnam, suggested a pattern which intellectuals, clearly, did not like. First, in both cases, the President moved subtly from one purpose to another in order to justify his action. In Vietnam, he had shifted from reprisal raids for civil insurrection to systematic bombings against foreign infiltration. In the Dominican Republic, he moved from a limited response to the American embassy's plea for protection of U.S. nationals to wider involvement to thwart a Communist uprising. Second, both at Pleiku and in Santo Domingo, Johnson attempted to cover his political position and international responsibilities by what he considered minimal action. In both cases, the President's effort to protect himself politically worked to his disadvantage with most intellectuals.

The intelligentsia's criticism mounted because of what Johnson did and how he explained himself. Like the Spanish-American War of 1898, Johnson's foray into the Dominican Republic aroused little *general* controversy because it ended quickly and with a modicum of American success. The public had a short memory in foreign affairs. Not so the intellectuals who added Johnson's intervention in Santo Domingo to the mix of grievances fostering their reradicalization.[54]

Partisan Review launched a series of essays addressed to that process. The title: "Is There a New Radicalism?" Nat Hentoff and Michael Harrington opened the symposium by answering "Yes." Hentoff asserted:

There are . . . the beginnings of a consensus about the irrelevancy of most traditional American radical styles and a corollary recognition— often more visceral than ideological—of both the root failures of the present society and the prospects of a far worse "society of technical necessity" (using Jacques Ellul's term) unless there is a fundamental change in values as well as in institutions.[55]

In terms of foreign policy, Hentoff assumed that new radicals opposed "unilateral and quite hypocritical involvements like our presence in South Vietnam." He believed that a "spirit of expanding humanism" should supplant the "Cold War game of dominoes" and that "the only realistic way to change our foreign policy is to build domestic political power first."

Harrington spoke more guardedly of a "small, but growing, minority . . . conscious of the need for basic transformations."[56] The transition from the Cold War era still portended "fearful 'ifs' of war and peace" beyond the control of the peace movement. With the superpowers still balancing their terrors and escalation of the Vietnam conflict threatening World War III, Harrington concluded that "it is in this international sphere that the Left of the Sixties is furthest from power."

Thereafter, the symposium degenerated into fashionable sparring over tactics. Yet all contributors to the series joined in what Irving Howe termed the "general weariness with chauvinism, hysteria, and mindless anti-Communism" (p. 342). All agreed that "confrontations with power forces" were the "effect and cause of the new radicalism" (Bayard Rustin, p. 526). All stressed that intellectuals needed new bases of power (Stephen Rousseas, p. 353, and Nat Hentoff, p. 372). But then, what else could they do but sever their umbilical link to the labor proletariat, with AFL-CIO President George Meany calling critics of American policy in Vietnam and the Dominican Republic "intellectual jitterbugs and nitwits"?

> *If World War II was like* Catch 22, *this war will be like* Naked Lunch.
>
> Norman Mailer
> *Partisan Review*, 1965

By June, 1965, the 50,000 American troops in Vietnam were authorized for "combat support" and 20,000 more were on the way. President Johnson enjoyed unflinching support in the polls. His military escalation seemed a political masterpiece. Its genius eluded only the national press, which turned against what Tom Wicker of *The New York Times* called "the Second Empire,"[57] and the leftist intelligentsia, where the momentum begun by the teach-ins simply accelerated.

The Long Dark Night of the Soul

In that mood, intellectuals seized upon the announcement of a White House Festival of the Arts, scheduled for June 14, 1965. It looked like a unique chance to lodge their antiwar protest in the very residence of the Chief Executive. The Festival was conceived by Eric Goldman as a gesture toward the nation's foremost writers, poets, artists, musicians, and patrons of the arts. Instead, it turned into a platform for leftist intellectual opposition to the Vietnam War and furious Presidential reaction, which only widened the gap between the two.[58]

The crisis broke when the poet Robert Lowell wrote to President Johnson that he felt "conscience-bound" to decline his invitation to the Festival.[59] Goldman argued with Lowell to no avail that guests should apply no policy test to their host since the President had employed none toward them. He stressed that the intelligentsia and the Administration should work together to broaden appreciation for the arts. A contretemps would only insult the office and person of the President and foreclose Johnson's already meager receptivity to intellectuals. Lowell felt that his attendance would express support for official policy in the Dominican Republic and Vietnam, which he considered morally reprehensible. Accordingly, he had already sent his letter to *The New York Times*, which gave it front-page coverage on June 3.

The refusal of one of America's leading poets to appear at a cultural occasion hosted by the President of the United States had both immediate and continuing, real and symbolic significance. For many intellectuals, the man who stayed away dominated the Festival. Eric Bentley saluted the "historic importance" of Lowell's absence and likened that "critical act" to Yevgeny Yevtushenko's stand against Soviet anti-Semitism.[60]

Goldman singled out *The New York Review* as a prime instigator in the intellectuals' attack on President Johnson and his foreign policy during the Festival. He claimed that the journal's inner circle "had gone along with President Johnson in the early phase of his Administration, approving his domestic policies but with a marked distaste for his Administration in general and for him personally." He contended that "almost all became emotional and contemptuous opponents of Johnson's escalation of the Vietnam War."[61]

Robert Silvers, joint editor of *The New York Review*, learned of Lowell's action from Elizabeth Hardwick, the poet's wife and one of the *NYR* staff. Together with the poet Stanley J. Kunitz, Silvers drafted a telegram to President Johnson. They declared support for Lowell and affixed an impressive array of intellectuals' signatures.[62] Silvers stated later that the President was trying to "use" Lowell "to present a false front to the world that writers and artists are backing the Vietnam War." He believed that there was a "moral duty to attack the festival." He felt that "the plain politics of the situation" dictated making Lowell's withdrawal "hurt Johnson as much as possible with intellectuals and artists who voted for him in 1964."[63] Saul Bellow, Ralph Ellison, and Roger Stevens complained to Goldman of fierce denunciations and hints of professional blackmail from the New York intelligentsia because of their participation in the Festival.

Although Dwight Macdonald signed the Silvers-Kunitz telegram, he accepted his invitation from the White House and agreed to cover the Festival for *The New York Review*. During the events, he circulated a pro-Lowell petition which six guests signed. In his subsequent article, Macdonald asserted that the Festival tried "to give the Johnson Administration a cultural image, a consensus of artists and writers reciprocating 'the White House's great interest in the arts,'" but that the gathering lacked "practically the entire literary establishment, from Edmund Wilson to Thornton Wilder."[64] He bewailed the plight of Goldman, "caught like Polonius . . . between the fell and incensed points of mighty antagonists." As for the relationship between the intelligentsia and the Administration, Macdonald maintained that Johnson's policies were alienating the intellectuals from both the President and the public:

The President's "forward" policies in Vietnam and the Dominican Republic have not only . . . alarmed and disgusted the intelligentsia . . . so much as to split them off from him, but they have also produced another split, between the intelligentsia and the rest of the country, which is getting as marked as it was during the McCarthy era.[65]

Goldman concluded glumly that the White House Festival had been an "unmitigated disaster." To him, it seemed that the nation had reached a point "where one section of the population, filled with a sense of elitism and snobbery about its ability to take action, was in hopeless confrontation with another segment, equally filled with its own elitism and snobbery about its cultural superiority." The intellectuals "needed some sense that just because they had read Macdonald in *The New York Review* and could discuss Calder's 'Whale' knowledgeably, they had not attained final omniscience in public policy. . . ."[66] The President faced domestic and foreign challenges of such magnitude that he particularly needed the kind of insight he might have found when John Hersey read from *Hiroshima* how wars can get out of hand. Instead, Johnson exploded against "these people," "Don't they know I'm the only President they've got and a war is on?" Just as Goldman had feared, the intellectuals' attack offended Johnson personally and his notion of respect for the Presidency.

His sensitivity to the intellectuals was not new. The Texan had long suffered from comparison to his Bostonian predecessor. Many intellectuals played upon that sense of inferiority by elevating a Rabelasian caricature of Johnson's style to a matter of substance. Responding to a question on the "meaning of the split between the Administration and the intellectuals," Susan Sontag was to say later:

When (and if) the man in the White House who paws people and scratches his balls in public is replaced by the man who dislikes being touched and finds Yevtushenko "an interesting fellow," American intellectuals won't be so disheartened.[67]

Postscript: The President, finally, blamed Goldman for the behavior of the leftist intellectuals. He was convinced that "some of them tried to insult me by staying away and some of them tried to insult me by coming." Goldman lost what little influence he had enjoyed with the President and resigned in August, 1965. In his review of Goldman's *The Tragedy of Lyndon Johnson,* Walter Goodman characterized the Goldman tenure as an "arrangement . . . programmed for failure." He admitted that "there will be a tendency among the intelligentsia to conclude, not without relish, that Goldman only suffered the humiliation due to anyone who allows himself to be coopted by the enemy."[68]

Vice-President Humphrey persuaded Johnson to replace Goldman with John P. Roche, chairman of the Department of Politics at Brandeis University and former chairman of Americans for Democratic Action. Roche's prowar position and disdain for liberal war critics put the sincerity of Administration desires to communicate with the dissident intelligentsia further into question.[69] Irving Howe wrote that "the appointment of the egregious John P. Roche as the President's advisor on intellectual affairs is a sufficient sign of official contempt."[70] Professor Roche exacerbated the problem of intellectual disaffection by "berating the customers."[71] He stated in an interview with Jimmy Breslin:

These alienated intellectuals? Who are they? Mainly the New York artsy-crafty set. They're in the *Partisan Review* and the *New York Review* and publications like that. The West Side jackal bins, I call them. They intend to launch a revolution from Riverside Drive. Names, there are plenty of names who write for them. Alfred Kazin writes, then Irving Howe, Dr. Spock, Norman Mailer. . . .[72]

CONTROVERSY OVER PEACE TALKS

No matter how satisfying the protest at the White House was for some leftist intellectuals, most could still not forget the continuing escalation of the Vietnam War. For that reason, they focused on the issue of negotiations during the latter half of 1965.

"Negotiations" had long been a forbidden word in the Johnson White House. That changed, however, with the President's Johns Hopkins speech. Thereafter, the Administration stressed negotiations as an integral part of the Vietnam policy. The official strategy was to convince the Vietcong and the North Vietnamese by force of arms that continued fighting would be too costly and that they should seek a negotiated settlement.

Rather than applauding that new policy, intellectuals questioned the morality and viability of an approach they interpreted as peace through force.[73] To them, Johnson's policy on negotiations sprang from delusions about history, national interest, human psychology, and the balance of power and public opinion in Asia. They believed that American escalation hindered the possibilities for negotiations. On the one hand, it stiffened enemy morale and increased their gains. On the other, it tempted the Administration to believe that it could win by fighting. With Johnson invoking the lessons of Munich as he doubled the monthly draft call, *New Republic* writers asserted, "There is far more danger from escalation than there is of a 'Munich.'"[74]

There was a further ironic twist to the situation. Leftist intellectuals believed that the Administration was stalling on negotiations in 1965 because it thought it could win militarily in Vietnam, whereas it had avoided negotiations in 1964 because it feared a collapse of the Saigon regime and military defeat. The peace talks, once precluded by weakness in the U.S. bargaining position, seemed blocked just as conclusively by the Administration's new strength.[75]

Eugene V. Rostow's response to *The New York Review*'s "A Special Supplement: Getting Out of Vietnam" showed how the Administration and the Intellectual Left went their separate ways on the issue of negotiations. Their different attitudes toward Communism and China came into play. Rostow wrote:

The Long Dark Night of the Soul

The position of your authors recalls that of some liberal and left-wing isolationists at the time of the Nazi-Soviet pact in 1939. We can expect another "God That Failed" from some, and from others, the discovery that our action in Vietnam is not "an imperialist war" after all, but an heroic effort to protect the innocent people of Asia from domination by a despotism worse than that of Stalin.[76]

Hans Morgenthau rejected Rostow's statement as proof of the "new demonology in which China has replaced the Soviet Union as the source of all evil."[77] Like many of his colleagues, Morgenthau opposed the Vietnam War largely because he thought it would not only fail to contain China but would expand Chinese power. In a similar spirit, *The New Republic* editors discounted Rostow's stress on inflammatory Chinese rhetoric because Peking's denunciations were "matched by the prudence of their deeds."[78] That was more than most leftist intellectuals were prepared to say for the United States.

WAR IN THE PEACE CAMP

That consensus notwithstanding, all was not well in the peace movement by late 1965. Although most of the Intellectual Left joined in opposing Johnson's policy of escalation-cum-negotiation, it split more and more over how to express that dissent. The tension between the intelligentsia and politically active youth was just part of the story.

Even within the older, more established Left, literary and academic, there was division over what the war meant and what to do about it. Views ranged from the polite protest of writers for *The Nation* and *The New Republic* through the intermediate position of *Commentary, Dissent,* and *The Public Interest* to the "radical chic" of *The New York Review*—and to journals beyond the purview of this book. Lines of argument were to rigidify over time into fierce political alignments.

True to its heritage since 1914, *The New Republic* expressed the liberal intellectuals' view on antiwar dissent. Its writers wanted President Johnson to seek a negotiated settlement. At the same time, they understood the political pressures on him. The journal's editors focused nervously on the "Republicans who stand ready to lambaste the Democrats either for being too 'soft' or too 'hard.' "[79] Edgar Snow admitted that "practical politicians do not risk the national self-esteem by correcting mistakes which still enjoy voter confidence."[80]

Because most liberal intellectuals interpreted Johnson's delay on negotiations as a reflection of his political dilemma and the war as an aberration from a generally honorable foreign policy, they approached the idea of a "peace movement" cautiously. They hoped to persuade the President through "reasonable" means that he would have support for American withdrawal from Vietnam. They wanted to create a counterweight to what the polls seemed to be telling Johnson in late 1965. To them, protest meant well-publicized marches like those which encouraged John Kennedy toward a test-ban treaty with the Soviet Union in the early 1960s.

Slightly to the left of the liberal writers were the self-styled democratic radicals. Irving Howe, the editor of *Dissent*, best personified their position.[81] Like his liberal colleagues, he stressed the largely domestic determinants of Johnson's war strategy. He considered the President a politician for whom "the matter of right and wrong cannot be separated from an estimate of political possibilities and a measure of the conflicting forces that bring their weight to bear upon the government."[82] He marveled at the "President's mania for admiration and 'consensus' "—"almost a caricature of national character." In view of Johnson's sensitivity and public indifference to foreign affairs, Howe believed that a vocal and organized intelligentsia could wield disproportionate influence:

Intellectuals, having lost much of their political bite, have gained in political influence; perhaps now, if they bite a little harder, it will be worth having the influence. Protests, teach-ins, counterproposals do not go unheard.[83]

The "Joint Statement on the Vietnam Protest Movement," drafted by Howe, Michael Harrington, Bayard Rustin, and Lewis Coser, defined the "democratic-radical" or "coalitionist" approach.[84] Its point of view served as a counterpoise throughout the Johnson period to the radicals' opposition to the Vietnam War or what Howe called the "authoritarian Left." In that statement, democratic radicals stressed the "legitimacy of protest against a policy that has never been seriously debated in Congress or candidly presented to the country." They dismissed Johnson's argument that dissent prolonged the war by encouraging the enemy. They condemned the Administration for overreacting to protests: "A nation tracing its origins to the Boston Tea Party ought not to become so jittery over the possibilities of a few burned cards."

What of support from the people at large? Given their premise of growing popular uneasiness about the Vietnam War, the democratic radicals believed that the peace movement could succeed with a "reasonable program of 'demands' appropriate to the present situation" and geared to larger numbers of people. They opposed explicit or covert support to the Vietcong. That was "both a tactical necessity and a moral obligation, since any ambiguity on this score makes impossible, as well as undeserved, the support of large numbers of the American people." They resisted making the draft the central issue of the anti-Vietnam movement. To do so would blur the "crucial difference . . . between individual moral objection and a political protest movement" and "forego in advance any possibility of affecting U.S. policy in the immediate future." They considered recourse to civil disobedience a legitimate but *ultimate* expression of dissent. For example, they questioned the protesters' right to stop troop trains in California, since that involved "an action by a small minority to revoke through its own decision the policy of a democratically elected government—which is something very different indeed from public protest against that government's decision or efforts to pressure it into changes of policy." Such "symbolic" interference only underscored the "impotence" of the peace movement and alienated potential adherents: "A 'revolutionary' tactic in a decidedly non-revolutionary situation is likely to do little more than increase the isolation of those who undertake it."[85]

Democratic radicals were among the first on the Intellectual Left to stress—and continue to stress—the tension between political and moral considerations raised by protest against the Vietnam War. They thus anticipated a growing division among leftist intellectuals between liberals and democratic radicals on the one hand and radicals and revolutionaries on the other over the problems of political responsibility and strategy for the peace movement. Since most Americans in 1965 still favored the "bad" Vietnam policy, they asked intellectuals to face "the conflict between the democratic idea as the will of the majority and the democratic idea as the embodiment of certain values."[86] The editors of *Dissent* contended that recourse to resistance implied that intellectuals had given up on the possibility to affect the public on the Vietnam question. David McReynolds, field secretary of the War Resisters' League, felt that popular acquiescence to government policy in Vietnam and the Dominican Republic obviated discussion of "democratic politics." He reacted like a modern Thoreau who believed that it was more important to uphold the moral law than to submit to the government. Lewis Coser warned *Dissent* readers, however, against those radicals who gratified their consciences at the expense of a Weberian ethics of political responsibility. He claimed, "To subsume the political under the ethical leads to political futility."[87]

Commentary deserves comparable billing with *Dissent* in any discussion of democratic radicals, even though its writers would probably never have used that term to describe themselves. *Commentary* is additionally important for showing how the Indochina conflict took its toll within one of the most important parts of America's interlocking intellectual elite—the New York "family."

Norman Podhoretz, editor of *Commentary,* took special pride in his role in the political wars of the 1960s. The Vietnam War became the focal point in those intellectual skirmishes, particularly between *Commentary* and *The New York Review.* Though Podhoretz said that he had opposed U.S. involvement in Vietnam since 1962, he did so on political grounds. It was a neo-containment position he attributed to Hans Morgenthau. He stated that "there have been war crimes, but the war itself is not a criminal war."[88] His view of Vietnam, in opposition to that of writers for *The New York Review* like Jason Epstein,[89] pushed the two men and their journals further and further apart during the 1960s. While Vietnam radicalized *The New York Review,* it "deradicalized"—Podhoretz's own term—*Commentary.* That was particularly true of Podhoretz himself and his wife, Midge Decter, a frequent writer for *Commentary* and subsequently literary editor of Norman Cousins's *Saturday Review/World.* According to Podhoretz, the "anti-Americans" emerged as the enemy in the 1960s, just as the "un-Americans" had done in the previous decade of *Commentary.* If the radicalized intellectuals were to become isolated within U.S. society by the 1970s, Podhoretz was to assume an even lonelier perch within the Intellectual Left.

SHIFT TO THE LEFT

The first real precursor of that political isolation came on November 27, 1965. The occasion was the antiwar March on Washington, sponsored by the National Committee for a Sane Nuclear Policy (SANE).[90]

At first the event reflected little more than the then prevailing doldrums of the protest movement. The thirty thousand marchers attracted to Washington hardly undercut the Johnsonian consensus. The meeting of the march's organizers only emphasized the tensions between radical and liberal dissidents. Their infighting on procedure and organization recalled the sectarianism of the 1930s. To young militants, it seemed clear that the liberals' emphasis on respectability would not dissuade the President from his course. Worse, it would impede the radicalization which they thought massive marches and civil disruption could engender.

At that point, Carl Oglesby, president of SDS and the program's only "movement" speaker, electrified the gathering with his speech on "Liberalism and the Corporate State."[91] He thus gave that march and the peace movement in general a new thrust. Oglesby rejected compromise, condemned liberals for supporting the "system" despised by the New Left, and said of the liberal Establishment:

We do not say these men are evil. We say rather that men can be divided from their compassion by the institutional system that inherits us all. People become instruments. Generals do not hear the screams of the bombed, and sugar executives do not see the misery of the cane-cutters; for to do so is to be that much *less* the general, that much *less* the executive.[92]

Oglesby's charge recalled Bernard Fall's censure of "depersonalization" and Anatol Rapoport's contention that "it is no longer necessary to be evil in order to do evil." It demonstrated again that the intellectuals' opposition to the Vietnam War arose primarily from moral considerations and that the Administration and the intelligentsia disagreed on how the United States should fulfill American values.

To those who condemned Oglesby for sounding anti-American, he retorted: "Don't blame *me* for *that*! Blame those who mouthed my liberal values and broke my American heart."[93]

His speech signaled the ascendance of radicalism in the peace movement. Thereafter, emphasis was to rest on radical reconstruction of the American society. Liberalism supplanted conservatism as a prime target for many leftist intellectuals. Radical critics came to blame liberals for the *embourgeoisement* of blacks, the decay of the cities, the bureaucratization of the universities, and the distortion of national priorities. They eventually condemned liberals for the Vietnam War and its contribution to the foregoing complex of problems. Tom Hayden was to be typical when he subsequently absolved "Birchite generals" and rednecks, only to turn against "Democratic bureaucrats" and "affluent liberalism."[94] In that sense, Hayden personified the radicalizing peace movement which became the collective battering ram against America's liberal superstructure.

Liberal admonitions began to sound tepid and establishmentarian, compared to the more romantic call to the barricades. Many in the Intellectual Left, craving the total commitment that implied, could not resist the summons. Mailer and Macdonald were back in the march of events, quite literally, for the first time in fifteen years. It seemed that much of the Intellectual Left was coming home again.

Staughton Lynd's response to the democratic radicals' "Statement on the Vietnam Protest Movement" reflected the post-SANE radicalized sentiments aglow on the Intellectual Left by late 1965. Lynd defended extreme forms of protest as a stimulant to more moderate dissent. He saw nothing wrong in desiring a Vietcong victory in South Vietnam or flying Vietcong flags in protest marches in America. He upheld the connection between using civil disobedience in both the civil rights and peace movements: "Isn't the effort in the one case as in the other to make the nation live up to concepts which it had endorsed in the abstract but which it had failed to practice?"[95] If blocking troop trains was an illegitimate act of a small minority, he wondered about the President's "Tuesday luncheon club—a very small minority indeed —who revoked through their own decision the policy to which they had pledged themselves in the 1964 election campaign."[96] Lynd's expression of the radical intellectuals' view on dissent represented a step beyond the protest strategy of the liberals and democratic radicals. It lagged only behind the violence, revolution, or anarchy advocated by the outer reaches of the Left— beyond the scope of this book.

Response to a statement "On Vietnam and the Dominican Republic" demonstrated in yet another quarter the radical turn in the leftist intellectuals' reaction against Johnson's Vietnam policy.[97] The statement itself in *Partisan Review* was restrained in tone and argument. Its signers lamented "the increasing and often self-defeating military involvements" of U.S. policy in Vietnam. However, they also asked that critics base their opposition to the war on "more than the apolitical assumption that power politics, the Cold War, and Communists are merely American inventions." In their estimation, neither the policies of the United States nor those of North Vietnam, Communist China, or the Vietcong promoted the signatories' desire for "a world in which free societies can exist." "Military action," they asserted, "can be a substitute for political foresight only if we propose to police the whole world; and to imagine that we can do that is to lack even hindsight." They concluded that "the time has come for some new thinking."

Respondents to the *Partisan Review* statement were united in opposing both the Vietnam War and that journal's declaration of opinion. Its moderation and anti-Communist emphasis were especially offensive. Marshall Cohen stated:

The Administration's not infrequent displays of disingenuousness, ineptitude and wrong-headedness are the more pertinent objects of criticism. I had hoped that *Partisan Review* was entering a period in which it would show less zeal in policing the American Left than it has on some occasions in the past. Do you take it for your Caribbean?[98]

Marcuse considered the *Partisan Review* statement "outspoken in its opposition to the American policy at the same time making assumptions which all but invalidate this opposition."[99] Harold

Rosenberg had refused to sign the original statement because "what comes through is the intellectual format of the paralyzing anti-Communist *Realpolitik* of the McCarthy days."[100] Macdonald opposed the declaration because "it asks American intellectuals to reopen a question many of us have come to consider closed: whether there is any justification, moral or in terms of national self-interest, for President Johnson's recent military adventures in Santo Domingo and Vietnam." New thinking? Macdonald's was done; if anyone was to indulge in reformulations, "Let McGeorge do it."[101]

Mailer responded with greatest length and venom, invoking antiwar animus, alienation from pop culture, and the horror of nuclear devastation. To him, *Partisan Review*'s words "read like they were written in milk and milk of magnesia." For all their "somber dubiety" and reservations, they constituted support for the war. Mailer condemned the journal for liberal rhetoric and a rationalization of the Administration's policy, which were worse than the war itself. As far as Mailer could determine, "We have an accelerating war whose justification by the Establishment is that there is final and historic honor in fighting an unpopular war if the cause is grave and just." He advocated U.S. withdrawal from Asia and disparaged *Partisan Review*'s concern with Communism because a "Communist bureaucrat is not likely to do any more harm or destroy any more spirit than a wheeler-dealer, a platoon sergeant, or a corporation executive overseas."[102] He concluded that, if World War II had been a cruel absurdity, the Vietnam conflict was an obscenity: "If World War II was like *Catch-22*, this war will be like *Naked Lunch*."[103]

Finally, Susan Sontag considered the *Partisan Review* declaration a "presumptuous reading of the language of the earlier statements." She agreed that petitions and ads taken out in *The New York Times* were only a gesture and did not supply information or sustained analysis. She admitted that "the existence of I. F. Stone putting out his *Weekly* and writing in *The New York*

Review is probably worth more than all the statements put together." But, in analyzing the experiences for herself and her fellow intellectuals, she stressed that "the statements do have a certain primitive educational effect—if only on the people who are moved to sign them, and then find themselves 'having' a position, having 'taken' a stand." She concluded by stressing the need for more emotional appeals against foreign policy because of the necessity to re-educate America:

Apart from the sustained analysis of American foreign policy that can be conducted by informed students of world affairs like George Lichtheim and Oscar Gass and Hans Morgenthau (it would be foolish for the average intellectual or writer to claim competence in these matters), there is a place for a more emotional kind of appeal and attempt at re-educating America, as represented by the earlier petitions and statements.

She continued:

Most Americans are possessed by a profound chauvinism that is existential rather than ideological: they really do not believe that other countries, other ways of life, *exist*—in the way that they, and theirs, do. . . . Whatever challenges this chauvinism, which is the basis of American consensus on foreign policy, is good—however simplified and unelaborated.[104]

Partisan Review's statement, in short, struck most leftist intellectuals as proof that *PR* itself most needed the "new thinking" it urged on its readers. A victim of its anti-Stalinist heritage, *Partisan Review* turned out to be as vulnerable as the Johnson Administration to the views of the reradicalized Intellectual Left.

STATUS AT YEAR'S END

The magazine's plight bespoke a deeper disarray among intellectuals in late 1965. After the bombardment of North Vietnam and the subsequent spring of teach-ins, the intelligentsia had emerged quickly as a political force opposed to the Vietnam War and its progenitive "system." Yet 1965 ended with dissension hard on the heels of the leftist intellectuals' new sense of political unity and group awareness. They harbored a variety of "reality worlds" revolving around a hot war fired by the Cold War. They were divided among themselves and isolated from their President and the people. Evaluating the situation for *The New Republic,* Tom Wicker saw opposition to the President only "among the obnoxious Klansmen and their ilk . . . and a handful of students and academics and pacifists . . .—groups linked by nothing but their positions on the opposite outer edges of the political spectrum."[105] How conclusive Johnson's political triumph with the public and over the intelligentsia would be in "the Second Empire" remained to be seen.

HOMAGE TO THE HAWK

Wherever the standard of freedom and independence has been or shall be unfurled, there will be America's heart. . . . But she does not go abroad in search of monsters to destroy. She is the well-wisher to the freedom and independence of all. She is the champion and vindicator only of her own. . . . She well knows that by once enlisting under other banners than her own . . . she would involve herself beyond the power of extrication, in all wars of interest and intrigue . . . which assume the colors and usurp the standards of freedom. The fundamental maxims of her policy would insensibly change from liberty to force.

John Quincy Adams
Quoted by George Kennan in Senate
Vietnam hearings, February 10, 1966

In China, 1966 was the Year of the Horse. To American leftist intellectuals, it seemed more like the Year of the Hawk. The Johnson Administration widened U.S. involvement in Vietnam with increased military appropriations, air bombardments, and troop levels. Efforts toward peace came to naught, despite the intercessions of U Thant, Pope Paul VI, Indian Prime Minister Indira Gandhi, and former British Prime Minister Anthony Eden, Earl of Avon. The American military presence in Thailand became explicit. Shortly after the Honolulu Conference with South Vietnamese leaders (February 6–8), President Johnson disavowed any desire to escalate the war. At the same time, he stated that additional troops would be sent as required. On June 29, American planes conducted the first of continuing attacks on oil installations around Hanoi and Haiphong. While visiting Saigon in August, Richard Nixon suggested that 500,000 American troops were needed to shorten the war. On November 5, Secretary McNamara said that the number of American troops in Vietnam would continue to grow. During the Christmas holidays, Harrison Salisbury of *The New York Times* contradicted the Administration by reporting from North Vietnam that American planes had bombed civilian targets.

BOMBING VERSUS NEGOTIATIONS

Intellectual cynicism festered as the Administration continued to escalate bombing while devoting what was alleged to be *pro forma* attention to negotiations. The more Johnson talked about talks, the further they seemed from his real policy priority, the belief in and need for military victory in Vietnam. It was neither the first nor last time critics were to seize on the gap between official action and rhetoric—under Johnson and Nixon.

The New Republic's editors termed the bombing pause (December 24, 1965–January 31, 1966) "a bit of blackmail, as if the President were saying 'sit down or I'll knock you down.'" Like the North Vietnamese and Russians, they suspected that the entire "Johnson peace offensive" was a "Texas trick."[106] At midsummer they wrote: "Secretary McNamara and Secretary Rusk are still reaching out like somnambulists for the Holy Grail of military victory, and one doesn't negotiate a victory. . . ."[107] To underscore the same point, *The New York Review* featured the "untold story" of U Thant's attempt to launch negotiations in late 1964, even though Eric Sevareid had broken the story a year before.[108]

Three examples of contradictory public diplomacy fed the intellectuals' suspicions about the Administration's real resolve to end the war peaceably. First, President Johnson announced the resumption of American air strikes against North Vietnam on January 31 at the same time he told Arthur Goldberg, U.S. ambassador to the United Nations, to ask that the Security Council seek an international conference to end the war. The abrupt reversal of policy, plus the inconsistency of the announcements, angered critics. Philip Ben wrote:

What had earlier seemed a futile initiative, but one at least dictated by good intentions, now seemed a cynical maneuver, aimed not at mobilizing international opinion for Mr. Johnson's effort to get the other side talking, but at giving something to "doves" at home, the "hawks" having been rewarded by the resumption of the raids.[109]

Johnson's preoccuption with balancing domestic factions hampered the credibility and viability of his Vietnam policy. That was true abroad, where observers could hardly appreciate Johnson's subterranean political motivation, and at home, where intellectuals viewed his quest for consensus as crass manipulation of the public.

Second, many leftist intellectuals believed that President Johnson used the hastily summoned Honolulu Conference to upstage the nationally televised Vietnam hearings before the Senate Foreign Relations Committee (January 28–February 18, 1966).[110] To counter the testimony of witnesses like Lieutenant General James M. Gavin and Professor George F. Kennan, President Johnson declared that those who "counsel retreat" from the war "belong to a group that has always been blind to experience and deaf to hope."

105

Third, Ambassador Goldberg presented a peace plan to the United Nations on September 22 at the same time Secretary McNamara announced intensified bombardment of North Vietnam and President Johnson disclosed his participation in the Manila Conference for war allies. *The New Republic* editors wondered how anyone could "reconcile UN Ambassador Arthur Goldberg's hopes for peace talks with Defense Secretary McNamara's brisk preparations for heavier fighting."[111] To many dissidents, the Manila Conference only postponed peace in Vietnam since the participants barely mentioned negotiations and never discussed a bombing halt. Administration leaders seemed to speak at cross-purposes, with hawks in the ascendant. Comparing the Goldberg statement with the Manila communiqué on October 25, *The New Republic* observed that "the meaning of Manila is that the U.S. and its 'Asian allies' . . . prefer to 'win the war'; and in Mr. Johnson's ugly phrase to 'bring back that coonskin on the wall.' "[112]

Increased bombing was related to this credibility gap on negotiations. Intellectuals opposed the air warfare on several counts. First, as noted above, they believed that it thwarted peace talks. Second, they thought that the Administration knew that it had oversold the benefits of bombing but did not dare admit its mistake. They interpreted the situation as a tragifarce. The government only worsened it by regularizing bombing near Hanoi and Haiphong and then denying the shift in policy from delaying North Vietnamese supply lines in transit to destroying them at their source.[113]

Third, intellectuals continued to contend that bombing increased the enemy's resistance and the infiltration it was designed to combat. I. F. Stone and Bernard Fall noted that even General Edward Lansdale, the Air Force's most experienced antiguerrilla expert, said that indiscriminate bombing helped Vietcong recruitment.[114]

Fourth, expanded American bombing made intellectuals wonder when the Chinese might decide that they had to respond militarily to U.S. intervention. As they pondered what they considered Washington's abysmal record in understanding Peking, intellectuals feared that the Johnson Administration could miscalculate Chinese intentions. They believed that the government was either misinterpreting China's toughening line on the Vietnam War or creating a self-fulfilling prophecy of eventual conflict with China.[115] They bemoaned the Administration's tendency to repeat the mistakes of pre-1933 American policy toward the Soviet Union. Jean Lacouture wondered "whether some leaders in Washington are committed not to 'self-determination' but to preserving South Vietnam as a military base for the containment of China." He referred to the essay in which George Lichtheim suggested that the main American objective was to maintain a strong presence in Vietnam for the day when Communist China would possess a nuclear force.[116]

Finally, contrary to official assertions, many critics stressed that Asians feared the United States more than they feared China. Alex Campbell, managing editor of *The New Republic*, concluded after a trip through the Far East that Asians were "less shocked by China's possession of nuclear weapons than they were by this country's use of them in Japan. . . ."[117] For all these reasons, intellectuals were elated when the Senate Foreign Relations Committee opened its "China hearings" in March, 1966.

LEADERS ALOOF

I would almost say that my country is like a conquered province with foreign rulers, except that they are not foreigners and we are responsible for what they do.

Paul Goodman
Like a Conquered Province, 1966

As the year progressed, however, many intellectuals believed that the Johnson Administration was isolating itself more and more from criticism, hardening its positions, and confusing or alienating the nation through contradictory statements and news management. The President's reluctance to hold press conferences and his use of the Tonkin Gulf Resolution to circumvent debate on the war particularly offended liberal writers.[118] The Administration's refusal to recognize the Vietcong and its defense of the Saigon regime in the face of widespread Buddhist rebellion suggested to critics that American diplomacy had fallen "victim to its own myths."[119] Lacouture claimed that "in the light of Mr. Rusk's performance the diplomacy of J. F. Dulles must be reconsidered and credited with an admirable flexibility."[120]

When President Johnson used the midterm election campaign to condemn protest as disloyalty to "our boys," *The New Republic* complained that officials "lecture, moralize and strike at straw men, but they do not come to terms with the real points the critics have been making."[121] The President seemed to lack that extra dimension of statesmanship which might ease the country out of a war he had magnified into a point of national honor.[122] Worse, he appeared to use his power over public information to slant news in his favor. The impression of "managed news," in turn, became a *cause célèbre* among intellectuals. Ronald Steel explained how critics interpreted Johnson's public diplomacy as a perversion of American democracy:

There is now a growing belief that the Tonkin Gulf incident . . . was, if not entirely fabricated, almost certainly provoked by the U.S. Government. Whatever the merits of the war, this is not a policy which can be shrugged off lightly, for it is central to the whole concept of government by consent. An Administration which deliberately manipulates the press and the Congress thereby manipulates the people as well. Whatever this may be, it is not democracy as it is understood by Americans.[123]

With Bill Moyers's resignation and Harrison Salisbury's charge that Washington was filled with men who "lived only for some crowning disaster which would bury all the smaller errors of the

108

past,"[124] the Johnson Administration struck most intellectuals by the end of 1966 as a beleaguered company of misled and misleading men.

Part of the problem perceived by the leftist intellectuals may have stemmed from a conscious decision taken by the Administration. Secretary of State Rusk stated later that "we decided not to create a war psychology on Southeast Asia" because "too many megatons were lying around to arouse the American people." The Administration preferred an undeclared war that would not embroil the Soviet Union or China. Rusk admitted that "history may question whether democracy can do in cold blood what it can't do in hot blood."[125]

John Roche raised the same question in his defense of the "liberal approach of flexible response over isolationism or massive retaliation." He felt that Johnson's refusal "to whoop up yahoo chauvinism" generated "the new liberal McCarthyism, which has loosed more hate in the U.S. than 'old Joe' could ever have dreamed of."[126]

On the other hand, Roche may simply have missed the point with the Intellectual Left. The Administration's failure to explain its Vietnam policy clearly and consistently was the major problem, not the alleged abstention from propaganda. Steel wrote:

A skeptic might be more receptive to the arguments in favor of this war if they were presented with less passion and more reason, if it were possible to feel that beneath the morass of figures and platitudes the Administration had a really clear grasp of issues. . . .[127]

Even Herman Kahn, director of the Hudson Institute, was to recommend later "much better formulation and exposition of our goals, strategies and tactics so that we ourselves understand what we are doing, the world understands and many existing myths and misconceptions are clarified."[128] The President's insistence on internal secrecy and random communication unnerved the intellectuals and preserved options at the expense of credibility.

Moreover, what little the Administration did say displeased the

Intellectual Left. The rhetoric with which the Administration presented its Vietnam policy drew heavily from Cold War terminology. It justified the U.S. commitment in terms of a historic defense against Communist attack. John Kenneth Galbraith typified antiwar critics resentful of leaders who claimed that the future of human liberty would be decided in Saigon. Such leaders did not persuade; they merely limited by their words their own freedom of action.[129]

Even if the Administration did not intend to create a war psychology at home, the references to "national honor" and the ultimate Chinese Communist threat contributed to just that. When the Johnson Administration claimed that the American Experiment depended on the outcome of the Vietnam conflict, a national commitment as binding as any declaration of war was created in the mind of both the general public and the Administration. For intellectuals wary of the consequences of that approach during and after the war, Administration rhetoric constituted a classic coupling of oversell at home with overkill abroad. Tocqueville had long ago identified this American propensity in public diplomacy.[130]

Daniel P. Moynihan, later bruised for his leaked memo to President Nixon on "benign neglect" in rhetoric, referred to the comparable problem in the Johnson era:

. . . The choice of words is in a significant sense a choice of government: certainly an immense influence on the process of governing and one to which too little attention is paid. The great liberal failing of this time is constantly to over-promise and to over-state and thereby constantly to appear to under-perform. . . . Surely, in some measure the disaster of Vietnam was brought on by the messianic rhetoric of the Cold War.[131]

By condemning the American tendency to identify political matters with a transcendent moralism, Edmund Stillman and William Pfaff had anticipated the rhetorical dimension of the moral controversy that raged during the Johnson era: "Everywhere diplomacy suffers from the degradation of language and the parallel failure to sense the reasonable limits of political action."[132]

The public pronouncements of the Johnson Administration struck many intellectuals as Engine Charlie Wilson's "What's good for General Motors . . ." gone global. They seemed to presume that what America wanted was what other nations wanted or should want. For intellectuals, official language began to sound about as realistic as Orwellian doublethink. In his critique of Johnson's "defensive" rationale for U.S. action in Vietnam, Henry Steele Commager recalled that "even Hitler claimed that his assault on Poland was 'defensive.' "[133]

Johnson's preoccupation with domestic political considerations explained part of the rhetorical excess which grated on intellectual sensitivities. Since the intelligentsia did not count as a primary constituency, Johnson rarely geared his addresses to it. He was the supreme political animal. He thus couched his Vietnam policy statements in the anti-Communist and patriotic terms which he thought appealed to most voters and which, significantly, he himself believed. Susan Sontag remarked of the President's attitudes on foreign policy, "Johnson is, alas, all too representative."[134] Yet, as opinion polls increasingly showed, the discrepancy between rhetoric and reality was undermining confidence for both the general and the attentive publics.

DOMESTIC FALLOUT

An ominous mood was apparent across the nation in 1966. *The New Republic*'s redoubtable TRB remarked, "This is the only U.S. conflict we know of where a father and son sit down together to figure out the best way of avoiding the draft."[135]

With that in mind, more and more leftist intellectuals focused that year on the domestic impact of the war. *The New Republic* stressed the *economic* implications of the Vietnam War. Though

Johnson asserted in his 1966 State of the Union message that "we can continue the Great Society while we fight in Vietnam," the magazine's editors refuted his confidence with the President's own statistics: "In the coming fiscal year we are going to spend ten times faster on the war in Vietnam than on all Great Society programs."[136] TRB was so intent on progressive legislation that he sided with incumbent Democratic supporters of the Great Society against peace candidates in the midterm elections of 1966.[137]

In like manner, *The New Republic* led many critics in identifying the *political* straws in the wind as early as 1966. TRB concluded that the national mood did not augur well for the President. He seemed doomed to become a scapegoat for popular frustration with the war.[138] The formation of the "No Wider War Committee" by Richard Goodwin to help Robert Kennedy suggested that, without a break in the Vietnam conflict, Johnson's future in the 1968 Presidential election looked "less evident."[139]

Most important for many leftist intellectuals were the *moral* implications at home of what they considered an immoral war abroad. Referring to U.S. air raids on civilian targets, *The New Republic* editors declared: "Morally speaking, we may be bombing *ourselves* back to the Stone Age."[140] Edgar Z. Friedenberg argued that "the war in Vietnam . . . is generating a vast contempt for legitimate authority."[141] More intellectuals recalled John Quincy Adams's warning against the perversion of liberty through foreign entanglement. The imperial mantle weighed heavily on Washington. Intellectuals wondered whether the burden could or should be borne—and, if so, at what price?

Yet, anyone reviewing the journals of 1966 could ask whether leftist intellectuals were more upset by the cost of the Vietnam War or their own frustration in failing to stop it. The majority seemed to suffer more from their own political malaise.

Even liberal critics admitted that "the frustration of the dissenters is understandable."[142] Hans Morgenthau contended that "the Julius Caesar of the American Republic" had reduced all countervailing powers to "virtual and seemingly permanent impotence."[143]

Younger militants eschewed "patterns of Old Left popular front electoral action." That was particularly true after the 1966 Congressional elections revealed for them the political weakness of the peace movement. *Studies*'s coverage of Robert Scheer's unsuccessful campaign in the Berkeley area typified the literature of frustration on the far Intellectual Left.[144] After experiences like that in California, many more radical writers urged the "movement" to shun electoral "sellouts" and change American foreign policy through a revolutionary restructuring of society. Many were later to oppose the convergence of the peace movement and Eugene McCarthy's campaign because they had been hit hard by the midterm rout of 1966.

The tally was particularly galling since it did not show the people or their President the anxiety which many leftist intellectuals believed the war was causing across the country.[145] Worse, the vote showed that the citizenry was *not* notably upset. How could the critics demand an end to the war in the name of "the people" when there was no apparent mandate at hand? That dilemma plagued the Intellectual Left thereafter in the Johnson period. Some radical dissidents, out of sheer frustration and more than a little elitist presumption, found an intriguing if awkward solution. They disavowed "the people" and rationalized their shift with the claim "We know best."

Radical frustration rose with the growing belief that antiwar demonstrations only bolstered the system by proving that it allowed dissent and by demoralizing the demonstrators with proof of their powerlessness. It seemed the ultimate travesty that the United States Information Agency presented films of war protests to illustrate freedom of speech in America. Edward Richer decried the "illusory ambitions" of the peace movement dictated by American culture:

113

The Long Dark Night of the Soul

We have been maneuvered, with some cooperation of our own, into a position analogous to what the White Liberals were to the civil rights movement . . . We are the Vietnamese people's White Liberals![146]

The fitting *dénouement* to the intellectuals' antiwar frustration in 1966 was the acclaim for *MacBird!*, a satirical play on contemporary politics by Barbara Garson. *Partisan Review* called it the season's *cause célèbre*. Some attributed its reception to the intellectuals' vulnerability to youthful sensibility in the 1960s. The novelist and critic Harvey Swados admitted: "What is new is what is happening; what is new is what is young; and one of the greatest dangers for an intellectual is to risk being labeled square for not having swiftly saluted what is new."[147] Yet a further statement by Swados suggested how the intellectuals' feeling of powerlessness vis-à-vis the Vietnam War may have been even more important in determining their reaction to *Mac-Bird!*:

Not only are we impotent to change the course of events, we remain free to register our complaints about that course. Not only do we remain free, we profit . . . from the continuation and intensification of a war that feeds a fevered military prosperity. Our shame is double: on the one hand we are ashamed of our impotence, on the other we are ashamed of what our country [is] doing to a tiny nation that . . . would gladly accept our bounty if it came in the form of CARE packages rather than napalm. . . .[148]

Dwight Macdonald approved the "impeccable bad taste" that pervaded *MacBird!* It was, he said, "just what the subject calls for, precisely the approach most congruent to the atmosphere of Washington under the Presidency of Lyndon Johnson. . . ."[149] Though perhaps understandable, much of the Intellectual Left's reaction to *MacBird!* suggested a lapse into nihilism and dissociation from the government which, in turn, imperiled the exercise of political or moral responsibility expected of the intellectuals. Their response showed that the war had given vent to a *Schadenfreude* that went beyond Johnson's Vietnam policy, the Pentagon, or Cold War propaganda. It was no coincidence that *The New York Review* published a long supplement that summer attacking the official Warren Report on President Kennedy's assassination and advancing the same conspiratorial theory suggested in *MacBird!* The radical intellectuals' response to that play and the 1966 elections and their growing rejection of liberalism presaged the move from political frustration to political alienation. It was an important way station in the depoliticization of the Intellectual Left.

Third Stage: The Vietnam War
Seen as a Reflection of Political Illegitimacy
—From January, 1967 through December, 1968

When the narrow-minded rule, the broadminded can only beseech. They will prevail in the long run, but what consolation is that for them or for the suffering world they would heal?

Editors of *The New Republic*, 1967

Drawing by David Levine. Reprinted with permission from *The New York Review of Books*. Copyright © 1966 The New York Review.

Leftist intellectuals continued to dissent from Johnson's Vietnam policy in 1967. The issues which had dominated their writing since 1965 remained: opposition to the bombing, concern about Chinese intervention, worry about the domestic cost of the war, disdain for the President's public diplomacy, and the need for a negotiated settlement. But if only because they were the same issues, a different kind of dissent hit the headlines. Old issues took on newly pejorative meanings. The Intellectual Left began to speak more often and more openly of political illegitimacy.

FAMILIAR REFRAINS

First, a review of the issues.

Intellectuals continued to reject American bombing of North Vietnam because, according to them, it thwarted peace talks and failed to accomplish its expressed goals—and because official denials of civilian casualties from American bombing contrasted so sharply with reports from North Vietnam. Defense Secretary McNamara's statements before Senate committees on January 23 and August 25, 1967, and his proposal to build an electronic anti-infiltration barrier just south of the Demilitarized Zone seemed to confirm their worst suspicions. Air warfare had apparently neither weakened North Vietnamese will nor curtailed enemy infiltration. Both McNamara's testimony and Harrison Salisbury's reporting from Hanoi impressed intellectuals by clashing with McGeorge Bundy's defense of the government's bombing policy.[1]

The Intellectual Left concluded that President Johnson persisted in bombing because of contradictory advice within the Administration and, even more important, because of his reading of American public opinion. Sixty-seven percent of those polled in early 1967 supported continued bombardment. However, critics of the war interpreted that high percentage as a reflection of public frustration with the conflict and the desire to end the war quickly, not as support for bombing.[2] They feared that the President used such surveys, together with the allegedly Adminis-

117

tration-manipulated Senate hearings on bombings, to rationalize his hard line in Vietnam and neutralize antiwar sentiment in the United States.[3]

The intelligentsia and the Administration continued to diverge in their evaluation of a possible Chinese response to American involvement in Southeast Asia. Although China seemed to lurk at the bottom of both groups' strategic concerns, their time projections differed: Intellectuals stressed the short-term danger of provoking Chinese intervention by American aggression in Vietnam, while government officials emphasized the long-term need to contain Chinese Communism by American firmness in Indochina. Three events in 1967—the Senate Foreign Relations Committee hearings (January), the downing of American planes by Chinese fighters (April 24, June 26, and August 21), and Secretary Rusk's "billion Chinese" news conference (October 12)—heightened the intellectuals' fear that the Johnson Administration might miscalculate Chinese intentions. Critics warned against facile comparisons with the Korean conflict. They recalled that Dean Rusk had also predicted that the Chinese would not enter the Korean War.[4]

As 1967 wore on, Administration spokesmen confirmed more openly what President Johnson had long hinted: Vietnam was part of a larger effort to checkmate China. The enormousness of the American commitment in Southeast Asia suggested to intellectuals that Johnson could not leave the region without sacrificing personal and national prestige. Intellectuals feared that official preoccupation with "face" might precipitate an inadvertent nuclear confrontation with China. The dilemma recalled Reinhold Niebuhr's warning fifteen years before against preventive war. President Johnson personified those "true believers" who "are always so preoccupied with their virtues that they have no residual awareness of the common characteristics in all human foibles and frailties and could not bear to be reminded that there is a hidden kinship between the vices of even the most vicious and the virtues of even the most upright."[5]

The Long Dark Night of the Soul

The New Republic persisted in leading the chorus of protests against the domestic economic consequences of the Vietnam War.[6] For that journal's writers, it was not just a matter of arithmetic and budgetary shuffling. The Indochina conflict evoked mourning for the hopes raised by Johnson and dashed by his war. TRB wrote:

This is worse than Camelot. There the bright young prince was made a radiant folk hero by a crazy bullet. Here a man whom we conceive to have a genuine vision of social justice is destroying himself bit by bit.[7]

Intellectuals found the Administration's public diplomacy increasingly contradictory and out of touch with reality. They objected to Johnson's State of the Union message in 1967 because the President came no closer to answering their questions on Vietnam. Many intellectuals interpreted General William Westmoreland's dramatic appearance before Congress on April 28, 1967, as part of Johnson's effort to reinforce the attack on war critics and to prepare the way for more military escalation.[8] They considered the Administration misleading in its claims of other nations' support in the war effort. No country, they felt, came close to supplying the 500,000 troops and $30 billion per year provided by the United States. Official optimism grated on the intellectuals. When Vice President Humphrey exclaimed, "By all measures . . . we are winning militarily," they dismissed that and all similar statements as part of the forthcoming election campaign. They contended that, if anything, Washington was intensifying pressure for encouraging reports in the face of contradictory evidence.[9]

The Tet offensive launched on January 30, 1968, by the North Vietnamese and Vietcong against U.S. military positions, South Vietnamese towns, and the American embassy was to expose the discrepancy between the officials' optimism and the critics' skepticism. *The New Republic* editors wrote:

The big offensive . . . came as no surprise to people who had been studying the months-long buildup of the foe's military strength. Unfortunately, those in the know do not seem to have included General William C. Westmoreland, Ambassador Ellsworth Bunker, the White House, the Pentagon, or the State Department. The knowledgeable people were mostly journalists, foreign and American, whom the officials are always loftily dismissing as rumormongers, liars and hippies who refuse to get on the team.[10]

Official credibility sank so low among intellectual commentators that few trusted the Administration's statements on the North Korean capture of the *Pueblo* or on American planes flying over China. Observers asked, "Who any longer believes the official excuses?"[11] Finally, although some writers stressed North Vietnamese opposition to negotiations, most leftist intellectuals blamed the Johnson Administration. The President seemed bent on military victory.[12] The South Vietnamese elections of September 3, 1967, struck many as a "cry for peace" ignored by the White House.

Theodore Draper's special supplement for *The New York Review* demonstrated best the division between the Administration and the leftist intelligentsia on negotiations in 1967.[13] It was one of the most significant pieces in the decade's antiwar literature. Draper argued that the latest failure to start talks reflected a *pattern* of official disinclination to negotiate. The fate of the Johnson–Ho Chi Minh correspondence (February, 1967) simply fit into the record of the previous two years. Draper contended that the "conditional unconditional" had dominated the American negotiating position during 1965: Rusk's "antennae" had to detect signs of North Vietnamese unilateral withdrawal as the prerequisite for negotiations. Since 1966, "reciprocity" had been the *leitmotif* of American policy: The United States would stop bombing North Vietnam only when Hanoi curtailed its military action in South Vietnam.

Draper condemned the "hypocrisy" of both the "conditional unconditional" and "reciprocity." "What," he asked, "could 'reciprocity' mean between a strong, rich power like the United

States and a weak, poor power like North Vietnam?"[14] President Johnson had accused his critics of "moral double-bookkeeping" because they did not equate Vietcong terrorism with American bombing. That charge provoked what became a prototypic position of the American Intellectual Left, deserving full quotation:

... The moral equation here is ... complicated by two questions: (1) whether the terror and counter-terror of Vietnamese against Vietnamese should be put on the same level as the violence and counter-violence of a foreign power against Vietnamese, and (2) whether the scale of destructiveness of a few mortar shells balances that of a sustained downpour of 1000-pound bombs. The *scale* of destructiveness cannot ... be disregarded in this consideration of "moral double-bookkeeping."[15]

The Administration countered press reports by asserting that American bombs were meant for military targets only. In view of the extraordinary expenditure of U.S. ordnance in North and South Vietnam, Draper wondered "whether the inevitability of the consequences was not more important than the deliberateness of the motivation":

One who fires a machine gun into a crowd in order to kill a single person can hardly protest that he did not mean to injure anyone else "deliberately"—especially if he misses his intended victim, as sometimes happens in the bombing of military targets. The indirect but unavoidable byproducts of a course of action cannot be exempted morally.[16]

In a related vein, Mary McCarthy wondered why the American "paramilitary intellectuals" in Vietnam could condemn a Vietcong bomb in a theater as an atrocity and excuse U.S. bombardment of a village as "different." How could they argue that the VC action was deliberate and the American accidental?[17] Miss McCarthy charged that "foreknowledge of the consequences of an action" argued the "will to do it." She added that repeated denial suggested "an *extreme and dangerous dissocia-*

tion of the personality."[18] It was a process of dissociation which extended from the lowest field soldier who seemed to have no control over his precision weaponry to President Johnson, who, "escalating, feigns to have no option in the war and to react, like an automat, to 'moves' from Hanoi." Miss McCarthy also attributed a "certain psychological truth" to the rationalizations of American policymakers:

Johnson and his advisers, like all Americans, are the conditioned subjects of the free-enterprise system, which . . . appears to function automatically, requiring no consent on the part of those involved in it. A sense of compulsion, dictated by the laws of the market, permeates every nerve of the national life.[19]

There was a familiar ring to Miss McCarthy's charge. Her argument about "dissociation" recalled the references of Fall, Rapoport, and Oglesby to American detachment from "evil" during the Vietnam experience. Arthur Miller had alluded earlier to the same phenomenon. He had related the general theme of accountability for evil in his play *Incident at Vichy* to the specific "evil" of U.S. intervention in Vietnam: "The prisoner crying out in agony is *our* prisoner."[20] He wondered why his fellow countrymen could not or would not recognize the connection.

Draper and McCarthy simply expanded the points of unintentional evil, depersonalization, and moral responsibility into a critique of the entire system. It was small comfort indeed that the American was both a willful and unwitting bully in Vietnam when the conclusion forced U.S. intellectuals to confront the moral tyranny of their own "free" society.

MOVE TO RESIST—AND WHY

The very persistence of the differences between the intelligentsia and the Administration bred a frustration above and beyond that occasioned by those points of contention. The exponential despair, in turn, fed the intellectuals' ever growing tendency to judge Johnson's Vietnam policy in moral terms. A war which many intellectuals defined as "immoral" justified the next step in their reaction: transition from *dissent* to *resistance*. Although some liberal critics did not make that change and some of their more revolutionary colleagues went beyond it, most leftist intellectuals responded to *The New York Review*'s "Call to Resist Illegitimate Authority." They did so for one or all of the following reasons: susceptibility to the initiative of youth, frustration with the lack of official responsiveness to criticism, belief in the relationship between domestic and foreign violence, and a reawakened sense of moral responsibility.

A REJUVENATING JUVENIPHILIA

The switch to resistance in 1967 had almost as many causes (and consequences) as it had adherents. One of the most intriguing was its attraction to leftist intellectuals in quest of political and moral rejuvenation. It was in this respect that the interaction between activist youth and the Intellectual Left, first noted during the teach-in days of 1965, showed yet another nuance. Antiwar protest provided both groups with a metamorphic experience. If they could not overcome their sense of powerlessness vis-à-vis the Johnson Administration, they could at least feel reborn through confrontation with that regime.

Existential cant? Perhaps. Yet there is much that is persuasive in a piece done by Robert Lifton at about that time.[21] He argued that the U.S. youth movement of the 1960s expressed the psychological themes of a new intellectual prototype or "protean man." He wrote that "protean man's affinity for the young . . . has to do with his never-ceasing quest for imagery of rebirth."[22] Viewed from that perspective, Norman Mailer's reference to antiwar confrontations as "rites of passage" acquires new meaning. So does Susan Sontag's stress on the importance and "moral imperative" of what she called her "transformative" trip to Hanoi in 1968. For some, the change was painful. Paul Jacobs of the Center for the Study of Democratic Institutions admitted as much:

Re-radicalization is being brought on by the continuation of the war in Vietnam. . . . Re-radicalization is a traumatic experience . . . usually there is much more at stake, personally, than when the original commitment was made.[23]

Others, like Dwight Macdonald, relished the emergence from political retirement imposed by the 1950s. He rejoiced in the personalization of politics invoked by the young. Still others, like Andrew Kopkind, who redefined the intellectual as a "street organizer," and Howard Zinn, who touted the "historian as an actor," gloried in equating political authenticity with the extent of one's alienation and willingness to perform existential acts of defiance.[24]

Whatever their motivation or reaction, many leftist intellectuals latched on to the campus vanguard to make their mark against the war. Mitchell Goodman, novelist and one of the "Boston Five" in the Dr. Benjamin Spock conspiracy case, admitted: "The kids invented the 'Resistance' movement, we came along behind."[25] Like most American intellectuals, Goodman had been apolitical until jolted by campus peace action in early 1965. He first encountered the resistance movement while teaching at Stanford University, where he was impressed by David Harris's stand against the draft.[26] Goodman's subsequent appeal for mass civil disobedience to stop the war launched the idea of adult support for draft resisters.

Journals like *The New York Review* shifted to the position anticipated by *Studies on the Left*. Paul Goodman confessed to his peers in *The New York Review*: "We are certainly in an embarrassing position to be looking to the young to make our will effective. I am ashamed to be so powerless. . . ."[27] The intelligentsia, with its sense of mission fired by young activists, moved to support draft resisters by signing "complicity pledges" in which they promised to share the dangers of prosecution for challenging the law. Efforts comparable to Mitchell Goodman's soon spread. Representative examples were Support in Action, started by writers Grace Paley and Paul Goodman; Clergy and Laymen Concerned about the War in Vietnam, begun by the Reverend William Sloane Coffin of Yale and Professor Seymour Melman of Columbia; and Resist, initiated by Professor Noam Chomsky of M.I.T. and critic Dwight Macdonald.

Whether the intellectuals were justified in resistance may never be clear. Intellectuals themselves have debated that kind of act throughout U.S. history. Thoreau had raised the same question in his essay on "Resistance to Civil Government" in 1849, retitled "Civil Disobedience" after his death. Bayard Rustin had challenged Staughton Lynd on the same point in 1965. As chairman of the Vietnam Day demonstration in Washington on April 17, 1965, Lynd had written:

It seemed that the great mass of people would simply flow on through and over the marble buildings, that our forward movement was irresistibly strong, that had some been shot or arrested nothing could have stopped that crowd from taking possession of its government. Perhaps next time we should keep going. . . .[28]

Bayard Rustin questioned the demonstrators' right, "even symbolically," to take control when public opinion still sided with the Administration on Vietnam. He found "putschism" in such visionary activism which "otherwise has no meaning except in a personal existential sense that is beyond the concern of politics and irrelevant as a guide to the outcome of social struggle."[29]

Mary McCarthy argued in 1967: "If the opposition wants to make itself felt politically, it ought to be acting so as to provoke intolerance."[30] Some could say—and did—that Miss McCarthy's position exemplified the characteristic failure of leftist intellectuals to understand the national milieu and its distance from revolution.

To that point—though in quite another context—Susan Sontag made a telling admission:

. . . Revolution in the Western capitalist countries seems to be an activity expressly designed never to succeed. For many people, it is an *asocial* activity, a form of action designed for the assertion of individuality against the body politic. It is the ritual activity of outsiders, rather than of people united by a passionate bond to their country.[31]

Perhaps unwittingly, Miss Sontag betrayed why the American Intellectual Left has been frustrated since its emergence and how powerlessness reclaimed its accustomed victim in the 1960s.

Yet who could know for sure? The record of intellectual commentary during the Johnson era raised countless such questions that persist. When Emerson asked Thoreau why he had gone to jail, Thoreau answered, "Why did you not?" In like manner, as if in answer to Rustin, Lynd had reminded his audience at the Berkeley teach-in in May, 1965, of the university-based resistance in Nazi Germany: "They kept the spirit of truth alive."

It is neither an idea nor an intellectual trend but rather what Michael Harrington then called "people in movement" that synchronize hope with actuality. Although the leftist intellectuals seemed unable in the short run to rouse the populace against the Vietnam War as an index to systemic illegitimacy, time and that generation teethed politically on Mills and Marcuse might yet put "people in movement." Victor Hugo once proclaimed: "There is nothing so powerful in all the world as an idea whose time has come. . . ." It is the lot, the sublime mission, and the immediate misfortune of the intellectuals most often to be precursors, to anticipate the coming.

The Long Dark Night of the Soul

UP AGAINST THE WHITE HOUSE WALL

That millennium seemed distant indeed by mid-1967. Or so the Intellectual Left thought as it appraised the impact of the peace movement on the Johnson Administration. Leftist intellectuals had responded to Chomsky's call "to speak the truth and to expose lies,"[32] only to find that "the truth does no good." It was apparently not enough to maintain a "merely honorable intellectual and moral position":

What have the intellectuals done when they have proven carefully to those who already agree with them that our government lies, that intellectuals who join the government to try to exert influence end up lying too; and that when this task of learning the truth and exposing the lies has been done, the question remains, what then?[33]

Writers repeated a despairing refrain. Robert Wolfe, *Studies* editor, blamed the "failure of the strategy of exposure" on capitulation to "token liberalism."[34] Paul Goodman premised his support for We Won't Go, a mass movement for draft resistance to stop the Vietnam War, on the futility of protest in Johnson's America.[35] Hans Morgenthau concluded that "the democratic state is in a blind alley, and so is American democracy."[36] Chomsky expanded on his essay "The Responsibility of Intellectuals" to stress "resistance":

The logic of resorting to resistance as a tactic for ending the war is fairly clear. There is no basis for supposing that those who will make the major policy decisions are open to reason on the fundamental issues, in particular the issue of whether we, alone among the nations of the world, have the authority and the competence to determine the social and political institutions of Vietnam.[37]

Chomsky intended resistance as a tactic to help stop the war and as a means to resolve the larger dilemma of powerlessness which underlay the Vietnam experience. By involving adults in draft resistance and expanding the peace movement, he hoped to increase the economic and political costs for the "system." He wanted to make it impossible for the government to ignore the protesters. Like many radicalized intellectuals, he placed his faith in the "unpredictable effects of a really large-scale repression" of youth and in a citizenry that raised "questions about the range of meaningful political action."[38] He had no faith in the electoral process alone. If by some "miracle" a choice were to be offered in the 1968 election, he questioned how seriously one could take the campaign promises of any "peace candidate" after the experience of 1964. Johnson's "betrayal" still festered within the Intellectual Left.

In a sequel to her series on Vietnam, Mary McCarthy chastised liberal critics like Arthur Schlesinger, Jr., Richard Goodwin, John Kenneth Galbraith, Senator J. William Fulbright, and George Kennan for committing the error of "an opposition that wants to be statesmanlike and responsible, in contrast to the 'irresponsible' opposition that is burning its draft card or refusing to pay taxes."[39] For her and an increasing segment of the radicalized American intelligentsia, the "mirage of an honorable exit"—"the Middle Course" of Schlesinger's *The Bitter Heritage*—was "the deceptive premise of the liberal opposition." She defined the role of the U.S. intellectual as making Americans understand that the war was wrong and turning that understanding, whenever possible, into the language of action.

According to Miss McCarthy, freedom was no longer a political value. It was instead a mode of self-expression as significant as psychodrama, kinky sex, or ceramics. She rationalized her turn to resistance by asserting the "uselessness of our free institutions" to stop the Vietnam War:

A feeling of having no choice is becoming more and more widespread in American life, and particularly among successful people, who supposedly are free beings. . . . In national election years, you are free to choose between Johnson and Goldwater and Romney or Reagan. . . . Just as in American hotel rooms you can decide whether or not to turn on the air conditioner . . . but you cannot open the window.[40]

The Long Dark Night of the Soul

Because the war was debated as a minority pastime and tolerated by the majority, Miss McCarthy concluded that the opposition could have political impact only by provoking intolerance. She advocated acts ranging from tax refusal to the operation of an underground railroad for protesting draftees. She referred those discouraged by the failure of conventional dissent to the precedent of the Abolitionists. Like Chomsky and his political mentors, Macdonald and Muste, she reverted to the tradition of American transcendentalism. She advised that each individual find his or her own mode of opposition to the war: "From each according to his abilities, but to be in the town jail, as Thoreau knew, can relieve any sense of imaginary imprisonment."[41]

THE "EVIL LINK"

That imprisonment was all too real, according to many leftist intellectuals. They became even more convinced that violence at home and abroad stemmed from the same cause, the collapse of democracy. Worse, they felt powerless to halt the trend. Recalling the Newark race riots during the summer of 1967, Jack Newfield said:

. . . One cannot speak of Black Power, or the riots or even Vietnam, in a departmentalized vacuum. They are all part of something larger. We have permitted political power in America to pass from the people to a technological elite that manipulates the mass media and hoards nuclear weaponry. Representational democracy has broken down.[42]

The war served as an "evil link between internal and external violence" and every statement about the war said something about America. Radical critics coupled "the institutional demands that induced the war—the politics and economics of anti-Communism"—with those "that kept the underclass in its place—the politics and economics of racism."[43] For them, the black insurrections of the 1960s betrayed the liberal assumption that the American system could absorb the demands of its alienated underclass. They believed that those in power could neither understand nor satisfy those demands. It was necessary to "extend democracy radically." The civil and foreign wars had contrived "to murder liberalism—in its official robes."⁴⁴ There were few mourners on the far Intellectual Left.

CAPTIVE TO CONSCIENCE

To resist was to take a moral stand. That, finally, was why most leftist intellectuals turned to resistance. Bernard Fall, as previously noted, was instrumental in awakening their conscience. He chided American leftist intellectuals for their moral default on the Vietnam question. He condemned their failure to speak out against war atrocities as their French counterparts had in the case of Algeria. Fall's critique prompted Marcus Raskin, coeditor with Fall of the influential *Vietnam Reader*, to think in terms of the French intellectuals' morally premised "Statement of the 121" when Raskin and Arthur Waskow drafted the "Call to Resist Illegitimate Authority." That "call" circulated throughout the peace movement. In so doing, it reaffirmed the intellectuals' traditional mandate to serve as society's conscience.

MARCH ON THE PENTAGON

Although "Vietnam Week" (April 8–15, 1967) marked the move from dissent to resistance among many young protesters, events in Washington on October 19–21 symbolized the transition for most leftist intellectuals. Noam Chomsky, for example, was inspired to write "On Resistance" for *The New York Review* after participating in that march. The draft-card turn-in at the Justice Department that weekend contributed to the indictment of Dr. Benjamin Spock, the Reverend William Sloane Coffin, Jr., Mitchell Goodman, Michael Ferber, and Marcus Raskin for conspiracy. The trial of the "Boston Five" was to become a rallying point in the intellectuals' response to the Vietnam War.⁴⁵ Paul

Goodman interpreted the October demonstrations as a "test of legitimacy," a "populist" groundswell against the "usurper" in the White House.[46] Goodman reflected the Intellectual Left's tendency not only to justify resistance as a challenge to illegitimate authority but also to equate the will of the protesters with that of the American masses. The atmosphere reminded Goodman and his friends of the eve of the French withdrawal from Algeria. There was the same spirit, the same coalition of the young, the intellectual, and the black (Algerian/Negro).

Gifted as Goodman was, another writer rose above the rest to record the turn in intellectual sensibilities. Future historians must consult Norman Mailer's *The Armies of the Night* to understand how and why the American Intellectual Left moved to "resistance" against Johnson's Vietnam War and, in fact, to comprehend the radicalized intellectual consciousness of the 1960s. That "interior" history of the March on the Pentagon (October 21, 1967) served a unique function. It synthesized the major themes in Mailer's writing and those behind the psychopolitical development of contemporary U.S. leftist intellectuals. It drew on the social criticism of the 1930s and the sickness of society portrayed in his *The Naked and the Dead* (1948), the problem of alienation presented in "The White Negro" (1957), and the sense of the writer as a public personality in *Advertisements for Myself* (1959).

The value of Mailer's novel/history of the October march lay in what it conveyed about the "rite of passage" for one prototypic writer, the Intellectual Left itself, and a troubled nation. By acting as both protagonist and narrator, Mailer made the confrontation at the Pentagon one with national and individual implications.

On the *national* level, the Vietnam War confirmed Mailer's grimmest suspicions about "the diseases of America, its oncoming totalitarianism, its oppressiveness, its smog."[47] He concluded from the war that "the center of America might be insane." Vietnam was the necessary outlet for a suppressed schizophrenia caused in Christian citizens worshiping the mystery of the Son of God and working for the American Corporation, whose center was the detestation of mystery, the worship of technology. Mailer defined the Pentagon as the symbolic center of the national schizophrenia. Thus, the need to inflict a real and symbolic wound on the Pentagon. He envisaged the March on the Pentagon as "the first major battle of a war which may go on for twenty years," a cross between Gettysburg and the storming of the Bastille. Hence, the title suggested by Matthew Arnold's "Where ignorant armies clash by night" in "Dover Beach" and the theme which Robert Lowell embellished in his poetic celebration of the experience he shared with Mailer.[48] Mailer believed that the resistance of a courageous minority might thwart totalitarianism and reaffirm what he called repeatedly his love for America.

The process of affirmation also operated on a *personal* level for Mailer. It involved the moral choices confronting men of conscience and the need of many to define themselves existentially through action. In many respects, Mailer's reaction was representative for the Intellectual Left. He joined the peace movement and agreed to march only grudgingly. He did so for reasons as varied as those prompting the general repoliticization of the 1960s: the "happy confidence that politics had again become mysterious," the example of young Americans who hated hypocrisy and flaunted a Cuban political aesthetic, and the need to be committed to a "cause"—in this case, the preservation of an American Dream imperiled by the nightmarish trappings of the Vietnam War. With Mailer, the last factor seemed most compelling. Through the rite of passage provided by the March on the Pentagon, he expunged the "rim of corruption" corroding his idea of himself and gloried in a new "clean sense of himself." After being arrested and imprisoned, he felt a "confirmation of the contests of his own life" and "closer to that freedom from dread which occupied the inner drama of his years."[49]

What was important to Mailer and about Mailer was that the act of resistance unified the philosopher and the man of action. He found at least one means whereby the intellectual could feel morally "alive" and part of the body politic. His solution met a common need among American intellectuals to clarify identity through confrontation, whether physical or spiritual. Furthermore, like many of his colleagues, Mailer had long been "imprisoned with a perception which will settle for nothing less than making a revolution in the consciousness of our time."[50] For growing numbers of leftist intellectuals, resistance against the Vietnam War provided a confrontation which transformed them and renewed their recurring commitment to "making a revolution in the consciousness of our time."[51]

The tragedy for the Intellectual Left was that the Johnson Administration and the public were not ready for that kind of transformation. Such a change rested on the assumption that the Vietnam War was obscene, that internally generated totalitarianism was a real possibility, and that there was a moral dilemma in deciding how or whether to commit civil disobedience to preserve legitimate government. In the unlikely event that they had read Mailer or *The New York Review*, most Americans would have found such sentiments nonsense.

Yet most intellectuals felt, in Mailer's words, a "responsibility to educate a nation" and reunite "the two worlds of America." They recognized the difficulty of their task in the face of the Vietnam experience of the 1960s. Resistance against the war at least helped the intellectuals through that ordeal—rather like psychic outlaws pursuing the American Dream.

RESISTANCE TO RESISTANCE

Though compelling as a ritualistic brief for resistance, *The Armies of the Night* did not reflect the sentiments of all leftist intellectuals. Many diverged from its prescription for action. In short, the transition from dissent to resistance met its own resistance within the intellectual community. It was a logical extension of prior war in the peace camp.

The schism within SANE exemplified both this new crisis and the old, continuing tension between liberal and radical intellectuals. Despite the shift to radical initiative during the SANE-organized March on Washington of November 27, 1965, most of the SANE board still balked when Dr. Spock, co-chairman of the organization since 1963, urged participation in antiwar events planned for April and October, 1967. For most of the year, SANE rehashed the "exclusionist" dilemma. It debated, for example, whether to associate with groups like David Dellinger's National Mobilization Committee to End the War in Vietnam. Thirty years before, many leftist intellectuals had called for "clearest differentiation" from their Communist colleagues. In like manner, SANE liberals in the 1960s opposed any affiliation which might jeopardize support for the peace movement. Norman Cousins, then editor of *Saturday Review* and co-founder of SANE, expressed the viewpoint of the anti-Spock forces: "The only way to get out of Vietnam is through a political settlement. But if SANE becomes linked with the extreme left, that will destroy its usefulness in pressing for such a settlement."[52]

That position struck many radical opponents of the Vietnam War as passé. Started in 1957 by a coalition of Quakers, pacifists, and liberals seeking a nuclear test ban, SANE seemed too middle-aged and middle-class for many after 1965. A new generation—unmindful or ignorant of the Moscow trials and the Hitler-Stalin pact or even the Berlin blockade and the Soviet invasion of Hungary—was challenging elders it blamed for abetting the Cold War, condoning McCarthyism, and allowing the Vietnam War. That group had experienced little to merit excluding any person or party from its ranks. In fact, the New Left ascribed many of the problems of the 1960s to the "exclusionist" mentality of corporate liberalism and anti-Communism. For that reason,

The Long Dark Night of the Soul

Dr. Spock gave up his SANE co-chairmanship to become an officer of the National Conference for New Politics and the "Establishment" darling of draft resisters reared on his *Common Sense of Baby and Child Care*.[53]

Whatever the long-range wisdom of the radical view, the liberal faction of SANE enjoyed a short-term vindication. Subsequent public reaction against radical "peaceniks" seemed to justify the liberals' concern with "clearest differentiation" from an apocalyptic fringe. It bolstered their scorn for the alleged existential gratification of some radicals' direct activism. One could argue that there is no necessary correlation between emotional satisfaction, sometimes the most conspicuous benefit of confrontation, and political effectiveness. Mailer's "rite of passage" too easily became a political blind alley.

Writers of democratic-radical persuasion continued to remind the Intellectual Left of the range of political and moral considerations raised by "resistance." Again, Irving Howe took the lead. He condemned the shift from dissent to resistance as "adventuristic." He promoted the statement on protest strategy in *The New York Review*, which asserted that foreign policy could be changed by pressure from *within* the political system. To act otherwise might "poison" the national mood and give the Administration a "new pretext or opportunity to unleash repressive acts."[54] It was the same reasoning which had characterized democratic-radical views on the peace movement since 1965. That argument recurred in a *Dissent* statement which honored draft refusal as a matter of conscience but opposed it as counterproductive politics.[55]

Theodore Draper, Michael Walzer, Michael Harrington, and Robert Pickus extended the case against civil disobedience by stressing the *moral* relevance of political tactics. They argued that the utility of dissent (writing and speaking against the war) versus resistance (violent or nonviolent "direct action") should be judged according to its objective. By 1967, the peace movement harbored three groups with potentially contradictory aims: those trying to end the war by converting the American public, those hoping to save their own souls through a "politics of gesture," and those backing the Vietnamese Communists and favoring "victory in the Third World."[56] Since the writers mentioned above all placed highest priority on ending the war, they tested the morality of the intellectuals' protest according to that criterion. To antagonize Americans by what Harrington called "middle class tantrums," just as many were turning against the war, struck democratic radicals as antipolitical.

In that context, antipolitics was immoral. As Walzer observed, "No one can be morally justified in acting (however heroically) in ways that defeat his own stated purposes."[57] Draper considered Chomsky deluded by the belief that resisters could affect the "cost of American aggression" for a government spending thirty billion dollars a year in Vietnam. He condemned Mailer's celebration of revolution since most Americans would reject peace if it also meant revolution. Those intellectuals who didn't care whether they were losing touch with the American people could not complain if the American people lost touch with them. They risked turning into a "morally self-satisfied but ultimately impotent cult."[58]

Paul Goodman's declaration of support for resisters, "We Won't Go," drew fire from *New York Review* readers on comparable grounds.[59] Respondents objected to Goodman's "uncritical worship of the young" and his tendency to fit their action into his own scheme for a populist upheaval in the United States. With most citizens "as square as the pages of *The New York Times*," protesters might better attract support by offering to end the slaughter of American men than by promising an anarchist millennium. Critics wondered whether Goodman, who rationalized resistance on moral premises, had faced the "moral issue" involved in the minority's assumption of the majority's prerogatives. Goodman's response that "some of us think we are living in a pre-revolutionary period if only because the unique problems of modern times are not susceptible to old formulas" begged the question.

Two exchanges in *The New York Review* underscored further the tensions brought out by this new war in the peace movement. Both showed radicalism moving toward antipolitics and liberalism waning in persuasiveness.

The first debate arose over Professor Henry Aiken's review of *A Critique of Pure Tolerance*—a collection of essays by Barrington Moore, Jr., Robert Paul Wolff, and Herbert Marcuse.[60] Moore explained that he had been prompted to write because he was "terrified by the consequences of fascism, communism and now of liberal democracy as revealed by current American policy in Vietnam."[61] Aiken considered Moore "deracinated by recent American foreign policy"; the Vietnam War had alienated him from the entire political system. Although sharing Moore's anguish over the war, Aiken feared that deracination might afflict many liberal Americans if there seemed no way within the political system to right wrongs. Aiken adhered to his liberal contention that "the evils that we all endure and sometimes condone in our imperfect liberal democracy are not caused by our liberal democratic principles . . . but by our disloyalty to them. . . ." Some radicals, like Carl Oglesby, had already said just that. Yet, unlike the radicals, Aiken was encouraged by the dissent aroused by the war: "No political order that permits a debate so ranging and so prolonged, in time of unclear but present danger, can have wholly lost its integrity."[62] More to the point, he opposed disruption of "liberal democracy" lest it lose what value it had and lest critics mourn its passing from behind bars.

Diana Trilling condemned Mary McCarthy's stance on Vietnam for the same reasons. When Miss McCarthy cited liberal critics like Kennan and Schlesinger as examples of how obsession with political "solutions" could divert intellectuals from their main moral duty, namely protest of the war, Mrs. Trilling wrote:

One . . . wonders whether Miss McCarthy, jealous as she is for the special domain of intellectuals, has let herself realize that by limiting the political role of intellectuals . . . she deprives them of an historical privilege they have claimed with some authority—the right to propose and even direct the positive operations of government.[63]

Miss McCarthy retorted that "the imminent danger for America was not of being "taken in" by Communism—she felt accused of having forgotten the lessons of the 1930s—but of being taken in by itself. She would resist that process even if it meant the worldwide triumph of Communism.

Her declamation bordered on moralistic presumption, as irresponsible in its way as the Administration's public diplomacy. To some, Miss McCarthy implied that she preferred to spend seven years at hard labor for dissidence, like Andrei Sinyavski and Yuli Daniel, rather than write for *The New York Review*.[64] Yet, others might counter, who can know yet whether Miss McCarthy showed an exaggerated distrust of politics or a flair for foresight?

Finally, to no one's surprise, writers like those at *The New Republic* shunned the shift to resistance. They concentrated instead on seeking Johnson's "voluntary withdrawal from renomination" and looking for an alternative within the Democratic Party.[65]

Even with that approach, they tangled with fellow liberals. *The New Republic* writers condemned the Americans for Democratic Action (ADA) for the "negative boost" given President Johnson by that organization's decision not to question then (September 24, 1967) whether Johnson should be renominated.[66] *The New Republic* sided with the young within ADA who opposed the "hands-off attitude" of Galbraith, Schlesinger, Goodwin, Moynihan, and others on the national board. Allard Lowenstein, the charismatic vice-chairman of ADA, was leading a Conference of Concerned Democrats to oppose Johnson and finding "overwhelming" approval across the country.

Moynihan rationalized ADA restraint on the grounds of liberal complicity in Vietnam decision-making, the very reason radicals condemned both liberalism and restraint:

> The violence abroad and the violence at home . . . [constitute] an especial problem of American liberals because more than anyone else it is they who . . . presided over the onset of the war in Vietnam and the violence in American cities. . . . It is this knowledge . . . that requires of many of us a restraint in a situation that gives to others the utmost play to the powers of invective and contempt, the plain fact being that if these men got us into the present situation, who are we to say we would have done better?[67]

Since Moynihan believed that "President Johnson will almost certainly be re-elected in 1968," that the national government would remain in the same "liberal" hands, and that the Vietnam War would continue for many more years, he proposed that "liberals see more clearly that their essential interest is in the stability of the social order." Applied to foreign affairs, his "politics of stability" meant that liberals should "make it politically worthwhile and possible for the administration to disengage." Furthermore, liberals should make clear that "we do in fact love peace more than we love the Vietcong."[68]

Although many liberal writers could accept Moynihan's position as a statement of "political realities" or an acknowledgment of collective guilt, it failed, in their eyes, to meet the challenge confronting the Democratic Party. By November, most declared for Senator Eugene McCarthy.[69]

Encouraged as they were by Senator McCarthy's "gallant" gesture, *New Republic* writers confessed by the turn of the year that "the U.S. . . . has slipped out of rational control." They stated that "as of this moment, a great many Americans don't much care who gets nominated or elected." No wonder, they thought, if the nation had to choose between Lyndon Johnson and Richard Nixon. Each was "a monument to incredibility."[70]

Thus, the "resisters" and the resisters to the "resistance" on the

The Long Dark Night of the Soul

Intellectual Left converged in a sense of shared powerlessness. Beneath the rhetoric, most resistance was only a variation on dissent as a means of pressure against institutions and individuals within the political system. Both reaffirmed that one still cared about the direction of society and believed it could be saved. The danger in 1968 lay in the sequel to more frustration for both dissenters and resisters, in the temptation for intellectuals to follow some alienated critics still further along the path of radicalization to revolution or anarchy. Reradicalization taken to that extreme risked the inversion of politicization for an Intellectual Left caught in the political dilemma of its own moral commitment.

MARCH 31, 1968

Lyndon Johnson's television address on April Fool's Eve broke this gloom of the Intellectual Left like a thunderclap. After renewing the San Antonio formula for bombing halts and the Manila formula on negotiations, he stated, to the astonishment of all but his closest advisers, that he would neither seek nor accept renomination to the Presidency.

Because the leftist intellectuals had focused so much of their opposition to the Vietnam War on Johnson himself, his speech almost single-handedly retrieved them from political despair. Andrew Kopkind proclaimed "a sense of breathing space in the society, at last, a hope that the next months will not bring the boot heel down on everyone who is trying to resist."[71] Most intellectuals eased into an era of political euphoria—despite discordant reminders that U.S. bombers had resumed action over North Vietnam four hours after the President's speech; contentions that "Johnson's refusal to seek another term does not change things fundamentally";[72] and assertions that Asians viewed Johnson's address as a "confession of the bankruptcy of the entire U.S. policy toward Vietnam."[73]

Most intellectuals attributed Johnson's renunciation of office in large part to the peace movement. In fact, Johnson's decision drew from many factors: the effect of the Tet offensive (January 30–February 6, 1968), Eugene McCarthy's strong showing in the New Hampshire primary (March 12), Robert Kennedy's subsequent entry into the Presidential race (March 16), the deepening "dollar crisis," the policy reappraisal of advisers like Clark Clifford, and the more personal pressure suggested in Mrs. Johnson's *A White House Diary*. Yet democratic-radical and liberal critics of the war reveled in the apparent vindication of dissent. Irving Howe exulted over the "triumph for democratic processes and values":

Surely a major reason for Johnson's decision was a belated but strong response to growing public pressure and disenchantment. The complaints one heard about American campuses that dissidents aren't listened to, and have no choice but "alienation" or exile or urban guerrilla tactics, seem now to be utterly wrong or, at the very least, wildly premature.[74]

Even more radical intellectuals seemed exhilarated by the prospect of a choice. There was an instructive contrast between the despair of *Partisan Review*'s symposium "What's Happening to America?" (Winter, 1966–Spring, 1967) and the optimism of a forum on the nature and future of American democracy sponsored by the Theatre for Ideas (TFI).[75] What emerged from that panel presentation—moderated by critic Nat Hentoff and featuring Marcuse, Mailer, and Schlesinger—was that a range of war critics had had their faith in American democracy restored by the success of the McCarthy campaign and Johnson's resignation.

Mailer answered "Yes" to Hentoff's opening question: Can we be optimistic about the processes of democracy after what has been happening politically? He stressed the miraculous change in mood less than half a year since he had marched on the Pentagon:

If this question had been asked six months ago, the consensus . . .
would have been altogether more pessimistic. In fact, it's hard almost
to conceive of a forum of this sort in New York City with this panel
six months ago. It's obvious that there's been an extraordinary shift in
the tempo of events. When McCarthy began to run, no one believed
that he had a chance. We were all drenched with a sense of defeat. . . .
Suddenly we've had this incredible phenomenon.[76]

Mailer was intrigued and encouraged by the belief that "the old
forms that were able to contain us ever since the Second World
War are just not working." He had written in *The Armies of the
Night* that "the center of America might be insane." By the
spring of 1968, he felt that the movement toward revolution had
begun by exposing the "madmen," the men in power.

Schlesinger expressed the same sentiment in liberal parlance:
"President Johnson accepted the case of his critics and we have—
rather than a choice between the worst among the Presidential
possibilities—a choice from among the best."[77] Only Marcuse
demurred from the prevailing optimism. He believed that the
democratic process had made itself felt only up to the point
where the will of the people might threaten the framework of
society. Given the concentrated power in a society where the
majority was "standardized" and "manipulated," he foresaw no
immediate prospect for real change.

MIGRATION TO MCCARTHY

Most intellectuals celebrated their sense of political emancipa-
tion that spring by shifting from discussion of the Vietnam War
per se to promotion of Eugene McCarthy for President. They
centered on McCarthy, not so much for what he was but for
what he had made possible and for what needs they projected
into him.

McCarthy had dared to challenge Johnson and his Vietnam
policy. He impressed the leftist intellectuals with his gesture of

moral rectitude, the act that was both real and symbolic in political impact. Robert Lowell, arch McCarthy supporter, drew upon the Senator's own poetry to convey the image of the brave trailblazer intellectuals particularly admired—and proved prophetic in the process:

The Tamarack tree is the saddest tree of all; it is the first tree to invade the swamp and when it makes the soil dry enough the other trees come and kill it. . . .[78]

The Minnesota Senator touched one of the bases of intellectual opposition to the Vietnam War when he repudiated the Cold War approach to American foreign policy. For him, Vietnam was "no accident." It was, instead, the product of containment doctrine institutionalized into a "University of the Cold War."[79] Hubert Humphrey had emerged as that school's "most ardent apologist," defending the war and every assumption which produced it. McCarthy challenged those articles and institutions of faith. He delighted critics by quipping, "We don't declare war any more, we declare national defense."[80] He stressed accountability over acquiescence in diplomatic decision-making. Thus, McCarthy put postwar emphasis on anti-Communism, military power, and "America's moral mission in the world" on the line for reaction.

Intellectuals lunged at the bait. Morgenthau applauded McCarthy's refusal to deceive himself or others.[81] Kennan thanked McCarthy for representing an alternative to Johnson's Vietnam policy at a time when Administration officials persisted "like men in a dream . . . seemingly unable to arrive at any realistic assessment of the effects of their own acts."[82]

By making Vietnam and U.S. foreign policy part of campaign debate, McCarthy helped diffuse the intellectuals' frustration with both the war and the "system." McCarthy was to liberalism what the New Deal had been to capitalism. Franklin Roosevelt's program saved free enterprise by applying intrasystemic reforms and luring many intellectuals into the effort. The McCarthy phenomenon represented change *within* the Establishment and rallied intellectuals to support a "system" many had written off. It was no accident that McCarthy was promoted to prominence by Allard Lowenstein, "a refugee from the New Deal hoping to make the dream work again."[83]

Although the lemminglike rush of intellectuals to the McCarthy movement showed their genuine dissatisfaction with what America had become, the speed and near unanimity with which they embraced that "liberal" solution raised questions about the depth of their avowed radicalism or their evaluation of McCarthy—or both. Part of the reason was disarmingly clear. Many intellectuals simply ignored the man and endorsed an image corresponding to what they wanted. As David Riesman admitted: "There is a tendency in all of us . . . to read ourselves into a condition we 'need' and hence on the part of some of his [McCarthy's] following, to see him as more radical than he is."[84] Irving Howe could support McCarthy as a means of "releasing the sentiments of the left-liberal community," while Murray Kempton could praise him as a revolutionary evangelist lacking complicity with the past.[85] To each according to his need.

Andrew Kopkind was one of the few to challenge the radicalized chimera conjured up by his colleagues. He reminded them of McCarthy's dreary record of sellouts in the Senate. He warned them that McCarthy was as devoted to the Establishment as was Robert Kennedy or Richard Nixon:

Neither Kennedy nor McCarthy will even think of breaking up the concentration of corporate power which is at the heart of America's undemocracy and produces the effects of imperialism and racism which the candidates decry. . . . What it will take to do all that is a politics independent of a Kennedy or McCarthy or Nixon Administration; radicals have their work cut out for them.[86]

Yet, in fairness to the intellectuals, there was more to their support for McCarthy than wish transference. The Senator's main support came from the spiritual heirs of Adlai Stevenson. The older ones had never particularly liked the Kennedys. The younger ones righteously scorned Robert Kennedy for his "opportunistic" entry into the Presidential race *after* the New Hampshire primary. Many remembered as McCarthy's finest hour his nomination of Stevenson at the Democratic convention in 1960. Not so many recalled that McCarthy's second choice had been Lyndon Johnson. Intellectuals admired McCarthy for his aversion to what they considered the baser instincts of the political animal, just as they had once identified with Stevenson "because he didn't seem really to *like* politics."[87] Robert Lowell even admitted that he preferred McCarthy "first for his negative qualities: lack of excessive charisma, driving ambition, machinelike drive, and the too great wish to be President."[88]

In backing McCarthy, intellectuals revealed that tendency for the antipolitical which recurred throughout the 1960s—whether in the explicit renunciation of politics pervading *The New York Review* or the implicit repudiation of power and "the people" prompting the extremes of "resistance." The very qualities which goaded McCarthy to his crusade and endeared him to the intellectuals blunted the political clout necessary to win the Presidency or end the war. Like many of the intellectuals themselves, McCarthy was sometimes too much the purist to accommodate himself to political compromise.

Furthermore, McCarthy could no more reunify the divided intelligentsia than he could unite the nation. It was not that McCarthy split the Intellectual Left or even the Democratic Party to which many intellectuals belonged. The Vietnam War had already exposed the anachronism of old coalitions and loyalties. McCarthy, while appreciating the moral thrust of the intellectuals' malaise, lacked the will and capacity to resolve factionalism on the Left. He was destined to disappoint all leftist comers. It was less his fault than theirs. McCarthy had emerged the knight gallant of the peace movement after being the third choice in Lowenstein's "Dump Johnson" campaign. The wonder of the Mc-

Carthy phenomenon was that intellectuals fixed on him when they should have been asking, Why only McCarthy? Galbraith had said in August, 1967, "This is a year when the people are right and the politicians are wrong." But 1968 underscored the politicians' power and popular base and the intellectuals' lack on both counts.

Why? Did the Intellectual Left have in the Thomas More of Minnesota the wrong man for that season? The question only breeds more of the same. What other candidate could have made a difference? Could McCarthy have won the nomination and the election with less poetry and more politicking? Or did the reaction four years later against George McGovern—against his compromise or his dalliance with Mayor Richard Daley—suggest otherwise? Were the intellectuals, in fact, doomed to wait for America to catch up with their Dream? In that answer, as noted before, lies the larger intrigue of the intellectuals' opposition to the Vietnam War.

SUMMER OF DISCONTENT

Senator Robert Kennedy's death on June 6, following that of the Reverend Martin Luther King on April 4, ended the brief respite of political euphoria. The assassinations revived the fears of madness loose in the land. They returned intellectuals to a more gloomy assessment of the situation at home and in Vietnam. William Phillips of *Partisan Review* mourned Robert Kennedy's death as the loss of "a symbol of the legitimacy of dissent."[89] The future again looked blackly uninviting to those for whom the slain leaders had represented the "charisma of change." *The New Republic* editors claimed that the fight begun by McCarthy and Kennedy was not over, but wondered: "What does a generation that has watched the successive slaughter of good men become?"[90]

Johnson's television address on March 31, North Vietnam's approval of preliminary discussions on April 3, and the initiation of peace talks in Paris on May 13—together with the sobering effect of the assassinations—contributed to reducing domestic criticism of the Vietnam War. Most Americans agreed gratefully to requests for quiet during the Paris negotiations. The Johnson Administration succeeded in capitalizing politically on that period. The call for less antiwar activity helped deflect the impact of McCarthy and gave Humphrey and Nixon pretexts for not clarifying their own positions on the war.

In effect, intellectuals also acceded to the moratorium on war dissent. There was little reference in their journals from April through June of 1968 to discrepancies in the Administration's position in Paris. Despite North Vietnamese de-escalation to meet Johnson's precondition for a bombing halt, the Administration persisted in bombing and in fact stiffened its San Antonio formula.

By summer, however, *The New Republic* dropped its restraint on criticism and took the Johnson Administration to task for its continuing intransigence on bombing.[91] Its editors supported Senator McCarthy's effort to talk directly with the Hanoi delegation in Paris despite the Administration's objections.[92] For its part, the Administration argued that dissent threatened the peace negotiations, just as it had insisted before that dissent hurt the war effort.

CONTRACONVENTIONAL IN MIAMI AND CHICAGO

Cynicism mounted in intellectual circles as it became clearer that the Establishment would prevail. *The New Republic* reprinted an item from its issue of July 2, 1924:

. . . There is a growing popular feeling that politics as now conducted is futile and unreal—that it is an occupation full of sound and fury, signifying nothing.[93]

The simmering mood of the summer came to a boil with the nominating conventions in August. On their eve, liberals and radicals alike made their final pleas to the "system." *The New Republic* published a special adless issue to appeal to Democratic Party delegates to renounce Humphrey or to ask Humphrey himself to step out of the race. In a remarkable admission for that journal, its editors wrote that Humphrey's nomination would make it "extremely difficult to effectively counter the arguments of those who contend in September that the politics of confrontation is the only way left to resist a system that has proved its corruption in Vietnam."[94] *The New York Review* carried a petition demanding "an open convention and meaningful choice."[95] Both appeals proved to be cries into the void. The very predictability of the Republican convention in Miami and the viciousness of the Democratic gathering in Chicago seemed to confirm the intellectuals' worst suspicions about contemporary American politics.

"Chicago" was a particularly striking juncture for the Intellectual Left. It clearly underscored its isolation from the Mayor Daleys and their masses. Arthur Waskow claimed that "Chicago proved that America is now governed by force, not consent." He called for a leftist coalition against "the four terrifying years of war and repression that now seem to be in prospect."[96] Elizabeth Hardwick concluded that "few had realized until Chicago how great a ruin Johnson and his war in Vietnam had brought down upon our country."[97]

Writers William Styron and Arthur Miller, covering the Democratic convention as "delegate challengers" for McCarthy, provided a unique perspective on the proceedings. Styron characterized the event as a "shame that most people who witnessed it will feel to their bones for a very long time."[98] Miller compared the mood within the Amphitheater to a session of the All-Union Soviet. The machinery of state mobilized to give Johnson what he wanted and to deny the voters' verdict in the primaries.

Above all, Miller stressed that an issue even larger than Vietnam was dividing the convention: "a split in the attitude toward power, two mutually hostile ways of being human."[99] Like many estranged intellectuals, Miller thought the Johnson government out of phase with the public and wondered "what had to happen before the powers realized they were not living in this time and in this place."[100]

Though demoralized by the Democratic convention, most older intellectuals conceded that young radicals stood to suffer most from the first broken heart of political affairs. Chicago confirmed militant youth's contention that "the basic institutions of liberal politics—the unions, the convention system, the mass media and the Democratic Party itself—are undemocratic."[101] To paraphrase Bob Dylan, they had nothing to live up to. When the Theatre for Ideas met in September, 1968, Tom Hayden proclaimed, "The system has been tried and found wanting."[102] Murray Kempton, fellow panelist and liberal columnist, dismissed Hayden by saying, "I think that Americans have a terrible temptation to use a kind of Faulknerian language to talk about what are Booth Tarkington experiences." TRB of *The New Republic* was probably closest to the mark when he wrote of young activists, "We need them more than they need us."[103]

Finally—perhaps inevitably?—Mailer strutted to center stage. Just as *The Armies of the Night* gave the best verbal still shot of the literary Left's turn to resistance in 1967, so did his *Miami and the Siege of Chicago* show its political stance in late 1968. For him and much of the Intellectual Left, the Chicago convention provoked the final and fitting paroxysm of response to Johnson's Vietnam policy.

Like most commentators, Mailer found little interesting or appealing about the Republican convention. He left Miami without knowing if Nixon was "a rudder to steer the ship of state or an empty captain above a directionless void, there to loose the fearful nauseas of the country."[104]

The Long Dark Night of the Soul

In contrast, the Democratic convention impinged upon Mailer's imagination. He left with what he considered a clear sense of the nominees and political forces. He evaluated the Chicago gathering in terms of the premise "politics is property." Convention politics depended, not on the art of the possible or the will of the people, but on an exchange of property. Mailer maintained that Johnson used Humphrey to vindicate his ego, the last vestige of his property. Humphrey succumbed to Johnson's interest rather than lose his own claim to property, the nomination. McCarthy betrayed his fanaticism by abstaining from the rules of exchange. Hence the fascination of that nonpolitician for Mailer and gang.

The political dynamics inside the Amphitheater thus pegged, Mailer concentrated on the war in the streets and parks. For him as for most leftist intellectuals, the confrontation between protesters and police was "the murderous paradigm of Vietnam."[105] He sympathized with the militant youth who resisted the schizophrenia and hypocrisy on which American society seemed built: "These children were his troops." Yet Mailer admitted that he could not relate to them or make "the essential connection" between tear gas and blood in Chicago and Vietnam that he had experienced in Washington the preceding October.

The difference was instructive. First, true to the dictates of the intellectual's role, Mailer sought but missed in Lincoln Park the symbolic inspiration of the March on the Pentagon. He wrote:

The justifications of the March on the Pentagon were not here. The reporter was a literary man—symbol had the power to push him into actions more heroic than himself. The fact that he had been marching to demonstrate against a building which was the living symbol of everything he most despised—the military-industrial complex of the land—had worked to fortify his steps.[106]

Second, the scope of devastation in Chicago forced Mailer to reassess his "true engagement." Was it to revolution or the stability of the nation? What price was he willing to pay for his life and America to go on? When he avoided confrontation, he wasn't sure whether he "was in danger of deteriorating, or becoming sufficiently tough to be able to take a backward step." It occurred to him that "a revolutionary with taste in wine has come already half the distance from Marx to Burke." A profound part of him "detested the thought of seeing his American society . . . disappear now in the nihilistic maw of a national disorder."

If one can take Mailer at his word—a debatable proposition— his response to Chicago reflected an important change from his earlier existential bravura. The Yippies fought out the extremes of Mailer's own fantasies and Mailer found himself detached from their struggle. He discovered the division within himself— insidious liberalism?! Like the radicalized intelligentsia he reflected, Mailer was humbled and puzzled by the revelation.

It was an inglorious demise to radical fervor befitting the course of events inside the Amphitheater. The "future storefront of the Mafia" [Humphrey] was nominated to oppose the "probable prince of the corporation" [Nixon]. Some said that Humphrey had promised everything but Muriel to preserve the vestiges of his political ego. After one hour of debate on the Vietnam plank in the party platform, "Lyndon Johnson was vindicated by the same poor arguments which had originally implicated him."[107]

For Mailer and the Intellectual Left in general, it had been a long war to lose. Basic emotion had been aroused for too little. All the possibilities seemed to evaporate into nothing much at all. Events were back in control. It seemed just possible to many leftist intellectuals that "one was at the edge of that watershed year from which the country might never function well again."[108]

DREARY POSTSCRIPT

As the emotional revulsion from Chicago abated within the intellectual community, that sector tried to regroup itself politically. It foundered on the realization that no party, with the possible exception of the Peace and Freedom Party, bespoke the sentiments stirred by the Vietnam experience. There seemed little the leftist intellectuals could do in a party which Hubert Humphrey tried to return to 1948—lest they, too, "beat on, boats against the current, borne back ceaselessly into the past."[109] It was the traditional dilemma of the American Intellectual Left that its ideas were expressed more frequently in word or gesture than through the electoral process.[110]

The political system gave intellectuals "the glum sensation of choicelessness." They felt that each dissenter from Administration policy was a helpless minority unto himself, "exercising options which are really non-options."[111] The editors at *The New Republic* considered Humphrey's efforts to dissociate himself from the Administration's Vietnam policy weak, desperate, and ineffective.[112] Gore Vidal scored Nixon as the "litmus-paper man of American politics" because he accommodated to the political milieu rejected by the intellectuals.[113] Even SANE pronounced both Nixon and Humphrey "unacceptable."

In their frustration with the lost, last hope offered by McCarthy, most intellectuals urged a clear renunciation of the only party that might have served their interests. Their calculations ranged from the desire to discredit the Democratic Party so badly that it would have to rebuild according to their will, to the belief that Nixon had a better chance to disengage the nation from Vietnam. No one, they reasoned, could accuse *him* of selling out to Communism.

Many intellectuals could not bear to vote. They hoped that staying home would, if not hurt Humphrey, at least assuage their consciences. Mary McCarthy explained that "the refusal to vote is conceived as a protest, an expression of total disgust, and not just on the part of liberals who, like me, used to vote for Norman Thomas to register dissaffection."[114]

She was typical of many leftist intellectuals who resented the "moral compulsion" to support Humphrey or the argument that there was no other choice, given the fact of Nixon. That strategy had worked in 1964. The liberal voter, afraid then that Goldwater would escalate the Vietnam conflict, had felt *forced* to vote for Johnson. Not so in 1968. Humphrey just antagonized most intellectuals when he warned, in the very tones Johnson had used against Goldwater, that Nixon would widen the war.

The fact that neither major Presidential candidate seemed willing or able to diverge from Johnson's Vietnam policy only fed the intellectuals' frustration. They continued to protest the Administration's blindness to de-escalatory signals from Hanoi and the persistence in bombing, the "symbolic" issue of the Paris negotiations.[115] Johnson's announcement of a bombing halt on October 31, just before the election, struck intellectuals as the apt dénouement to a Vietnam policy geared to domestic political calculations.

Still other leftist intellectuals agonized over the question of the "lesser evil." In that spirit, Paul Goodman opted for Richard Nixon: "Dick Nixon (!) . . . is the post to which they hitch the chariot of State when the horses are tired."[116] Hans Morgenthau disparaged the quest for the "lesser evil" since both candidates portended evil, "different in kind but not in degree." Yet he believed that the threat of George Wallace forced a choice upon responsible voters, "not between their intrinsic merits but between their respective abilities to contain Wallace." With that in mind, as well as the eventual hope for a restructured Democratic Party, he wrote:

. . . American democracy seems to be best served not only by Nixon's victory in 1968 but by a defeat of the Democratic Party so drastic as to amount to the disavowal of its present leadership, philosophy and policies and to render inevitable the radical transformation of its philosophy and structure.[117]

He argued that the popular base of the Democratic Party had been so decimated by Vietnam that it would never recover the way the Republican Party had done after the electoral debacle of 1964.

Despite his work on both the McCarthy and Kennedy campaigns, Michael Harrington was one of the few to choose Humphrey because of "straight lesser-evilism."[118] Murray Kempton resisted the plea to support Humphrey on those grounds. He felt that the Vice President had forsworn political decency by embracing Mayor Daley. Kempton spoke for many leftist intellectuals when he asserted that the controlling fact of politics in 1968 was the belief that many Americans were ashamed of their country. They were confused by a recent history determined by assassinations and by institutions too distorted to represent the popular will. The only honorable choice for the future lay in what Kempton called "politics of conscience":

> We must struggle for every candidate who fought against this time when there is nothing to vote for at the top of the line, that alone gives us a chance for another time when there will be a face there again.[119]

Finally, there was a tendency for the Intellectual Left to apply moral absolutism to the Presidential campaign. Making Humphrey rather than Nixon the main target recalled the 1930s. Then radical intellectuals had found in the liberal "an enemy who shared enough of their own values to be despised for not sharing them *à outrance*."[120]

After Nixon's victory, intellectuals resigned themselves to a repressive Republican interregnum. Apparently sensing the despair of the intellectual community and trying to counter political paralysis, *Partisan Review* reprinted Leon Trotsky's essay of 1912, "Concerning the Intelligentsia." Trotsky had scolded Russian intellectuals who succumbed to depression under the recovered Czarist government following defeat by Japan and the Revolution of 1905, and had urged them to use that time as a mere prelude to revolution.[121]

Other liberal writers tried to come to terms with political reality.[122] However, most intellectuals seemed uncertain of themselves and their mission. The intelligentsia was torn between considering itself liberal or radical, rather like Mailer battling with himself in Lincoln Park. Most intellectuals felt more alienated than ever from the national mood. Their moral opposition to Johnson's Vietnam policy had not converted their fellow countrymen. The tragedy for intellectuals lay in the fact that 1968 *did* reflect the will of the people. Richard Nixon found himself in the enviable position of the French general shouting to his troops: "I must follow them; I am their leader!"

Thus, when Professor Zbigniew Brzezinski spoke to a convention of intellectuals at the end of 1968, he unwittingly conveyed the Intellectual Left's bleak view of its status in America: "If my colleagues and I all drop dead today, there'd be big obituaries tomorrow, but no social effect."[123]

Epilogue

*We must get it out of our head that this is a doomed
time, that we are waiting for the end, and the rest of
it. . . . Things are grim enough without these shivery
games. . . . We love apocalypses too much.*

Saul Bellow
Herzog, 1964

Drawing by David Levine. Reprinted with permission from *The New York
Review of Books.* Copyright © 1969 The New York Review.

Long "dark night of the soul"?[1] To some extent, American intellectuals have always felt that darkness was about to fall. Miracu-
lously or mysteriously, it never has done so.

The Long Dark Night of the Soul

Yet, for the intellectual elite—like the rest of us—perception is often more compelling than reality. The prospect by 1969 *was* bleak because it *looked* that way to the intellectuals. Never mind that Johnson was out. Nixon was in. We, they thought, are the public conscience. How could the people have let *us* down?

It was elitism with a vengeance, and with little avail for the needs of the new decade. The 1970s required a President and an intelligentsia with the will to restore a sense of national legitimacy. Each, ironically, spoke of a "new American revolution" and "power to the people." Each meant something different. Each, perhaps, meant nothing much at all.

The My Lai disclosures hit and disappeared from the headlines before the public got the message the intellectuals thought they should. Writers like Mary McCarthy were left thinking, "We will be lucky . . . if failure, finally, is the only crime we are made to confess. . . ."[2] The publication of the "Pentagon Papers" in 1971 proved to Gabriel Almond's "attentive public," if not to its mass counterpart, that Vietnam was no fluke. The tragedy of that war, as far as most intellectuals were concerned, was that "the system worked."[3] Concomitantly, the government lost their allegiance.

The nation's Intellectual Left reached that conclusion only in stages. Its literature shows that it shifted gradually from stress on pragmatic questions of national security to emphasis on moral issues that challenged the authority of the Johnson Administration. The war was first a lapse in judgment, then an exercise in immorality, and finally a reflection of political illegitimacy.

No society, particularly one like that of the United States, which depends on mutual respect between the government and the governed, can survive or develop without a claim to legitimacy—that intangible mandate for authority. Military reverses have always tended to undo both the least and the most stable of governments. The examples of Czarist Russia after humiliation at Japanese hands or the Hohenzollern regime following defeat by the Allies come to mind. War involves the entire national identity

—real and symbolic. Consequently it bears on the very basis of legitimacy.

Though the United States did not lose the Vietnam War in the 1960s, it did not win it either. The fighting just dragged on. Nightly telecasts seemed to confirm the government's ineffectiveness. The man on the street did not talk in terms of lost legitimacy or distorted priorities. Yet he may have meant the same thing when he complained about corruption in politics, crime in the streets, and filth in the air.

Partly because of that mood, the intellectuals often seemed to achieve disproportionate influence during the decade. They seized the war as their weapon and poised for the *coup de grâce* to national legitimacy. How lasting or serious is the wound? With lingering U.S. involvement in Southeast Asia and with few answers to the questions raised during the Johnson era, the wound could fester for some time. Public cynicism—witness the subsequent reaction to "Watergate"—was just one symptom of a more pervasive malaise. Though there was no necessary relationship between the way successive Presidents treated separate tests of political legitimacy, revulsion against Nixon's handling of Watergate fed, in part, on disillusionment fostered by Johnson's Vietnam policy. There was a wry irony to a statement made by Spiro Agnew and quoted by the Washington *Post* after the Vice-President's resignation in 1973:

The last decade saw the most precipitous decline in respect for law of any decade in our history. Some of those who call each other "intellectuals" helped to sow the wind, and America reaped the whirlwind.

INTELLECTUALS IN REVIEW

The Intellectual Left has had and will continue to have much to say about the return of the nation's political health. Their record from the last decade already holds some insight. It tells, for example, a great deal about sentiments and changes within intellectual ranks. It reflects the leftist intellectuals' rapport (or lack thereof) with Main Street, their posturing at a political Fountain of Youth, and their equivocation at the seat of power. To recapitulate and comment. . . .

SPLIT ON THE CHARLES

Not all leftist intellectuals were alienated from the "system." Not every writer reacted the same way to the war—or at the same time. If Johnson lacked consensus, so did the Intellectual Left. Dissensus more often prevailed, despite the intellectuals' general movement toward repoliticization and reradicalization and the fact that the war awakened their sense of community as intellectuals. The new historiography both set the stage for criticism of Johnson's Vietnam policy and pitted revisionists against traditionalists when the war came. Vietnam revived the recurrent battle between U.S. liberals and radicals. The role of certain liberals within the Kennedy and Johnson Administrations raised questions about when an intellectual ceases to be a critic of power. The war underscored the clash between "humanist" intellectuals and the technocrats.

The division was so acute that a single university often became a microcosm of conflict within the entire Intellectual Left. At the Massachusetts Institute of Technology, Ithiel de Sola Pool, political scientist, confronted Noam Chomsky, linguist. Pool blamed his colleagues for discounting the CIA as "the epitome of evil rather than recognizing their brothers in the search of knowledge."[4] Chomsky condemned the "new mandarins" who proposed "to move a nation" with counterinsurgency and computerized kill ratios. He attributed the dereliction of academic intellectuals vis-à-vis Vietnam to their behavioralist conception of man. In its claim to specialized expertise, behavioralism camouflaged the mandarins' aspirations to power and minimized the importance of moral considerations.

The Long Dark Night of the Soul

Some concluded from such exchanges that twentieth-century specialization of knowledge will yet render the humanist intellectual irrelevant. The leftist intellectuals' opposition to the Vietnam War may have been a rear-guard exercise in futility against the Age of Technology. If so, the Intellectual Left went out with a commendable whimper.

LOST RAPPORT WITH MAIN STREET

Poll data from both Gallup and the ballot box indicate that leftist intellectuals failed to convert the country to their way of thinking in the 1960s. They changed neither hearts nor minds with regard to the Vietnam War and a restructuring of U.S. society.

Their failure was not for lack of shared concerns. At home, most Americans recoiled from the assassinations of respected leaders and cities reduced to combat zones. Abroad, they puzzled over the U.S. role as world policeman and agonized over the tension between a moralizing tradition in public diplomacy and the actual exercise of imperial power. Both intellectuals and their fellow countrymen felt a growing sense of powerlessness in a mass society teetering in a world imbalance of terror.

Opinion samplings indicated that Vietnam was the main concern of all Americans during most of the Johnson Administration. However, long after the President lost the support of the Intellectual Left by bombing North Vietnam in early 1965, he kept the allegiance of the public. With Johnson's popularity up ten points in polls after the March on the Pentagon in October, 1967, Norman Mailer remarked: "When it came to sensing new waves of public opinion, LBJ was the legendary surfboarder of them all." Influential as the intellectuals were in ousting Johnson, the public's eventual renunciation of the war on pragmatic grounds encompassed neither the moral outrage which underlay the intellectuals' response to the war nor the re-examination of American foreign policy which the critics hoped would prevent future Vietnams. Despite the peace movement, Americans, when asked "who would do a better job in handling the Vietnam War?" still preferred Hubert Humphrey to Eugene McCarthy, 47 to 29 percent.[5] Why?

Any group which wants to affect public opinion must at least start by enlisting established points of view. The United States of the 1960s was primarily a conservative, consensual society. With regard to the Vietnam War, it had to be approached on *its* terms before it could become more concerned about the Nuremberg principles than food prices. It associated peace protests with campus kooks and saw no reason to believe that the nation needed radical revision. The hard-hat reacted to violence at home and frustration abroad by voting for Nixon's "low profile," not more disruption from "resistance."

Rather than understanding or addressing the public mood, the Intellectual Left couched its argument in bombast bound to turn off widespread support. Its recurrent loathing for Midcult and the "tyranny of the majority" showed. Indeed, radical dissent from the middle class had preceded and would survive the war. The discrepancy between public and elite perspectives made too many radical intellectuals turn discussion points into non-negotiable demands, yet another reflection of *The Paranoid Style of American Politics.*[6]

Even according to the leftist intellectuals' own dialectic, a revolutionary situation never existed during the Johnson era. To suggest that it did merely served to antagonize the real-life *Joe* or Archie Bunker. He felt threatened enough by change without the intellectuals' feeding his paranoia. No matter what one called the American majority in 1968—hidden, silent, imagined, emerging, or real—the Center was in control and was concentrating on "law and order." By 1969, campus disorders replaced Vietnam as the main concern of the American people. No statistics then justified taking a new coalition on the Left seriously. Many radical intellectuals exaggerated public frustration, miscalculated its basis, or disregarded all evidence and surrendered themselves to an orgy of apocalypticism. They diverged from more moderate colleagues who cautioned against provocation lest repression rear from its rightist lair. In so doing, they split the peace movement and undermined what little political power the Intellectual Left had.

Thus, although the Vietnam experience brought out the shared powerlessness of the populace, it revealed crucial differences between the political impotence of the popular majority and the intellectual minority. Since the public and the intelligentsia differed in both their evaluation and their response to the Vietnam War, their division outweighed potential rapport and simply reinforced the traditional estrangement of American intellectuals. In effect, the people disowned or delegitimated their own symbolic legitimists. Whether another Daniel Ellsberg can ever put the Vietnam War itself on trial and so raise the public consciousness, as the Intellectual Left would have it, remains unclear.

DALLIANCE AT THE FOUNTAIN OF YOUTH

Youth was the vanguard which took intellectuals in tow during the 1960s. The Intellectual Left drew from the moral outrage and activist approach of politicized students the substance and style of its own radicalization. Paul Goodman was typical. Though aghast before the Manichean nightmare of youngsters who culled the elect and the damned according to their own precepts, he could never break from the belief that the young would be his and the nation's salvation. Raymond Aron discerned the same phenomenon in the Parisian intellectuals' rush to the barricades in 1968. He disparaged "the enthusiasm shown by grown men who thought they were living, or reliving, a revolutionary epic."[7] In like manner, extrapolations from Jean-François Revel's *Without Marx or Jesus* found their mark in the American Intellectual Left.

American college youth, inspired to moral witness by the civil rights movement, helped restore a politics of conscience. That trend attracted intellectuals because of their perennial preoccupation with moral questions. There was, for example, an obvious continuity for some conscientious objectors from the 1940s who resurfaced to help college students resist the draft in the 1960s. For others, the act of will at Greensboro[8] set the crucial mode of the "transformative" experience. Stokely Carmichael had scolded white university youth for "coming alive through the black community" and the civil rights movement.[9] Yet the spectacle of Norman Mailer, Robert Lowell, and Dwight Macdonald marching on the Pentagon with a politicized Sergeant Pepper's Band attested to more than their empathy for the Cause. It suggested their quest for political relevance and rejuvenation through the youthful peace movement.

Some intellectuals' submission to what Robert Lifton called a "protean" sensibility[10] blunted their political impact and revived anti-intellectualism. First, as Richard Scammon and Ben Wattenberg stressed, the projected coalition of young, black, and intellectual—with the poor tossed in for egalitarian fillip—was little more than a figment of intellectual wish fulfillment in 1968. Though it was a start—as 1972 was to show—it could not stand alone as a political constituency. In fact, it was not clear whether it could be considered one bloc at all. The shift in the protesters' mood in Washington from August, 1963, to October, 1967, reflected how Vietnam exposed what Mailer called the black Achilles' heel of the New Left. With Martin Luther King of the SCLC in 1963, there had been an eager, if *too* polite, unanimity between the races. With John Wilson of SNCC in 1967, blacks openly disdained whites and withdrew to make their own demonstration elsewhere.

Second, many intellectuals renounced "rationality" as the demon behind the war. That tendency, together with their liaison with young and admittedly anti-intellectual dissenters, contributed to the travesty of intellectuals disparaging intellect. Vietnam reconstituted C. P. Snow's dilemma of the "two cultures" in such a way that the American intelligentsia skewered itself on the competing points of reason and passion. Radicalized intellectuals like Staughton Lynd appeared close to the Maoist doctrine of "red first, expert second." They condemned the purely academic mind to extinction in the name of liberation.[11] Diana Trilling made the point: Radical intellectuals assert that "a higher reasonableness will be reached by acts of unreason" and embrace the "ambiguousness" of the student revolution to blur "the ambiguousness . . . of our moral and intellectual times."[12]

In view of their experience during the Johnson era, many intellectuals began to wonder whether the life of the mind alone was a self-justifying *raison d'être.* The intellectuals' activist response to the Vietnam War in the 1960s may have wrought an overreaction to the privatized passivity of the 1950s. That about-face threatened, in turn, most productive mergers between scholarship and social relevance for the 1970s.

Youth was more the conduit than the culprit in this process. It was the intellectuals' view of power, defined as the public authority's capacity for effective action, which underlay their response to Johnson's Vietnam policy. Their problem was part of the general and continuing conflict between the critic and agent of authority.

The reaction of the dissident intelligentsia to the Administration only revealed more specific dimensions of the problem. The Vietnam War demonstrated the contrasting political perspectives which the government and the intelligentsia brought to bear on U.S. foreign policy. Even their historical references were instructive. Dean Rusk recalled the lesson of appeasement at Munich to justify U.S. action in Southeast Asia. Noam Chomsky invoked the ethic of war guilt at Nuremberg to condemn American intervention. Whereas officials in the Johnson Administration believed that they could not afford to lose in Vietnam, leftist critics came to feel that the nation could only lose by trying to win. Each side, given the context in which it thought and operated, believed what it said. Neither, however, undertook the serious examination the situation required: on the officials' part, a probe of Vietnam's value to the United States, or for the intellectuals, an inquiry into what kind of settlement was possible in Vietnam or what motivated decision-making in Washington. (The officials were to attempt the latter themselves, to some extent, in the "Pentagon Papers" exercise.)

Though lines of communication might have stayed more open with greater candor from the government and less cacophony from the intelligentsia, there was little chance for them to see eye to eye on massive U.S. involvement in Vietnam. The apparent official refusal to heed the intellectuals' protests simply undermined an already precarious relationship. The rudest shock had come with the first U.S. bombing of North Vietnam. The intellectuals considered that action a slap at their trust in Johnson's campaign promises in 1964. Combined with the American invasion of the Dominican Republic in 1965, that betrayal jeopardized what little rapport had existed between the intelligentsia and the Johnson Administration. Some intellectuals concluded from the experience of the Vietnam teach-ins that there was little chance for dialogue between the intelligentsia and the government. The "Lowell incident" at the White House Festival of the Arts, the two *Partisan Review* symposia, and Carl Oglesby's speech at the SANE March on Washington showed how 1965 became a watershed in relations. By 1966, even the pro-Great Society *New Republic* suggested that Johnson could serve his party and country best by forgoing the 1968 Presidential race. By 1967, dissent turned into resistance. With Chicago, the exclusion of the leftist intellectuals from power seemed clarified and, with the election of Nixon, sanctified.

By making Vietnam the measure of the legitimacy of the government, the intellectuals were brought full circle in their powerlessness. Their propensity to find in youthful sensibility a means of political perspective contributed to and reflected many intellectuals' unsatisfactory relationship with power. The intelligentsia's sense of political impotence was so acute by 1968 that Noam Chomsky, Paul Lauter, and Florence Howe concluded from the Boston draft-card "conspiracy" trial that the fundamental issue of their times was the rightful exercise of official authority. They could see no prospect for legitimate government in the United States.

Distressing as that conclusion was for American intellectuals, the fault lay neither in the "system" nor in the proverbial stars but largely within themselves. The intellectuals foundered in their opposition to Johnson's Vietnam policy primarily because of a dilemma inherent in their role as society's naysayers. They were condemned to powerlessness by the predictable tendency, especially among radical critics, to stress the contradiction between morality and politics. The failure of much of the Intellectual Left to maintain the necessary balance between the moral and the political lay at the heart of that community's response to the Vietnam War. It remains a continuing dilemma for the U.S. intelligentsia.

The intellectuals' preoccupation with moral truth inspired their stand against Johnson's Vietnam policy. It helped activate their repoliticization and reradicalization. Yet that very sequence presaged contradiction. Devotion to moral purity made many intellectuals shun political compromise. On the general level, the individual clashed with authority. It was entirely appropriate that anti-Vietnam resisters invoked the precedent of the Abolitionists. Both advocated immediate solutions that were more morally satisfying than politically practicable. Free the slaves, end the war—now!

166

The Long Dark Night of the Soul

That is not to disparage the objectives or the frustrations with the political system in either case, only the methods. Repoliticization, taken to the extreme of moralism, brought a counterproductive dissociation of politics and morality. Thoreau as prophet transcending the state anticipated Susan Sontag as counterrevolutionary.

Antipolitics, then, was not new to American intellectuals. It simply had not surfaced for some time. It is rarely apparent when things are going well—when there is public indulgence for the intellectuals, when they have jobs, and when the United States seems benignly pre-eminent in world affairs. The tradition reasserts itself when affairs go awry. It reappeared, for example, when Lyndon Johnson maligned the intellectual "Nervous Nellies" and the war soured. There were cries of "genocide" from intellectuals primarily when power began to wane. They had been quiet when the government seemed omnipotent and had clasped them to its treasury. Whereas the intellectuals' antipolitics has most often amounted to withdrawal—as in the 1950s—it took an activist turn in the 1960s. Intellectuals took to the streets and the broadsheets.

Enter a related phenomenon as old as the intellectuals' antipolitics: the ambiguity toward power. The intelligentsia was at once fascinated and repelled by power, as witness its mercurial relationship with both Kennedy and Johnson. It was not an accident that the Intellectual Left tried to discredit politics by associating it with power. Theodore Roszak stated: "Politics is the organization of power, and power is the enemy of life."[13] Ithiel de Sola Pool chided his colleagues in the Theatre for Ideas for "four fashionable clichés about power": "people are increasingly powerless in modern society, power in America is increasingly concentrated, it is more moral to be a critic than a member of the Establishment, and power is a bad thing."[14]

The case was not as clear-cut as either Roszak or Pool suggested. Although the leftist intellectuals of the 1960s talked a great deal about power, they did little to come to grips with it. They were caught in their own lines of logic. They both hated and denied power. Read: the authority of the Johnson Administration. Yet they acceded to its fact. They expected it to respond to their critique and fulminated against "illegitimate authority" when it did not. By stressing the immorality of the Vietnam War at the same time that they rejected all possibility of ending it by conventional political means, many radical intellectuals reached the height of self-defeating cynicism. With the conclusion that they could not achieve peace in Vietnam without revolution in America, radical intellectuals were powerless indeed. The split between those who chose to speak through power and those who preached against it betrayed the difference between those liberals in 1968 who heard a firecracker and those radicals who detected the crack of doom. No matter which sector of the American Intellectual Left historians come to vindicate the immediate effect of the estrangement between the dissident intelligentsia and the Johnson Administration was to leave both humbled by the experience. It was an ironic *dénouement* to the decade, ill serving the men of power or their critics—or a nation in need of their complementarity of perspectives on Vietnam.

Did that conclusion foreclose all contact between Morgenthau's truth and power? Again, the discrepancy between perception and reality was critical. The merger was impossible primarily if seen as such. An ironic twist to our times makes the point. After years of intellectual treks to Washington during Democratic administrations, it took Richard Nixon to give significant power to an intellectual. The scholarly credentials of Henry Kissinger are impeccable and his contributions to modern diplomacy indisputable. Yet, like the man who said, "That was no lady, that was my wife," many on the Left still claim that Kissinger is no intellectual but Metternich in mandarin guise.

The Long Dark Night of the Soul

The retort is telling. The leftist intellectuals suffered—and still suffer—from their problem with power. There was proof of it during the 1960s in their preference for critique over program, their use of ideology, their denunciation of liberalism, their revival of anarchism, their preoccupation with existential fulfillment, and their rhetorical excess. All indicated how the moral drive behind the intellectuals' opposition to Johnson's Vietnam policy spurred their repoliticization only to reverse that process. What followed was, in effect, the depoliticization of the intellectuals.

Furthermore, some intellectuals resorted to such extremes of resistance and so circumvented the will of "the people" whom they pretended to represent that they jeopardized the very cause of peace. "No one," as Michael Walzer observed, "can be morally justified in acting (however heroically) in ways that defeat his own stated purposes."[15] To do so, no matter the apparent lack of choice, betrayed the moral mission of society's self-proclaimed moral guardians.

PREFERENCE FOR CRITIQUE OVER PROGRAM

The intellectuals used Vietnam, in Susan Sontag's words, as their "ideal Other." It was the catalyst. It galvanized discontent and exposed contradictions throughout the political system. Yet the intellectuals never progressed from their "systematic criticism of America" to a coherent political program.[16] Nor, in fact, was their critique notably systematic. Little writing by the Intellectual Left of the 1960s went much beyond incensed revelation to comprehensive analysis of why the nation's leaders acted as they did and what that meant.

That is not to discount the value of exposé or moral gesture as such. It is simply to suggest that the intellectuals never resolved for themselves what they should or could do against the war or an allegedly dehumanized society. They never came to grips with the question raised by Staughton Lynd: "Is what's intended a moral gesture only, or a determined attempt to transform the American power structure?"[17] If a sociology of alienation explained the radical intellectuals' attempt to equate the function of politics with, as Lynd put it, "the building of a brotherly way of life . . . in the jaws of Leviathan," it did not excuse abdication from politics. Nor did it excuse the potential immorality of the intellectuals' morally premised renunciation of politics.

USE OF IDEOLOGY

The intellectuals' response to the Vietnam War revealed several types of ideology, most of which were antipolitical in effect. There were still some liberal adherents to "the end of ideology," whom C. Wright Mills condemned for their "intellectual celebration of apathy." There were those so traumatized by their flirtation with Communism in the 1930s that they overreacted with what Hal Draper called the "non-ideological hangup."

Perhaps most characteristic of leftist reaction in the 1960s was the radical intellectuals' infatuation with "participatory democracy" and "Guevarism." Those were the home-grown and imported reflections of pre-Marxist utopian socialism or Marxism as a humanist vision of the good society. Both dimensions appealed to intellectuals alienated from the bureaucratized nation that could produce the Vietnam War. Again, one does not question the sincerity of the intellectuals' desire for a more humanized society, only their politics—or lack of it. Like Soviet Communism imported in the 1930s, neither "participatory democracy" nor Guevarism was appropriate to American conditions. Equating Scarsdale with the Sierra Maestra could not stop evil or prevent the onslaught of worse. Whatever advantage riding the beast of revolution to discover the true nature of the situation—to paraphrase Mailer—produced in existential affirmation, that approach destroyed by dividing the Left and weakening intellectual opposition to an organized power structure.

RELIANCE ON MARGINAL GROUPS

Intellectuals erred in basing much of their "revolutionary" movement on two marginal groups—the students and the blacks. Margot Hentoff admitted belatedly the intellectuals' "neo-populist faith first in the blacks and then in the young as the instruments of purification, the trustees of a new morality."[18] The leftist intellectuals' dependence on such minorities was derived in part from their susceptibility to youthful sensibilities and their shared concerns about the war.

It drew more fundamentally from the American intellectuals' perennial vacillation between democratic aspiration and elite identity—their love of "the people" and loathing for the Average Man. The peace movement, as a mass in the vanguard, satisfied both tendencies. By 1968, however, it became clear that the coalition of the young and the intellectual was becoming an entity unto itself. It was a surrogate citizenry often insensitive to and replacing the recalcitrant populace. Because too few intellectuals could reconcile their image of "the people" with the political reality grasped by a George Wallace, they lost influence.

The intellectuals' failure was all the more galling because of the growing convergence of the Left and Right. Both Students for a Democratic Society and the Ku Klux Klan, for example, opposed the concentration of Federal power and worried most about FBI infiltration. Yet leftist intellectuals of the Sixties failed to speak effectively and so seize the opportunity offered by the growing complementarity of concerns across the political board.

The Long Dark Night of the Soul

FROM LIBERALISM TO ANARCHISM

The peace movement of the 1960s caught the Intellectual Left in a contradiction between the aims of its radical and liberal components. Their mutual critiques created a tautology which destroyed what they had in common. Furthermore, the liberal-radical split recalled both the factionalism of the American Left in the 1930s and the precedent set by the left-wing intelligentsia of Weimar Germany.

The dramatic revival of American intellectual interest in the Weimar Left during the 1960s was not accidental.[19] Interpretations of the past reflected the contemporary dichotomy between liberal and radical perspectives on political responsibility. There were obvious parallels between the *linke Intellektuelle* espousing *das andere Deutschland* and the American Left pursuing a "new America." More liberal American intellectuals drew from the Weimar precedent an equation between political responsibility and pragmatic moderation. They hoped to effect maximal social change with minimal rightist backlash. More radical intellectuals met their critics' charges of nihilism with the argument espoused in behalf of *Die Weltbühne*, the onetime counterpart of *The New York Review*: Society itself dictated the choices of politicized literati who foresaw in the 1920s that only a radical restructuring of the republic could prevent the decline to authoritarianism which occurred in the 1930s.

It is of more than passing interest that Herbert Marcuse, one intellectual mentor of the American radicals in the 1960s, had rejected the Weimar Republic outright in the early 1930s. Indeed, American intellectuals brought the points of the Weimar debate to bear directly in their response to the Vietnam War throughout the Johnson period. The fundamental division on strategy for the peace movement reflected disagreement between liberals and radicals on the need for a revolutionary change in the United States.

172

As passion superseded reason, it was psychologically consistent for the Intellectual Left of the Sixties to perceive the revolutionary struggle as not between liberalism and conservatism, as had been the case in the Fifties, but between radicalism and liberalism. The tendency during the 1968 election to "opt out" or back the Republican Party smacked of the naïve proposition, *"nach Nixon, uns."* Yippie provocateurs in Chicago, often supported by the radical Intellectual Left, had hoped that blatant repression would rouse the public to revolution. Instead, support for Mayor Daley unmasked the true political face of the citizenry. In the short run, powerlessness betrayed the intellectuals' nobility of intention. Contemporaries could only mourn a comparable abdication from political responsibility by the American Left of the Johnson era and the German Left of the Weimar Republic.

Allusions to anarchism betrayed further the sense of powerlessness among intellectuals and their growing distrust of authority during the Johnson period. Again, the proliferation of American literature on the subject was more than coincidence. Many intellectuals welcomed the revived interest in anarchism as a response to alienation. Yet it was generally a Bakuninist phase emphasizing agitation, direct action, and disruption. Those were traditionally ineffectual ways to seize or manage power.

EGO GRATIFICATION

The revival of existentialism was related to that of anarchism. Paul Goodman remarked that, thanks to students, "politics have been existentialized." Therein lay the value of the change he perceived at the political turning point for American intellectuals in 1965.[20] Still, real revolution required more political sophistication and less of the preoccupation with existential fulfillment which characterized so much of the radical intellectuals' response to Johnson's Vietnam policy. With passion and meaning valued over accomplishment, their political gestures were sometimes more personally therapeutic than socially effective.

All too often, the individual transformation or self-gratification gained through confrontation was the central experience. Andrew Kopkind's definition of the intellectual as a "street organizer"[21] and Howard Zinn's dedication to the "historian as an actor"[22] suggested the tendency. Irving Louis Horowitz asserted that, like the *fin de siècle* radicalism of Western Europe, American radicalism in the 1960s was "a reassertion of the priorities of egotism."[23] He argued that radical intellectuals drew on the passion and idealism of the decade's youth culture to absolve their sense of personal and political guilt. Encouraging or participating in resistance against the Johnson Administration helped some intellectuals to hedge against knowledge of their own political acquiescence or liberal hypocrisy in the 1950s and early 1960s. To avoid corruption, they rejected serious politics in favor of psychodrama. The regular gathering of the New York literary clan in a self-confirming "Theatre for Ideas" was its own apt indictment.

VERBAL FALLOUT

The shrill tone and vitriolic content of many intellectuals' statements in the 1960s gave the clearest index to their political failure. Indeed, one could trace the estrangement between the Intellectual Left and the Johnson Administration by the rhetorical escalation. The government's deepening commitment to the war expressed itself in increasingly Orwellian justification of the American mission. We are in Vietnam, said Johnson, "to wage the battle for peace." That kind of language infuriated the intellectuals almost more than the war itself. The critics wanted the Administration to address what they considered the real issues and not just to court voters.

The intellectuals, in turn, voiced their mounting desperation to end the war in verbal overkill to match the military variety in

Vietnam. Their all-out attack undercut their impact on public attitudes and politicians. Susan Sontag did not win over Middle America by proclaiming, "The white race is the cancer of human history." Nor did she reach a Walt Rostow, whose chief regret in 1969 was that the United States had not escalated the war earlier.[24] Since there could be no politics commensurate with Miss Sontag's stand, she held forth unencumbered by considerations of political consequence. Powerlessness grew by feeding upon itself.

It was one matter for the intelligentsia to sympathize with the moral outrage that motivated the students' politics of alienation. It was quite another to let that empathy excuse submission to the young militants' style to the exclusion of all other considerations. The verbiage of both public diplomacy and intellectual dissent served the interests of neither the government nor the intelligentsia and only widened the gap between the two. The nation still suffers from the rhetorical fallout.

NEW POLITICS

If the foregoing evaluation of intellectual opposition to the Vietnam War seems unduly harsh, a longer-term view may soften the critique. Therein *may* lie the recompense for the intellectuals' long dark night of the soul.

Although the intellectuals agonized in the apparent impasse between morality and politics and erred in their approach to power in the short run during the 1960s, they affirmed, by the very nature of their moral opposition to Johnson's policy, the new politics of conscience. Senator McCarthy wrote with some justification that a "general constituency of conscience was shown to exist in America."[25] Although U.S. intellectuals abused the political implications of their moral challenge to the Vietnam War, the principle of their protest redounded to their long-term credit and their continuing claim as the nation's naysayers.

175

If the split between liberals and radicals precluded a united intellectual front against the Indochina conflict, it still stimulated a healthful challenge to the postwar liberal consensus. Lionel Trilling had warned in the 1950s that it was "not conducive to the real strength of liberalism that it should occupy the intellectual field alone."[26] Liberalism unchallenged became complacent. The Vietnam experience spurred the beginning of a division between the "conscience" and the "class" wings of the Democratic Party. It replaced the bread-and-butter issues of the New Deal era with those of the quality of life and realignment of national priorities.

To some extent, it heralded George McGovern's coming of age in 1972 and the 180-degree turn from Chicago to Miami. It let the South Dakotan preach liberalism that was a cross between the New Politics and the Old Populism. The way was open—if not ready—for a radicalized liberalism that would redefine the relationship of individuals to government. Though Marcuse still rang truer than Charles (*The Greening of America*) Reich in his view of American political reality, there was and is hope that the "prophetic minority" may still come into its own.

NEW DIPLOMACY

Although intellectuals did not convince the public or the government by their moral case against the Vietnam War, they did set in motion some important new considerations for American foreign policy. First, the intellectuals' role in opposition to the war contributed to the decay of Johnson's consensus. Some gloated over the President's confession in 1969: "Vietnam has been the most frustrating of all the crises I have faced."[27] His decision not to seek re-election confirmed, at least in part, the need for foreign policy to accord with popular priorities. If the antiwar movement did nothing else, it ensured that no future American President could dismiss the lesson lightly—though dismiss it he might. Richard Nixon at least had to rationalize the Cambodian operation of 1970 and continued bombing elsewhere as "protective reaction" to save American lives and expedite the timetable of U.S. troop withdrawal from Vietnam.

Second, the intelligentsia's opposition to the Vietnam War revived the beneficial exercise of debate of American foreign policy. The collapse of the American Left after World War II and its disappearance into an anti-Communist sanctuary had left the assumptions of Cold War diplomacy unchallenged. Inspired by a younger generation not directly affected by Cold War experiences and pushed by the black and poor angered with a foreign policy which diverted welfare funds to war, the intellectuals came full round with Vietnam in the cycle of their own neglect of postwar foreign policy. Even allowing for "repressive tolerance," the growing attention to revisionist historiography suggested the beginning of a new "conventional wisdom" in the foreign-affairs Establishment.

Controversy rocked the Establishment itself. Members of the Council of Foreign Relations protested the appointment in 1971 of one of their own—William P. Bundy—to edit *Foreign Affairs*. Men like Richard Falk, Richard Barnet, and Ronald Steel questioned "rewarding" the man who had been Johnson's Assistant Secretary of State for East Asian and Pacific Affairs. Hamilton Fish Armstrong, the man Bundy replaced, remarked: "The war in Vietnam has been the longest and in some ways the most calamitous war in our history."[28] If the club membership did not change, at least its outlook began to. And, yes, Henry Kissinger and Richard Nixon made the belated pilgrimage to Peking.

"NEW AMERICA"

Finally, "radical chic" all but submerged the most fundamental undercurrent. More important than the potential long-range realignment of domestic forces and the readjustment of foreign policy was—and is—the intellectuals' obsessive quest after their meaning as Americans and the validity of the American Dream and their hunt for a "new America."[29] Norman Mailer asserted at the Berkeley teach-in of 1965:

America is a country which has never decided its true nature. It's a country in which every citizen is perpetually confronting the fact that he does not know if he's a member of a good country or a bad country . . . and so for that reason the psychology of a member of a minority group sits upon every American.[30]

The greatest significance of the intellectuals' antiwar protest lay in that minority's attempt to resolve the national torment in a reassertion of who we are and what we ought to be. They referred repeatedly to patriotism—though they obviously did not mean patriotism in the particularistic sense of "my country right or wrong." The very topics that dominated the Theatre for Ideas —the legitimacy of violence as a political act, the meaning of Chicago, the impotence of power—showed the participants' appreciation for a peculiarly American phenomenon. The United States is not a country; it is an idea, a political covenant. Hence the effort to retrieve its quintessence. Perhaps in that spirit and for that reason, Susan Sontag decided after her trip to Hanoi in 1968:

Probably no serious radical movement has any future in America unless it can revalidate the tarnished idea of patriotism. One of my thoughts in the closing days of my stay in North Vietnam was that I would like to try.[31]

The Johnson years brought hard times to the nation's leftist intellectuals. Literary allusions blur and conjure up images of dead souls in the long dark night. The experience prompted Mailer to conclude his *Armies of the Night*: "Brood on that country who expresses our will. She is America. . . ." His preoccupation with the national destiny was doubly illuminating. It explained why he may have come closer than any other American to expressing the significant mood of the 1960s, as F. Scott Fitzgerald did for the 1920s. Both fixed on the agony of a nation sprung from a "platonic conception of itself." Both sensed the delicate balance that defined the Dream.

If the intellectuals fell short of their immediate mission in the 1960s, there may be solace for the 1970s in Mailer's revelation while marching toward the Pentagon:

. . . The sense of America divided on this day now liberated some undiscovered patriotism in Mailer so that he felt a sharp searing love for his country in this moment and on this day, crossing some divide in his own mind wider than the Potomac.[32]

Such was the sentiment that pervaded and transcended the long dark night of the soul. It may be the stuff of hope for that "new America" and, perhaps, the redemptive value for the challenge to the war that betrayed the Dream.

Notes

Prologue

1. See the sequel to *Authors Take Sides on the Spanish War* (1937). Of the forty-seven American respondents to the new survey, all but four opposed "U.S. intervention" in Vietnam and did so on highly passionate, moral grounds. Cecil Woolf and John Bagguley, *Authors Take Sides on Vietnam* (New York: Clarion, 1967).

2. Louis Harris poll in the Washington *Post*, December 7, 1972.

3. According to Charles Kadushin: "By identifying and interviewing those who write for the leading intellectual journals, we have identified the American intellectual elite." Charles Kadushin, "Who Are the Elite Intellectuals?" *The Public Interest*, Fall, 1972, p. 110.

4. Seymour Martin Lipset, "American Intellectuals: Their Politics and Status," *Daedalus*, Summer, 1959, pp. 469–70.

5. Christopher Lasch, *The New Radicalism in America, 1889–1963* (New York: Alfred A. Knopf, 1965).

6. Richard Hofstadter, *Anti-Intellectualism in American Life* (New York: Alfred A. Knopf, 1963).

7. *The New York Review* and *The New Republic* were judged as pace-setters in politics and the *Partisan Review* and *The New York Review* as leaders in cultural affairs. Charles Kadushin, Julie Hover, and Monique Tichy, "How and Where to Find Intellectual Elite in the United States," *Public Opinion Quarterly*, Spring, 1971, pp. 1–18.

8. Several caveats: First, the four control journals will often be abbreviated as *TNR*, *PR*, *Studies*, and *NYR*, respectively. Second, the intent of this book is to emphasize group movement, while realizing that there is the germ of contradiction in every generalization. A primary reliance on printed material, furthermore, gives a built-in bias for the attitudes of the most powerful, noisy, articulate, or committed

—not necessarily the most representative. It is, at best, an excerpt from contemporary American intellectual history. It leaves to others to trace the course of particular individuals within the Intellectual Left. Third, nonpolitical scholars, technocrats within the government, conservatives like William F. Buckley, Jr., or revolutionary radicals like Eldridge Cleaver are discussed primarily as foils to the main group under consideration. Fourth, where liberals and radicals within the leftist intelligentsia diverge, that, too, is specified.

9. Daniel Ellsberg, *Papers on the War* (New York: Simon and Schuster, 1972), p. 9.

10. Arthur I. Waskow, *Running Riot: A Journey through the Official Disasters and Creative Disorder in American Society* (New York: Herder and Herder, 1970), p. x.

11. Miss Sontag wrote: "Radical Americans have profited from the war in Vietnam, profited from having a clear-cut moral issue on which to mobilize discontent and expose the camouflaged contradictions in the system. Beyond isolated private disenchantment or despair over America's betrayal of its ideals, Vietnam offered the key to a systematic criticism of America. In this scheme of use, Vietnam becomes an ideal Other." Susan Sontag, *Styles of Radical Will* (New York: Dell Publishing Company, 1969), p. 271.

12. Andrew Kopkind, "Are We in the Middle of a Revolution?" *The New York Times Magazine*, November 10, 1968, p. 54 ff.

13. Hans J. Morgenthau, *Truth and Power: Essays of a Decade, 1960–70* (New York: Praeger Publishers, 1970).

14. Theodore Roszak, "The Disease Called Politics," *Seeds of Liberation*, Paul Goodman, ed. (New York: George Braziller, 1965), p. 450.

15. Marcus Raskin, *Being and Doing* (New York: Random House, 1971), p. xii.

16. F. Scott Fitzgerald, *The Crack-Up*, Edmund Wilson, ed. (New York: New Directions, 1945), p. 75.

17. See also: Reinhold Niebuhr, "Vietnam: Study in Ironies," *TNR*, June 24, 1967, p. 11.

Notes, pages 14–17

Who They Were

1. Raymond Aron, Karl Mannheim, and Bertrand de Jouvenel all remarked on this problem in the introduction to George B. de Huszar's *The Intellectuals: A Controversial Portrait* (New York: The Free Press, 1960), p. 3. That text is one of the most valuable collections of essays on the subject: Sixty-eight writers discuss intellectuals from the perspectives of their emergence, nature, types, role, ideologies, and national variants. For a less ambitious counterpart, see: Philip Rieff, ed., *On Intellectuals: Theoretical Studies and Case Studies* (Garden City, N.Y.: Doubleday, 1969). For a useful sociological survey, note: Lewis A. Coser, *Men of Ideas: A Sociologist's View* (New York: The Free Press, 1965). A helpful collection is available in: Edward Shils, *The Intellectuals and the Powers and Other Essays* (Chicago: The University of Chicago Press, 1972). Otherwise, an abundance of articles exists in scholarly journals and appropriate selections will be cited throughout the text, as well as in the Bibliography under the heading "On and by Intellectuals."

2. Edward Shils, "The Intellectuals and the Powers," *Comparative Studies in Society and History*, October, 1958, p. 5. See also: Karl Deutsch, "American Intellectuals: Their Politics and Status," *Daedalus*, Summer, 1959, p. 490.

3. William Kornhauser, *The Politics of Mass Society* (New York: The Free Press, 1959), p. 189.

4. Charles Frankel, "The Scribblers and International Relations," *Foreign Affairs*, October, 1965, p. 4.

5. Quoted in an interview with Levertov and Goodman by James Finn, ed., *Protest: Pacifism and Politics* (New York: Vintage Books, 1968), p. 472.

6. Arthur Koestler, "The Intelligentsia," *PR*, Summer, 1944, p. 269.

7. Henry A. Kissinger, "The Policymaker and the Intellectual," *The Reporter*, March 5, 1959, pp. 34–35.

8. Hans J. Morgenthau, "Truth and Power: The Intellectuals and the Johnson Administration," *TNR*, November 26, 1966, pp. 8–9. See also: Morgenthau, *Truth and Power: Essays of a Decade, 1960–70* (New York: Praeger Publishers, 1970).

9. Ithiel de Sola Pool, chairman of the Department of Political Science at the Massachusetts Institute of Technology, was a member of the Defense Science Board of the Department of Defense, for which he conducted research in Vietnam, in 1966 and 1967. Samuel P. Huntington, chairman of the Department of Government at Harvard University, was consultant to the Policy Planning Council of the Department of State and to the Agency for International Development.

10. Noam Chomsky, "The Welfare-Warfare Intellectuals," *New Society*, July 3, 1969, p. 12.

11. Ronald Steel, "Recent Fiction," *NYR*, April 6, 1967, p. 8. The occasion was his vitriolic review of *American Strategy: A New Perspective*, by Urs Schwarz; *Escalation and the Nuclear Option*, by Bernard Brodie; and *Arms and Influence*, by Thomas Schelling.

12. Richard Hofstadter, *Anti-Intellectualism in American Life* (New York: Alfred A. Knopf, 1963), p. 429.

13. Benda wrote a controversial book often cited by American leftist intellectuals. Julien Benda, *The Treason of the Intellectuals* (*La Trahison des clercs*), translated by Richard Aldington (New York: William Morrow & Company, 1928).

14. Arthur M. Schlesinger, Jr., *The Crisis of Confidence* (Boston: Houghton Mifflin Company, 1969), p. 92.

15. Hofstadter, *Anti-Intellectualism in American Life*, p. 408. He observed further that only then did the nation provide the accouterments essential to a vital intelligentsia: libraries, a system of genuine universities, scholarly journals, publishing houses, expanding governmental bureaucracies, and wealthy foundations.

16. Christopher Lasch, *The New Radicalism in America* (New York: Alfred A. Knopf, 1965), p. ix.

17. Schlesinger, *The Crisis of Confidence*, p. 74.

18. Robert L. Beisner, *Twelve against Empire—the Anti-Imperialists, 1898–1900* (New York: McGraw-Hill Book Company, 1968), pp. xiv–xv. I. F. Stone recommended this book strongly in "Who Are the Democrats," *NYR*, August 22, 1968, p. 8.

19. Samuel Eliot Morison, Frederick Merk, and Frank Freidel,

Dissent in Three American Wars (Cambridge, Mass.: Harvard University Press, 1970), p. 95.

20. Hofstadter, *Anti-Intellectualism in American Life*, p. viii.

21. Norman Mailer, "The Great Society?" in *We Accuse*, James Petras, ed. (Berkeley, Calif.: Diablo Press, 1965), p. 17.

22. Alexis de Tocqueville, *Democracy in America*, Phillips Bradley, ed. (New York: Alfred A. Knopf, 1944), Vol. 2, p. 106.

23. Seymour Martin Lipset, "American Intellectuals: Their Politics and Status," *Daedalus*, Summer, 1959, pp. 469–70. The same point was made by David Riesman and Nathan Glazer in "The Intellectuals and the Discontented Classes," *PR*, Winter, 1955, p. 50, and by Melvin Seeman in "The Intellectual and the Language of Minorities," *American Journal of Sociology*, July, 1958, p. 28.

24. Hofstadter, *Anti-Intellectualism in American Life*, p. 7; Marcus Cunliffe, "The Intellectual: The United States," *Encounter*, May, 1955, p. 25.

25. Arthur Schlesinger, Jr., "The Highbrow in Politics," *PR*, March–April, 1953, pp. 162–65.

26. James B. Gilbert, *Writers and Partisans: A History of Literary Radicalism in America* (New York: John Wiley & Sons, 1968), p. viii.

27. The following general-interest periodicals come to mind and have been consulted extensively: *The American Scholar, The Atlantic Monthly, Commentary, Daedalus, Dissent, Foreign Affairs, Harper's, Monthly Review, The Nation, New Politics, The New Republic, The New York Review, The New York Times Book Review* and *Magazine, The New Yorker, Partisan Review, The Progressive, The Public Interest, Ramparts, Saturday Review, Studies on the Left, The Village Voice,* and *The Yale Review.*

28. Explained by Herbert Croly to Randolph Bourne, one of the frequent contributors to the early *NR* and an important figure in subsequent American intellectual history, June 3, 1914, and quoted by Christopher Lasch in *The New Radicalism in America*, p. 183. The chapter in that collection entitled "The *New Republic* and the War," pp. 181–224, is one of the most helpful treatments of the young *NR* and suggests precedents for later intellectual debates on American

involvement in war. See also: Charles Forcey, *The Crossroads of Liberalism: Croly, Weyl, Lippmann, and the Progressive Era, 1900–1925* (New York: Oxford University Press, 1961).

29. See Harrison's Preface in *The Faces of Five Decades: Selections from Fifty Years of the New Republic, 1914–1964*, Robert B. Luce, ed. (New York: Simon and Schuster, 1964), p. 11.

30. Carl Resek, ed., *War and the Intellectuals, Essays of Randolph S. Bourne, 1915–1919* (New York: Harper & Row, 1964), p. 7.

31. Ibid., p. 11. The source is Bourne's "The War and the Intellectuals."

32. Luce, *The Faces of Five Decades*, pp. 229–30.

33. Richard Strout of the *Christian Science Monitor* has been TRB for the last thirty years. "TRB" stands for "The Rover Boys." In an interview, April 8, 1971, Mr. Strout classified himself as a "Walter Lippmann liberal" but admitted that his own political stance has moved leftward over the years. Loyal to Johnson's domestic program, he came to oppose his Vietnam policy only "gradually" –and then on pragmatic or economic grounds. His "passionate moral objection" to the war developed primarily after Nixon became President.

34. Norman Podhoretz, *Making It* (New York: Random House, 1967), p. 111.

35. This is Irving Howe's shorthand for "the intellectuals of New York who began to appear in the 1930s, most of whom were Jewish." It was a term with continuing validity in the 1960s. Irving Howe, "The New York Intellectuals: A Chronicle and a Critique," *Commentary*, October, 1968, p. 30.

36. For his updated version of Bourne's "The War and the Intellectuals," see: Dwight Macdonald, "War and the Intellectuals: Act II," *PR*, Spring, 1939, p. 10.

37. Arthur Koestler, *PR*, Summer, 1944, p. 269.

38. Howe, *Commentary*, October, 1968, p. 38.

39. Gilbert, *Writers and Partisans*, p. 266.

40. Symposium, "Our Country and Our Culture," *PR*, May–June, 1952; pp. 282–84.

41. James Weinstein and David W. Eakins, eds., *For a New America* (New York: Random House, 1970), p. 6. Their collection of

essays from *Studies*, though admittedly "internal and partisan," provides one of the most useful insights into the young American Intellectual Left of the 1960s. Other radical journals of this genre include *New University Thought* and *Point Sixty*.

42. James Weinstein, "Socialist Intellectuals," *Studies*, September–October, 1966, p. 3.

43. Weinstein and Eakins, *For a New America*, p. 30.

44. Charles Kadushin, Julie Hover, and Monique Tichy, "How and Where to Find Intellectual Elite in the U.S." *Public Opinion Quarterly*, Spring, 1971, pp. 1–18.

45. Dennis Wrong, "The Case of the 'New York Review,'" *Commentary*, November, 1970, pp. 60–61.

46. Podhoretz, *Making It*, p. 322. This occurred despite Podhoretz's decision, upon assuming the editorship of *Commentary*, to reflect his own leftward movement with a new "ideological strategy" opposed to "hard anti-Communism" and what C. Wright Mills called "the American celebration."

47. Jason Epstein, "The CIA and the Intellectuals," *NYR*, April 20, 1967, pp. 16–21. His wife, Barbara, was one of *NYR*'s co-editors.

48. Irving Howe and Philip Rahv, "An Exchange on the Left," *NYR*, November 23, 1967, pp. 36–42. It evoked the fiery debate reminiscent of the 1930s and was remarkable for showing Rahv to the left of Howe, even though Howe's *Dissent*, together with Macdonald's *Politics*, had kept alive democratic socialism abandoned by Rahv and Phillips's *PR* during World War II and the Cold War.

49. Noam Chomsky, *American Power and the New Mandarins* (New York: Random House, 1967), pp. 5–9.

50. Hans H. Gerth and C. Wright Mills, eds., *From Max Weber: Essays in Sociology* (New York: Oxford University Press, 1946), p. 120.

What They Wrote: First Stage

1. Daniel P. Moynihan, "The Democrats, Kennedy and the Murder of Dr. King," *Commentary*, May, 1968, p. 22. Theodore Sorensen put the point of intellectual disengagement at February, 1965, when John-

son's bombing of North Vietnam "fundamentally altered John Kennedy's Vietnam policy." Theodore C. Sorensen, *The Kennedy Legacy* (New York: The Macmillan Company, 1969), pp. 213–14.

2. Such liberal intellectuals of the Establishment as Chester Bowles, Deputy Under Secretary of State; Averell Harriman, Assistant Secretary of State for Far Eastern Affairs; Roger Hilsman, head of the State Department's Bureau of Intelligence and Research; Michael Forrestal of the White House staff; and John Kenneth Galbraith, ambassador to India, were most noteworthy.

3. James A. Wechsler, "Vietnam: A Study in Deception," *The Progressive*, February, 1965, pp. 14–17. For a representative selection of critical American reporting from Vietnam, see the books by Malcolm Browne, David Halberstam, John Mecklin, and Robert Shaplen in the Bibliography. The writing of Neil Sheehan of the United Press International, Charles Mohr of *Time*, and François Sully of *Newsweek* was outstanding.

4. Midge Decter, "Kennedyism," *Commentary*, January, 1970, p. 27.

5. George Kahin and John Lewis were describing the Kennedy Administration when they wrote: "The idea seemed to be that, 'if the Americans expressed enough optimism, Diem would come to trust them and be more receptive to their suggestions' and that 'a sensitive Administration back home wanted to hear that it was winning the war.'" Kahin and Lewis, *The United States in Vietnam* (New York: Dell Publishing Company, 1969), p. 141.

6. Christopher Lasch, "UnAmerican Activities," *NYR*, October 6, 1966, p. 19.

7. Henry Fairlie, "Johnson and the Intellectuals," *Commentary*, October, 1965, p. 50.

8. Decter, *Commentary*, January, 1970, p. 24.

9. Theodore C. Sorensen, *Kennedy* (New York: Harper & Row, 1965), p. 623.

10. Arthur M. Schlesinger, Jr., *A Thousand Days: John F. Kennedy in the White House* (Boston: Houghton Mifflin Company, 1965), pp. 544–47, 986.

11. Theodore Draper, "The American Crisis: Vietnam, Cuba, and the Dominican Republic," *Commentary*, January, 1967, p. 34.

12. Symposium, "The Fate of the Union: Kennedy and After," *NYR*, December 26, 1963, pp. 3–12.

13. TRB, "LBJ's Triumph," *TNR*, May 2, 1964, p. 2.

14. Editors, "Darkness on the Mekong," *TNR*, (February 8, 1964), p. 4; Editors, "Can Khanh?" *TNR*, March 28, 1964, p. 4.

15. Editors, "Vietnam—No Exit?" *TNR*, March 7, 1964, p. 3.

16. Bernard Fall, "How Much Time Do We Have in Vietnam?" *TNR*, February 22, 1964, p. 11.

17. Editors, "Fire Alarm in Asia," *TNR*, July 4, 1964, p. 3.

18. Editors, "Blackmail in Vietnam," *TNR*, August 8, 1964, p. 4.

19. Murray Kempton, "The People's Choice," *NYR*, November 5, 1964, p. 3.

20. I. F. Stone, "McNamara and Tonkin Bay: The Unanswered Questions," *NYR*, March 28, 1968, p. 8.

21. Ibid., p. 11. In reviewing Roger Hilsman's *To Move a Nation*, John McDermott made much the same argument in: "To Move a Nation," *NYR*, September 14, 1967, pp. 4–10.

22. Philip Geyelin, *Lyndon B. Johnson and the World* (New York: Praeger Publishers, 1966), p. 187.

23. Ibid, p. 197.

24. Symposium, "Some Comments on Senator Goldwater," *PR*, Fall, 1964, p. 597.

25. Editors, "The CIA Analysis," *TNR*, September 12, 1964, p. 3, and Editors, "Vietnam—a Way Out," *TNR*, October 3, 1964, p. 5.

26. I. F. Stone, "The Making of a President," *NYR*, July 30, 1964, p. 3.

27. Kempton, *NYR*, November 5, 1964, pp. 3–4.

28. Editors, "The Wasted Year," *TNR*, November 14, 1964, p. 1.

29. Paul Goodman, "The Liberal Victory," *NYR*, December 3, 1964, p. 7.

30. Editors, "Escalation in Vietnam," *TNR*, November 14, 1964, p. 8.

31. Bernard Fall, "Vietnam 'Hawks' and 'Doves,'" *TNR*, January 16, 1965, p. 8. While Fall criticized the "unreality" of war hawks, he also dismissed the doves' belief that North Vietnam would give up all the political and military advantages secured at a heavy price for the sake of an "Indochina Common Market" or a "TVA on the Mekong."

He himself adopted a middle position and advocated negotiations since he believed "it would be as unrealistic to underestimate America's leverage on Hanoi as it would be to overestimate Peking's leverage on the guerrillas of South Vietnam."

32. Editors, "The President," *TNR*, January 16, 1965, p. 4.

Second Stage

1. Conversation with a high State Department official one week before Pleiku, quoted by Geyelin, *Lyndon B. Johnson and the World*, p. 216. For the sources on all background sketches of official decision-making—a peripheral concern of this book since it is treated so extensively elsewhere—see "U.S. Foreign Policy: Vietnam" and "Johnson Administration" in the Bibliography.

2. Bill D. Moyers, "One Thing We Learned," *Foreign Affairs*, July, 1968, pp. 657–64.

3. Editors, "Who's Signaling What?" *TNR*, February 20, 1965, pp. 5–6; Roger Morris, "Russia's Stake in Vietnam," *TNR*, February 13, 1965, p. 15.

4. Editors, "The White Paper," *TNR*, March 13, 1965, p. 5. See this article for an itemized rebuttal of the Administration's case.

5. I. F. Stone, "Vietnam: An Exercise in Self-Delusion," *NYR*, April 22, 1965, p. 4. The occasion was Stone's review of Malcolm Browne's *The New Face of War* and David Halberstam's *The Making of a Quagmire*, two books Stone saluted for showing the Vietnam War "as a challenge to freedom of information and therefore freedom of decision." See also: Stone, "A Reply to the White Paper," *I. F. Stone's Weekly*, March 8, 1965—distributed at the National Teach-in in Washington in May, 1965.

6. Hans Morgenthau, "War with China?" *TNR*, April 3, 1965, p. 14.

7. Inter-university Committee for Public Hearings on Vietnam, "Program for National Teach-in on the Vietnam War," distributed at the Sheraton Park Hotel, Washington, D.C., May 15, 1965.

8. Or so said one of its organizers, Kenneth Boulding, in "Reflections on Protest," *The Bulletin of the Atomic Scientists*, October, 1965, pp. 18–20.

9. From the abridged transcripts of a report distributed privately by Professor Anatol Rapoport at the University of Michigan and the first address before the National Teach-in by Professor Hans Morgenthau, included in Louis Menashe and Ronald Radosh, eds., *Teach-ins: U.S.A.* (New York: Praeger Publishers, 1967), pp. 159, 174. This text represents one of the most comprehensive, if *engagé*, collections on the teach-in movement.

10. Senator Fulbright admitted, "Maybe if we had held this inquiry earlier, the teach-ins on the university campuses would not have been so necessary." Quoted by James Reston, "Senator Fulbright's 'Teach-in,'" *The New York Times*, February 13, 1966.

11. Norman Podhoretz, *Making It* (New York: Random House, 1967), p. 216.

12. Jack Newfield, *A Prophetic Minority* (New York: The New American Library, 1966), pp. 27–28. A former SDS member and prominent New Left journalist, Newfield contended that Kennedy's encouragement to youth was critical to the emergence of the New Left then and that "if Nixon had won in 1960, . . . the earliest protests would have been crushed in a McCarthyite paroxysm and the New Left aborted."

13. Staughton Lynd quoted in Priscilla Long, ed., *The New Left: A Collection of Essays* (Boston: Porter Sargent Publisher, 1969), p. 6.

14. Staughton Lynd and Thomas Hayden, *The Other Side* (New York: The New American Library, 1966), p. 11.

15. Mailer, *The Armies of the Night*, pp. 90, 311–12.

16. For one of the most important primary documents on this subject, see: Dale L. Johnson's "On the Ideology of the Campus Revolution." It first appeared in *Studies on the Left* in 1961, and was reprinted in Paul Jacobs and Saul Landau, eds., *The New Radicals* (New York: Vintage Books, 1966), pp. 97–98. In his essay, Johnson asserted a relationship between the Cuban and campus revolutions premised on their pragmatic "ideology of dissent" and their "refreshing combination of humanism and rationalism." He argued that U.S. action toward Cuba demonstrated for American youth the "counter-revolutionary" nature of American foreign policy and that "U.S. imperialistic ventures have served to radicalize the dissenters"—especially those who had expected something different from the Kennedy

Administration. This book's evaluation of the impact of the Cuban experience on U.S. youth draws from essays like Dale Johnson's and from the open meetings of Harvard students fresh from sugarcane-cutting missions to Cuba in 1970.

17. LeRoi Jones, "Cuba Libre," *Home* (New York: William Morrow & Company, 1966), p. 53.

18. Norman Mailer, "The Letter to Castro," *The Presidential Papers* (New York: G. P. Putnam's Sons, 1963), pp. 67–75.

19. Richard Flacks, "Some Social Implications of the Teach-ins," *The Bulletin of the Atomic Scientists*, October, 1965, p. 21. This is *not* to state that all academicians opposed the Vietnam War. Many of the war's most ardent supporters, students and professors alike, came from the campus.

20. Jacobs and Landau, *The New Radicals*, p. 80.

21. Michael Harrington, *Partisan Review*, Spring, 1965, p. 194.

22. Peter Caws, "What Happened in Paris," *PR*, Fall, 1968, p. 521.

23. Among those appearing were: Isaac Deutscher (Marxist historian), Ernest Gruening (Democratic Senator from Alaska), Dr. Benjamin Spock (chairman of SANE), Norman Thomas (leading Socialist), Norman Mailer (novelist), I. F. Stone (journalist), David Dellinger (editor of *Liberation*), James Aronson (editor of *National Guardian*), Paul Krassner (editor of *The Realist*), Robert Scheer (*Ramparts*), Hal Draper (editor of *New Politics*), Staughton Lynd (historian), Bob Parris (SNCC leader), Mario Savio (Free Speech Movement, Berkeley), and Paul Potter (SDS president).

24. Susan Sontag, quoted by Menashe and Radosh, *Teach-ins*, pp. 345–46. For examples of poetry Read-ins for Peace, see: Walter Lowenfels, ed., *Where Is Vietnam?—American Poets Respond* (Garden City, N.Y.: Doubleday & Company, Inc., 1967).

25. Ibid.

26. Ibid, p. 34.

27. From a précis of his remarks delivered at the Columbia University teach-in, March 24, 1966, quoted by Menashe and Radosh, *Teach-ins*, p. 68.

28. Reply to Professor Scalapino's condemnation of the Berkeley

teach-in by Professors Morris Hirsh and Stephen Smale and Jerry Rubin, quoted by Menashe and Radosh, *Teach-ins*, pp. 30–32.

29. James Petras, ed., *We Accuse* (Berkeley, Calif.: Diablo Press, 1965), p. 159. The tape-transcript of the 36-hour "Vietnam Day" protest constituted what its organizers called "a statement of the new political anger in America" in the tradition of Emile Zola's *J'accuse.* Their program concentrated on structuring "moral impulses" to oppose the liberal Democratic Party Establishment, effect basic changes in society, legitimize radical discussion of foreign policy, and realign the American Left.

30. For the full text of the Williams statement, see: *The New York Times*, May 2, 1965.

31. Christopher Lasch, *The Nation*, October 18, 1965, p. 240. See also: Williams's address to the University of Wisconsin teach-in, April 1, 1965, quoted by Menashe and Radosh, *Teach-ins*, p. 48.

32. Ibid., p. 180. Bernard Fall elaborated on these same moral consequences of "depersonalization" in "Vietnam Blitz: A Report on the Impersonal War," *TNR*, October 9, 1965, pp. 17–21.

33. Lewis Coser, "The Visibility of Evil," *Journal of Social Issues*, January, 1969, pp. 101–9. For other statements on the neutralizing influence of television, see: TRB, "Bombing Our Way Out," *TNR*, June 3, 1967, p. 1, and Dan Wakefield, "Supernation at Peace and War," *The Atlantic*, March, 1968, p. 76.

34. An aside from a major foreign-policy address to the American Society of International Law, April 23, 1965.

35. Joan Wallach Scott, "The Teach-in: A National Movement or the End of an Affair?" *Studies*, Summer, 1965, p. 84. See also: Peter Lathrop, "Teach-ins: New Force or Isolated Phenomenon?" *Studies*, Fall, 1965, pp. 41–53; William A. Williams, "Pseudo-Debate in the Teach-in: Criticism Contained," quoted by Menashe and Radosh, *Teach-ins*, pp. 187–89.

36. Carl Oglesby, "The Teach-ins: A Student Response," *Dissent*, Autumn, 1965, p. 479.

37. For the text of Howe's 1965 essay, "New Styles of Leftism," see: Jacobs and Landau's *The New Radicals*, pp. 290–91.

38. Newfield, *A Prophetic Minority*, p. 132.

39. Hal Draper, "In Defense of the 'New Radicals,'" *New Politics*, Summer, 1965, p. 21.

40. Elizabeth Hardwick, "Selma, Alabama: The Charms of Goodness," *NYR*, April 22, 1965, p. 3.

41. Ibid.

42. Daniel Bell, *The End of Ideology: On the Exhaustion of Political Ideas in the Fifties* (New York: The Free Press, 1960), pp. 399–400.

43. Ibid., p. 400.

44. C. Wright Mills's "On the New Left" was the most famous rebuttal of Bell. See: *Studies*, 1961, pp. 63–72, and the earlier reference in this chapter. The debate between Daniel Bell and Henry David Aiken foretold the crisis of moralistic anti-establishmentarianism which befell the intellectuals' opposition to the Vietnam War. Daniel Bell and Henry Aiken, "Ideology—a Debate," *Commentary*, October, 1964, pp. 69–76.

45. Draper, *New Politics*, Summer, 1965, pp. 5–28.

46. Nathan Glazer, "The New Left and Its Limits," *Commentary*, July, 1968, p. 39.

47. For example, Howe argued against the liberal historian Arthur Schlesinger, Jr., at the Theatre for Ideas in 1966, in favor of public demonstrations and student protests but warned radical intellectuals against undue violence and Vietcong sympathy in those demonstrations. He applauded Schlesinger's statement of opposition to Johnson's policy in *The Bitter Heritage* but criticized him for omitting the role of American liberalism in U.S. foreign policy. Irving Howe, "A New Turn at Arthur's," *NYR*, February 23, 1967, p. 13.

48. Herbert Gans, "Rational Approach to Radicalism," *Studies*, January–February, 1966, pp. 37–46. Note the angry responses by Staughton Lynd and James Weinstein for a representative exchange of this genre. This point also relates to the wider issue of intellectual sensitivity to the views of the general public on Vietnam which emerged during the Johnson period.

49. David McReynolds, "Pacifists in Battle," *New Politics*, Summer, 1965, pp. 29–35.

50. Reinhold Niebuhr, *Reinhold Niebuhr on Politics* (New York:

Charles Scribner's Sons, 1960), pp. 139–51. Niebuhr argued that pacifism, a form of perfectionism, tended toward a relativist sense of justice and so rationalized its own often nonpacifist forms of coercion.

51. Arthur Waskow, "The New Student Movement," *Dissent*, Autumn, 1965, pp. 486–93. Normally a passionate worshiper of youth, Paul Goodman winced at students who protested being treated like IBM cards at the same time they defended Chairman Mao's "little red book." Paul Goodman, "The Black Flag of Anarchism," *The New York Times Magazine*, July 14, 1968, pp. 10–11, 13.

52. George Kahin, "Text of Speech at the National Teach-in on the Vietnam War," Washington, D.C., May 15, 1965, p. 9.

53. Hans Morgenthau, "Russia, the U.S. and Vietnam," *TNR*, May 1, 1965, p. 12.

54. Editors, "Deeper and Deeper," *TNR*, May 22, 1965, p. 5; William Phillips et al., "A Statement on Vietnam and the Dominican Republic," *PR*, Summer, 1965, pp. 397–98—plus stormy response in the following issue.

55. Symposium, "Is There a New Radicalism?" *PR*, Spring, 1965, p. 183.

56. Ibid., p. 194.

57. Tom Wicker, "One Year of LBJ," *TNR*, November 13, 1965, p. 17.

58. For Goldman's own account, see: Eric Goldman, "The White House and the Intellectuals," *Harper's*, January, 1969, pp. 31–45, or Chapter 16 of Goldman's *The Tragedy of Lyndon Johnson* (New York: Alfred A. Knopf, 1969), pp. 418–75.

59. Lowell wrote: "Although I am very enthusiastic about most of your domestic legislation and intentions, I nevertheless can only follow our present foreign policy with the greatest dismay and distrust. What we will do and what we ought to do as a sovereign nation facing other sovereign nations seem now to hang in the balance between the better and worse possibilities. We are in danger of imperceptibly becoming an explosive and suddenly chauvinistic nation, and may even be drifting on our way to the last nuclear ruin. I know it is hard for the responsible man to act; it is also painful for the private and irresolute man to dare criticism. At this anguished, delicate, and perhaps deter-

mining moment, I feel I am serving you and our country best by not taking part in the White House Festival of the Arts."

Of the 102 writers, artists, and critics invited, four others declined on Lowell's grounds: Robert Brustein, Alexander Calder, Jack Levine, and Paul Strand.

60. Eric Bentley, "The Treason of the Experts," *The Nation,* December 13, 1965, p. 469. Stephen Spender compared Lowell's attitude toward Johnson to the castigation of Castlereagh by Byron and Shelley in "Writers and Politics," *PR,* Summer, 1967, pp. 367–68.

61. Goldman, *Harper's,* January, 1969, p. 35.

62. The message read in part: "We would like you to know that others of us share his [Lowell's] dismay at recent American foreign policy decisions. We hope that people in this and other countries will not conclude that a White House arts program testifies to approval of Administration policy by the members of the artistic community. . . ." The signers were Hannah Arendt, John Berryman, Alan Dugan, Jules Feiffer, Philip Guston, Lillian Hellman, Alfred Kazin, Stanley Kunitz, Dwight Macdonald, Bernard Malamud, Mary McCarthy, Larry Rivers, Philip Roth, Mark Rothko, Louis Simpson, W. D. Snodgrass, William Styron, Peter Taylor, Edgar Varèse, and Robert Penn Warren.

63. Quoted by Goldman, *Harper's,* January, 1969, p. 35.

64. Dwight Macdonald, "A Day at the White House," *NYR,* July 15, 1965, p. 11.

65. Ibid., p. 15.

66. Goldman, *Harper's,* January, 1969, p. 45.

67. Susan Sontag in Symposium, "What's Happening to America?," *PR,* Winter, 1967, p. 54.

68. Walter Goodman, "Advising the President: II," *Commentary,* April, 1969, pp. 76–79.

69. John P. Roche, "The Liberals and Vietnam," *The New Leader,* April 26, 1965, pp. 16–20.

70. Irving Howe, "A New Turn at Arthur's," *NYR,* February 23, 1967, p. 13.

71. Editors, "Message to the Intelligentsia," *The Nation,* November 18, 1968, p. 517.

72. That interview was frequently and derisively quoted in intellec-

Notes, pages 92–94

tual journals. *PR* offered it tongue-in-cheek as Roche's "introduction to our readers" in "Washington, D.C.: The Bureau of Misplaced Persons," *PR*, Fall, 1966, p. 607. Hans Morgenthau condemned Roche's personal diatribes against John K. Galbraith and himself: "Those are the qualities not of the intellectual but of the demogogue." Morgenthau, *TNR*, November 26, 1966, p. 12.

73. Franz Schurmann, Peter Scott, and Reginald Zelnik, *The Politics of Escalation in Vietnam* (Boston: Beacon Press, 1966).

74. Editors, "War in Asia—Why?" *TNR*, August 7, 1965, p. 6, and TRB, "Papa Knows Best," *TNR*, ibid., p. 4.

75. Bernard Fall, "Vietnam: European Viewpoints," *TNR*, August 21, 1965, p. 13; Editors, "Delusions of Power," *TNR*, October 16, 1965, p. 6; and Editors, "Dare We Negotiate?" *TNR*, November 6, 1965, p. 5. For further reaction on negotiations in the intellectual community at that time, see: Jean Lacouture, "The Chance for Peace in Vietnam," *NYR*, October 14, 1965, pp. 37–38; Joseph Kraft's review of Lacouture's *Vietnam: Between Two Truces* and Victor Bator's *Vietnam: A Diplomatic Tragedy*, in "Understanding the Vietcong," *NYR*, August 5, 1965, pp. 7–9; and David Kraslow and Stuart Loory, *The Secret Search for Peace* (New York: Random House, 1968).

76. Eugene V. Rostow and Hans J. Morgenthau, "Getting Out of Vietnam" (letters), *NYR*, October 28, 1965, p. 39. The exchange stemmed from the supplement which included "Vietnam: Shadow and Substance," by Hans Morgenthau; "The American Dienbienphu," by Joseph Kraft; and "A Diplomatic Alternative," by Marcus G. Raskin and Bernard Fall, *NYR*, September 16, 1965, pp. 3–6. Rostow was Deputy Under Secretary of State during the Johnson Administration.

77. Ibid., p. 39.

78. Editors, "Hold That Tiger!" *TNR*, November 27, 1965, p. 5.

79. Editors, "Start Talking," *TNR*, September 4, 1965, pp. 5–6; TRB, "Vietnam Trap," *TNR*, July 3, 1965, p. 4.

80. Edgar Snow, "Deeper into the Trap," *TNR*, December 25, 1965, p. 18.

81. For the best summary of this position, see: Irving Howe, *Steady Work: Essays in the Politics of Democratic Radicalism, 1953–1966*

(New York: Harcourt Brace Jovanovich, 1966). That collection reflects Howe's twelve- to fifteen-year running attack on what he calls the "politics of authoritarian elitism." The book shows "a man on the left in dialogue with himself," seeking the middle course of a "radical renovation of society" without the sacrifice of "democratic values" and affiliating with socialism as "the best problem to which a political intellectual can attach himself."

82. Irving Howe, "I'd Rather Be Wrong," *NYR*, June 17, 1965, p. 3.

83. Ibid.

84. Irving Howe et al., "A Joint Statement on the Vietnam Protest Movement," *NYR*, November 25, 1965, pp. 12–13.

85. Ibid.

86. Symposium, "Vietnam and the Left," *Dissent*, Autumn, 1965, p. 395.

87. Ibid., p. 405. For comparative purposes, see: Symposium, "Civil Disobedience and 'Resistance,'" *Dissent*, January–February, 1968, pp. 13–25.

88. Quoted by Merle Miller in "Why Norman and Jason Aren't Talking," *The New York Times Magazine*, March 26, 1972, p. 104.

89. Jason Epstein is the husband of Barbara Epstein, one of the co-editors of *The New York Review*.

90. For an interesting account of that demonstration, see: Andrew Kopkind, "Radicals on the March: But Where to and by What Route?" *TNR*, December 11, 1965, p. 18.

91. Jacobs and Landau, *The New Radicals*, pp. 257–66.

92. Ibid., p. 263.

93. Ibid., p. 261.

94. Tom Hayden, "The Ability to Face Whatever Comes," *TNR*, January 15, 1966, pp. 16–18.

95. Staughton Lynd and Irving Howe, "An Exchange on Vietnam," *NYR*, December 23, 1965, p. 28.

96. Ibid.

97. Joint Statement, "On Vietnam and the Dominican Republic," *PR*, Summer, 1965, pp. 397–98. Those signing were: Eleanor Clark, Martin Duberman, Irving Howe, Alfred Kazin, Bernard Malamud, Steven Marcus, William Phillips, Norman Podhoretz, Richard Poirier, and Richard Schlatter.

98. Symposium, "On Vietnam," *PR*, Fall, 1965, p. 624.
99. Ibid., p. 646.
100. Ibid., p. 651.
101. Ibid., p. 635.
102. Ibid., p. 642.
103. Ibid., p. 641.
104. Ibid., p. 656.
105. Wicker, *TNR*, November 13, 1965, p. 22.
106. Editors, "Shooting for Peace," *TNR*, January 15, 1966, pp. 5–6; TRB, "Diplomacy by Megaphone," ibid., p. 4; Editors, "Walk, Don't Run," *TNR*, May 21, 1966, p. 6; Arthur Fraleigh, "How to Fail in Negotiations without Really Trying," *TNR*, January 1, 1966, p. 9.
107. Editors, "The Sleepwalkers," *TNR*, July 2, 1966, p. 1. Ronald Steel also contrasted *official* obeisance to a negotiated truce with the *actual* commitment to "victory" in *NYR*, October 6, 1966, p. 6.
108. Mario Rossi, "U Thant and Vietnam: The Untold Story," *NYR*, November 17, 1966, pp. 8–13.
109. Philip Ben, "Tragedy of Errors: The Humiliation of the United States in the Security Council," *TNR*, February 19, 1966, p. 9. See also: Editors, "So the War Goes On," *TNR*, February 12, 1966), p. 5.
110. Editors, "Getting in Deeper," *TNR*, February 19, 1966, p. 5. The Vietnam hearings, held by the Senate Foreign Relations Committee in February, 1966, and chaired by Senator J. William Fulbright, were tremendously encouraging to American intellectuals. See: TRB, "Vital Support in Vietnam," *TNR*, March 5, 1966, p. 4; Editors, "Whose History," *TNR*, March 12, 1966, p. 7; Alex Campbell, "Fulbright on Camera," *TNR*, May 21, 1966, pp. 19–22; I. F. Stone, "Fulbright of Arkansas: I," *NYR*, December 29, 1966, pp. 5–6; and Marvin Kalb, "Doves, Hawks and Flutterers in the Foreign Relations Committee," *The New York Times Magazine*, November 19, 1967, p. 56 ff.
111. Editors, "Vietnam—Garbled Signals," *TNR*, October 15, 1966, p. 5; Editors, "Eroding Goldberg," ibid., p. 7.
112. Editors, "The Coonskin," *TNR*, November 12, 1966, p. 7.
113. Bernard Fall, "The Air-Raids—Leftover Puzzles," *TNR*, July 16, 1966, p. 7; TRB, "'Embarrassments,'" *TNR*, November 5, 1966, p. 4; Editors, "The War," *TNR*, June 11, 1966, p. 7.

114. I. F. Stone, "Keep 'Em Flying," *NYR*, January 20, 1966, p. 4; Bernard Fall, "Vietnam: The Undiscovered Country," *NYR*, March 17, 1966, pp. 8–9; Editors, "Vietnam Must Choose," *TNR*, April 16, 1966, p. 6; Jean Lacouture, "Vietnam: The Turning Point," *NYR*, May 12, 1966, pp. 5–8.

115. Editors, "Defective Vision," *TNR*, March 19, 1966, p. 7; Ross Terrill, "China and Vietnam," *TNR*, October 29, 1966, pp. 16–20.

116. Jean Lacouture, "Vietnam: The Turning Point," *NYR*, May 12, 1966, p. 6. Lichtheim's article in *Commentary* (April, 1966) was in line with the fears expressed in that journal's "China Symposium" in February, 1966, before the Senate hearings. Symposium, "Containing China: A Round-Table Discussion," *Commentary*, May, 1966, pp. 23–41. One of the panelists, Richard Goodwin, suggested at that time that China was being used as an excuse because of the increasing level of commitment in Vietnam, p. 30.

Edgar Snow characterized American intervention in Vietnam as a "proxy war" with China in "China and Vietnam," *TNR*, July 30, 1966, p. 12.

117. Alex Campbell, "Who's Afraid of China?" *TNR*, April 9, 1966, pp. 13–15.

118. TRB, "Shocked Senators," *TNR*, February 12, 1966, p. 4; TRB, "Congress Wants to Know," *TNR*, February 19, 1966, p. 4.

119. Hans Morgenthau, "Johnson's Dilemma," *TNR*, May 28, 1966, p. 12; Alex Campbell, "Voices from Asia," *TNR*, April 16, 1966, p. 27; Joseph Kraft, "Politics in Vietnam," *NYR*, June 23, 1966, p. 8.

120. Jean Lacouture, "Vietnam: The Lessons of War," *NYR*, March 3, 1966, p. 3.

121. Editors, "Fooling the People," *TNR*, August 13, 1966, p. 5.

122. Reinhold Niebuhr, "Reinhold Niebuhr Discusses the War in Vietnam," *TNR*, January 29, 1966, pp. 15–16.

123. Ronald Steel, "A Visit to Washington," *NYR*, October 6, 1966, p. 5. The following articles stressed the same point: Don Oberdorfer, "Noninterventionism, 1967 Style," *The New York Times Magazine*, September 17, 1967, p. 28; Henry Brandon, "The View from Vietnam," *Saturday Review*, November 25, 1967, p. 16; Ward S. Just, "Notes on Losing the War," *The Atlantic*, January, 1969, pp. 39–44. Just wrote: "The principal philosophical difficulty was the

absence of a clearly-stated war aim; in an age of doubt and Tito, it is not enough to state that the enemy is Communist."

124. Harrison Salisbury, *Behind the Lines—Hanoi* (New York: Harper & Row, 1967), p. 238.

125. Stated by Secretary Rusk at the Fletcher School of Law and Diplomacy, September 25, 1969.

126. John Roche, "Can a Free Society Fight a Limited War?" *The New Leader*, October 21, 1968, pp. 6–11. According to Roche, Ho Chi Minh hit the most vulnerable point in the doctrine of limited war: domestic opinion. The Administration's rhetoric of limited war did little to reverse public frustration. What President could expect popular acclaim for requests to sacrifice for stalemate or a bargaining position?

127. Steel, *NYR*, October 6, 1966, p. 5.

128. Herman Kahn, "If Negotiations Fail," *Foreign Affairs*, July, 1968, p. 640.

129. John K. Galbraith, "The Galbraith Plan to End the War," *The New York Times Magazine*, November 12, 1967, p. 130.

130. Alexis de Tocqueville, "Why American Writers and Orators Use an Inflated Style," *Democracy in America*, Phillips Bradley, ed. (New York: Alfred A. Knopf, 1945), Vol. 2, pp. 85–86.

131. Daniel P. Moynihan, "The Democrats, Kennedy and the Murder of Dr. King," *Commentary*, May, 1968, p. 26.

132. Quoted in Robert Nisbet's review of *The New Politics* by Stillman and Pfaff, in "Foreign Policy and the American Mind," *Commentary*, September, 1961, p. 194. Nisbet himself stressed the difference between morality and moralism: the former "is a vastly different thing from that ontology which makes us see American political life as the image of universal good, and our foreign policy as a kind of avenging sword for the destruction of the Infidel." Ibid., p. 203.

133. Commager, *TNR*, April 6, 1968, p. 16. See also: Robert Heilbroner, "Grand Illusions," *NYR*, February 20, 1964, p. 9.

134. Sontag, *PR*, Winter, 1967, p. 53.

135. TRB, "Johnson and Moyers," *TNR*, December 24, 1966, p. 4.

136. Editors, "Paying for What?" *TNR*, January 22, 1966, p. 6.

137. TRB, "Playing on the War," *TNR*, March 12, 1966, p. 4; TRB, "Sick of Vietnam," *TNR*, June 25, 1966, p. 4.

138. TRB, *TNR*, December 24, 1966, p. 4.

139. Helen Hill Miller, "Kennedy in '68," *TNR*, October 15, 1966, p. 13.

140. Editors, "Trigger Happy," *TNR*, August 27, 1966, p. 7. For a range of opinions on the morality of American intervention in Vietnam, see: Staughton Lynd, "Reply," *Studies*, January–February, 1966, p. 48; Niebuhr, *TNR*, January 29, 1966, p. 15; Senator George McGovern, "Vietnam: A Proposal," *NYR*, July 6, 1966, p. 5; Ronald Steel and John P. Roche, "The Vietnam War—an Exchange," *The New Leader*, January 3, 1966, pp. 3–6.

141. Edgar Z. Friedenberg, "A Violent Country," *NYR*, October 20, 1966, pp. 3–4.

142. Editors, "Hung-up on Vietnam," *TNR*, December 10, 1966, p. 6.

143. Hans Morgenthau, "The Colossus of Johnson City," *NYR*, March 31, 1966, pp. 11–13.

144. Buddy Stein and David Wellman, "The Scheer Campaign," *Studies*, January–February, 1967, pp. 62–77.

145. Andrew Kopkind, "Goodbye to All That," *TNR*, November 19, 1966, p. 7.

146. Edward Richer, "Peace Activism in Vietnam," *Studies*, January–February, 1966, pp. 59–61.

147. Harvey Swados, "*MacBird!* Satire or Symptom?" *New Politics*, Summer, 1966, pp. 62–63.

148. Ibid., p. 63.

149. Dwight Macdonald, "Birds of America," *NYR*, December 12, 1966, p. 12. Robert Lowell and Robert Brustein praised the play with comparable enthusiasm.

Third Stage

1. McGeorge Bundy, "End of Either/Or," *Foreign Affairs*, January, 1967, pp. 189–201. Salisbury had written: "I could begin to see quite clearly that there was a vast gap between the reality of the air

war, as seen from the ground in Hanoi, and the bland, vague American communiqués with their reiterated assumptions that our bombs were falling precisely upon 'military objectives' and accomplishing our military purposes with some kind of surgical precision which for the first time in the history of war was crippling the enemy without hurting or damaging civilian life." Harrison Salisbury, *Behind the Lines— Hanoi*, p. 69.

2. TRB, "Yes, the Answer's No," *TNR*, April 22, 1967, p. 2.

3. Editors, "Bombing," *TNR*, September 9, 1967, p. 6.

4. Editors, "World War III?" *TNR*, May 27, 1967, p. 4; John Osborne, "When Did China Decide to Enter the Korean War?" *TNR*, June 3, 1967, p. 3.

5. Quoted from *The Irony of American History*, by Editors, "Some Olive Branch," *TNR*, December 23, 1967, pp. 5–6.

6. Editors, "State of the Economy," *TNR*, January 7, 1967, p. 11; Editors, "No Staying Power?" *TNR*, January 21, 1967, pp. 6–7; and TRB, "Thanks but No Thanks," *TNR*, January 20, 1968, p. 6.

7. TRB, *TNR*, April 22, 1967, p. 2; TRB, "The Other Johnson," *TNR*, June 24, 1967, p. 2.

8. Editors, "More, More," *TNR*, May 6, 1967, p. 6; Andrew Hamilton, "Westmoreland's Progress Report," *TNR*, December 16, 1967, p. 15. After interim denials, Johnson *did* announce that General Westmoreland would get those troops which he needed over and above the approved troop ceiling of 480,000.

9. David Halberstam, "Return to Vietnam," *Harper's*, December, 1967, p. 18; Bernard Fall, "The View from Vietnam," *NYR*, February 9, 1967, p. 13.

10. Editors, "Giap's Firecracker," *TNR*, February 10, 1968, p. 5.

11. Editors, "Tick, Tock," *TNR*, February 3, 1968, p. 6.

12. Editors, "Mini-Truce in Vietnam," *TNR*, February 25, 1967, p. 7; John McDermott, "The Pause That Refreshes," *NYR*, March 23, 1967, pp. 14–15; Noam Chomsky, "The Responsibility of Intellectuals" (letter), *NYR*, April 20, 1967, p. 34; and Mark O. Hatfield, "Hatfield on LBJ," *TNR*, May 6, 1967, pp. 17–18.

13. Theodore Draper, "How Not to Negotiate," *NYR*, May 4, 1967, pp. 17–29.

14. Ibid., p. 27.
15. Ibid., p. 19. Related to that argument was Draper's contention in behalf of the Vietcong that "political 'terrorism' does not have the same cultural roots or stigma in all countries" (p. 25). For a refutation of Draper's "partisan bias," see: Victor Bator, "How Not to Negotiate" (letter), *NYR*, July 13, 1967, p. 38.
16. Ibid., p. 19.
17. Mary McCarthy, *Vietnam* (New York: Harcourt Brace Jovanovich, 1967), pp. 85–86. Her series on her trip to South Vietnam, February, 1967, first appeared in *NYR*, April 20–May 18, 1967.
18. Ibid., p. 86.
19. Ibid., p. 101.
20. Arthur Miller, "Our Guilt for the World's Evil," *The New York Times Magazine*, January 3, 1965, p. 11.
21. Robert Lifton, "Protean Man," *PR*, Winter, 1968, pp. 13–27.
22. Ibid.
23. Paul Jacobs, "Re-Radicalizing the De-Radicalized," *New Politics*, Fall, 1966, p. 14.
24. Andrew Kopkind, "Soul Power," *NYR*, August 24, 1967, pp. 3–6; Howard Zinn, *The Politics of History* (Boston: The Beacon Press, 1970), p. 1. For example, Zinn asked: "In a world where children are still not safe from starvation or bombs, should not the historian thrust himself and his writing into history, on behalf of goals in which he deeply believes?" For more interpretation of such sentiments, see: Christopher Lasch, *The Agony of the American Left* (New York: Alfred A. Knopf, 1969), p. 181. Both Lasch and Keniston, author of *The Uncommitted*, detected the same underlying values in the 1950s and 1960s, with the cult of privacy of the former simply becoming the cult of community in the latter. Either way, the crowd was lonely!
25. Quoted by Jessica Mitford, *The Trial of Doctor Spock* (New York: Alfred A. Knopf, 1969), p. 31.
26. David Harris was the university's student-body president and husband then of the folk singer Joan Baez. He was imprisoned for draft evasion.
27. Paul Goodman, "Appeal," *NYR*, April 6, 1967, p. 38.

28. Quoted by Bayard Rustin, "The New Radicalism," *PR*, Fall, 1965, p. 536.

29. Ibid., p. 539.

30. Mary McCarthy, "Vietnam: Solutions," *NYR*, November 9, 1967, p. 6.

31. Sontag, *Styles of Radical Will*, p. 264.

32. Noam Chomsky, "The Responsibility of Intellectuals," *NYR*, February 23, 1967, pp. 16–25.

33. John Thompson, "Good Man," *NYR*, August 3, 1967, p. 19. The occasion for his essay was a review of Paul Goodman's *Like a Conquered Province*.

34. Robert Wolfe, "Editorial Statement: Beyond Protest," *Studies*, January–February, 1967, pp. 3–21.

35. Paul Goodman, "We Won't Go," *NYR*, May 18, 1967, p. 17.

36. Hans Morgenthau, "What Ails America?" *TNR*, October 28, 1967, p. 17.

37. Noam Chomsky, *American Power and the New Mandarins* (New York: Pantheon, 1969), p. 383. Taken from the chapter entitled "On Resistance," which first appeared in *NYR*, December 7, 1967.

38. Noam Chomsky, "An Exchange on Resistance," *NYR*, February 1, 1968, p. 29.

39. Mary McCarthy, *Vietnam*, p. 91.

40. Ibid., pp. 101–103.

41. Ibid., p. 106.

42. Jack Newfield, "Black Power," *PR*, Spring, 1968, p. 222. The same point was made by Hans Morgenthau in *TNR*, October 28, 1967, p. 21.

43. Robert Lifton, ed., *America and the Asian Revolutions* (New York: Aldine Publishing Company, 1970), p. 5.

44. Kopkind, *NYR*, August 24, 1967, p. 3.

45. Noam Chomsky, Paul Lauter, and Florence Howe, "Reflections on a Political Trial," *NYR*, August 22, 1968, pp. 23–30; Murray Kempton, Introduction, *Trials of the Resistance* (New York: Vintage Books, 1970).

Notes, pages 131–136

46. Paul Goodman, "A Causerie at the Military-Industrial," *NYR*, November 23, 1967, p. 18.

47. Norman Mailer, *The Armies of the Night* (New York: New American Library, 1971), p. 211.

48. Robert Lowell, "The March," *NYR*, November 23, 1967, p. 3.

49. Mailer, *The Armies of the Night*, pp. 132–33, 238.

50. Norman Mailer, *Advertisements for Myself* (New York: G. P. Putnam's Sons, 1959), p. 17.

51. For example, the idea of inner transformation and rededication to revolution dominated Susan Sontag's "Trip to Hanoi" in *Styles of Radical Will*, pp. 205–74.

52. Quoted by Walter Goodman, "Liberals vs. Radicals—War in the Peace Camp," *The New York Times Magazine*, December 3, 1967, p. 179.

53. For more on his position, see: Dr. Benjamin Spock, *Dr. Spock on Vietnam* (New York: Dell Publishing Company, 1968).

54. Joint Statement, "What Can We Do?" *NYR*, June 15, 1967, p. 8. The signers were: Lewis Coser, Michael Harrington, Richard Hofstadter, Irving Howe, Arnold Kaufman, Allard Lowenstein, Lenore Marshall, Seymour Melman, Stanley Plastrik, Bernard Rosenberg, Meyer Schapiro, and Norman Thomas.

55. Statement, "Students and the Draft," *Dissent*, May–June, 1968, pp. 193–96. Among the signers were: Lewis Coser, Michael Harrington, Irving Howe, Arnold Kaufman, Steven Kelman, Norman Podhoretz, Norman Thomas, and Michael Walzer.

56. Theodore Draper, "Vietnam and American Politics," *Commentary*, March, 1968, pp. 15–28.

57. Symposium, "Civil Disobedience and 'Resistance,'" *Dissent*, January–February, 1968, p. 15. In the same discussion, Pickus, founder of the World Without War Council of the United States, criticized men like Dwight Macdonald "who are rightly committed to civil disobedience but make common cause with those committed to insurrectionary violence on the latter's terms, thus robbing civil disobedience of its moral force and desired practical effect." Ibid., p. 19. See also: Michael Harrington, "Strategies for Opposition: The Draft—Tax Refusal—'Resistance,'" *Dissent*, March–April, 1968, pp. 119–30.

58. Ibid., p. 26.

59. James Shand et al., "We Won't Go," *NYR*, June 29, 1967, p. 30.

60. Henry David Aiken, "A Virtue in Question," *NYR*, June 9, 1966, pp. 10–12; Robert Paul Wolff, Barrington Moore, Jr., and Herbert Marcuse, *A Critique of Pure Tolerance* (Boston: The Beacon Press, 1965). The authors stated in the Foreword: "For each of us the prevailing theory and practice of tolerance turned out on examination to be in varying degrees hypocritical masks to cover appalling political realities." The tone of indignation rose sharply from Wolff's plea for a "new philosophy of community beyond pluralism and beyond tolerance," to Moore's stress on the intellectuals' duty for "destructive criticism of a destructive reality," to Marcuse's belief in the "natural right" of resistance against "the concreteness of oppression."

61. Barrington Moore, Jr. and Henry Aiken, "Varieties of Liberalism," *NYR*, January 26, 1967, p. 33.

62. Ibid., p. 34.

63. Mary McCarthy and Diana Trilling, "On Withdrawing from Vietnam: An Exchange," *NYR*, January 18, 1968, p. 5.

64. Diana Trilling, "Ideology and Vietnam" (letter), *NYR*, February 29, 1968, p. 33.

65. Editors, "Hitched to LBJ?" *TNR*, September 30, 1967, p. 5.

66. Editors, "ADA Defers," *TNR*, October 7, 1967, p. 5.

67. Daniel P. Moynihan, "The Politics of Stability," from his speech before the National Board meeting of the ADA, Washington, D.C., September 23, 1967.

68. Ibid.

69. Editors, "Gene McCarthy," *TNR*, November 18, 1967, pp. 7–8.

70. Editors, "Will We Make It?" *TNR*, January 6, 1968, p. 10.

71. Andrew Kopkind, "The Thaw," *NYR*, April 25, 1968, p. 5; Editors, "Two Cheers," *TNR*, April 13, 1968, p. 5.

72. Michael Ferber, "On Being Indicted," *NYR*, April 25, 1968, p. 4.

73. Ross Terrill, "A Report on the Paris Talks," *TNR*, July 13, 1968, pp. 15–16.

74. Irving Howe, "Sticking with McCarthy," *NYR*, April 25, 1968, p. 6; Irving Howe, "A Triumph for Democracy," *Dissent*, May–June,

1968, pp. 198–99. The same point was made by Daniel P. Moynihan in "The Democrats, Kennedy and the Murder of Dr. King," *Commentary*, May, 1968, pp. 15–29.

75. From an abridged transcript of the public session at the Friends Meeting House in Gramercy Park on May 3, 1968, published as "Democracy (Has, Hasn't) a Future . . . a Present" in *The New York Times Magazine*, May 26, 1968, p. 30 ff. For more discussions from the TFI, see: Alexander Klein, editor, *Dissent, Power, and Confrontation* (New York: McGraw-Hill Book Company, 1971).

76. *The New York Times Magazine*, May 26, 1968, p. 30.

77. Ibid., p. 31.

78. Quoted by Robert Lowell, "Why I'm for McCarthy," *TNR*, April 13, 1968, p. 22.

79. McCarthy quoted by Editors, "Two from Minnesota," *TNR*, June 8, 1968, pp. 10–11.

80. Quoted by Tom Wicker, "Report on the Phenomenon Named McCarthy," *The New York Times Magazine*, August 25, 1968, p. 24.

81. For his spirited endorsement of McCarthy and the Senator's *The Limits of Power*, see: Hans Morgenthau, "A Talk with Senator McCarthy," *NYR*, August 22, 1968, pp. 14–16.

82. George Kennan, "Introducing Eugene McCarthy," *NYR*, April 11, 1968, p. 15.

83. David Halberstam, "The Man Who Ran Against Lyndon Johnson," *Harper's*, December, 1968, p. 52.

84. David Riesman, "McCarthy and Kennedy—Some Very Personal Reflections," *TNR*, April 13, 1968, p. 21.

85. Irving Howe, "Sticking with McCarthy," *NYR*, April 25, 1968, p. 9; Murray Kempton, "Why I'm for McCarthy," *TNR*, May 25, 1968, p. 18.

86. Kopkind, *NYR*, April 25, 1968, p. 4.

87. Irving Howe, "Stevenson and the Intellectuals," *Steady Work*, p. 207. Max Ways made the same point about the intellectuals' attraction to Stevenson because of his "remoteness from the corruptions and compromises associated with the familiar use of power." Max Ways, "Intellectuals and the Presidency," *Fortune*, April, 1967, p. 212.

88. Lowell, *TNR*, May 13, 1968, p. 22.

89. William Phillips, "June 6, 1968," *PR*, Summer, 1968, p. 445.

90. Editors, "The Kennedy Cause," *TNR*, June 15, 1968, p. 3.

91. Zalin Grant, "Counting on Strength That's Not There," *TNR*, June 15, 1968, p. 12; Editors, "LBJ and the Paris Talks," *TNR*, August 24, 1968, p. 5.

92. Editors, "Who's Mischievous?" *TNR*, July 13, 1968, pp. 6–7.

93. Quoted by Editors, "Time Enough," *TNR*, June 22, 1968, p. 5.

94. Editors, "Calling All Delegates," *TNR*, July 27, 1968, p. 6.

95. Erich Fromm et al., "The People's Choice," *NYR*, August 22, 1968, p. 37. They stated: "We, citizens of the United States, representing as the primaries so clearly show, a popular majority of Democrats, opposed to the policies of the present Administration, call upon our fellow citizens to join with us in active support against the cynical disregard of the electorate's expressed wishes by the political bosses who are attempting to utilize the delegates to perpetuate themselves and their bosses. . . . We demand an open convention and a meaningful choice." The signers were: Erich Fromm, Erich Kahler, Dwight Macdonald, Herbert Marcuse, Ashley Montagu, Lewis Mumford, George Ward, and James Watson.

96. Arthur Waskow, "Opposition," *NYR*, October 24, 1968, p. 37.

97. Elizabeth Hardwick, "Chicago," *NYR*, September 26, 1968, p. 5.

98. William Styron, "In the Jungle," ibid., p. 11.

99. Arthur Miller, "The Battle of Chicago: From the Delegates' Side," *The New York Times Magazine*, September 15, 1968, p. 122.

100. Ibid., p. 128.

101. Jack Newfield, "New Politics: More Mood than Movement," *The Nation*, July 28, 1969, p. 71.

102. Quoted by John Leo, "Theatre for Ideas Explores Politics," *The New York Times*, September 22, 1968, p. 55. Hayden was quoted in the same spirit by Leo Whalen, "U.S. Postage from Chicago," *PR*, Fall, 1968, p. 526.

103. TRB, "A Kind of Bastille," *TNR*, September 7, 1968, p. 6.

104. Norman Mailer, *Miami and the Siege of Chicago* (New York: World Publishing Company, 1968), p. 82.

105. Ibid., p. 172.

106. Ibid., p. 144.
107. Ibid., p. 164.
108. Ibid., p. 158.
109. Quoted from F. Scott Fitzgerald, *The Great Gatsby* (New York: Charles Scribner's Sons, 1925), p. 182.
110. Noted by Irving Howe, Symposium, "How Shall We Vote?" *Dissent*, November–December, 1968, p. 472.
111. Mary McCarthy, "Notes on the Election," *NYR*, October 24, 1968, p. 3.
112. Editors, "Squaring the Circle," *TNR*, September 21, 1968, p. 11.
113. Gore Vidal, "The Late Show," *NYR*, September 12, 1968, p. 8.
114. Mary McCarthy, *NYR*, October 24, 1968, p. 3.
115. Richard J. Barnet, "The North Vietnamese in Paris: The Impasse," *NYR*, October 24, 1968, p. 18; George McT. Kahin, "Impasse at Paris," *TNR*, October 12, 1968, p. 24; and Jan Mirsky, "What They Don't Say," *NYR*, October 24, 1968, pp. 23–26. Mirsky's article on the North Vietnamese perspective developed from thirteen hours of discussion between the Hanoi delegation in Paris and George Kahin, Howard Zinn, Douglas Dowd, and the author. Its expression of North Vietnamese (versus American) assumptions and problems was significantly different from the perspective usually presented in the U.S. press.
116. Paul Goodman, "The Best Man" (letter), *NYR*, October 24, 1968, p. 37.
117. Hans Morgenthau, "The Lesser Evil," *NYR*, November 7, 1968, pp. 13–16.
118. Michael Harrington, Symposium, "How Shall We Vote?" *Dissent*, November–December, 1968, pp. 470–71.
119. Murray Kempton, "What's to Be Done? An Honorable Choice," *TNR*, November 2, 1968, p. 12.
120. David Riesman, "America Moves to the Right," *The New York Times Magazine*, October 27, 1968, p. 82.
121. Leon Trotsky, "Concerning the Intelligentsia," *PR*, Fall, 1968, pp. 585–86.
122. TRB, "The Next Four Years," *TNR*, November 16, 1968, p.

4; Editors, "Campaign '68," *The Nation*, November 18, 1968, pp. 514–16.

123. Quoted from the conference organized at Princeton University by the International Association for Cultural Freedom by the *Herald Tribune*, December 9, 1968, p. 7. For full coverage on that seminar, see: François Duchêne, ed., *The Endless Crisis* (New York: Simon and Schuster, 1970).

Epilogue

1. F. Scott Fitzgerald, *The Crack-Up*, Edmund Wilson, ed. (New York: New Directions, 1945), p. 75.

2. See: Mary McCarthy, *Hanoi* (New York: Harcourt Brace Jovanovich, 1968) and *Medina* (New York: Harcourt Brace Jovanovich, 1972).

3. See accounts such as that done by the head of the "Pentagon Papers" study: Leslie H. Gelb, "The Pentagon Papers and *The Vantage Point*," *Foreign Policy*, Spring, 1972, pp. 25–41, and "Vietnam: The System Worked," *Foreign Policy*, Summer, 1971, pp. 140–67.

4. Alexander Klein, ed., *Dissent, Power, and Confrontation* (New York: McGraw-Hill Book Company, 1971), p. 229. The statement came in Pool's afterword to a session of the Theatre for Ideas, May, 1969.

5. Louis Harris poll, August 22, 1968.

6. Richard Hofstadter, *The Paranoid Style of American Politics and Other Essays* (New York: Alfred A. Knopf, 1966), pp. 3–40.

7. Raymond Aron, *The Elusive Revolution: Anatomy of a Student Revolt* (New York: Praeger Publishers, 1969), p. xviii.

8. Refers to the first student sit-in at a F. W. Woolworth lunch counter in Greensboro, N.C., February, 1960.

9. Stokely Carmichael, "What We Want," *NYR*, September 22, 1966, p. 8.

10. Robert Lifton, "Protean Man," *PR*, Winter, 1968, p. 27.

11. Staughton Lynd, "Historical Past and Existential Present," *The Dissenting Academy*, Theodore Roszak, ed. (New York: Pantheon Books, 1968), pp. 92–109.

12. Diana Trilling, "On the Steps of Low Library," *Commentary*, November, 1968, p. 55.

13. Theodore Roszak, "The Disease Called Politics," *Seeds of Liberation*, Paul Goodman, ed. (New York: George Braziller, 1965), p. 450.

14. Klein, *Dissent, Power, and Confrontation*, p. 226.

15. Michael Walzer, Symposium, "Civil Disobedience and 'Resistance,' " *Dissent*, January–February, 1968, p. 15.

16. Susan Sontag, *Styles of Radical Will* (New York: Dell Publishing Company, 1968), p. 271.

17. Staughton Lynd, "The New Radicals and 'Participatory Democracy,' " *Dissent*, Summer, 1965, p. 333.

18. Margot Hentoff, "Notes from a Plague Year," *NYR*, November 7, 1968, p. 23.

19. Istvan Deak, *Weimar Germany's Left-wing Intellectuals: A Political History of the Weltbühne and Its Circle* (Berkeley, Calif.: University of California Press, 1968); Peter Gay, *Weimar Culture: The Outsider as Insider* (New York: Harper & Row, 1968); Ernst Pawel, "A Voice Before the Silence," *Commentary*, December, 1968, pp. 100–106; Carl E. Schorske, "Weimar and the Intellectuals," *NYR* May 7 and 21, 1970, pp. 22–27 and 20–25, respectively.

20. Paul Goodman, "Berkeley in February," *Dissent*, Spring, 1965, pp. 161–75.

21. Andrew Kopkind, "Soul Power," *NYR*, August 24, 1967, pp. 3–6.

22. Howard Zinn, *The Politics of History* (Boston: The Beacon Press, 1970), p. 1.

23. Irving Louis Horowitz, *Radicalism and the Revolt Against Reason: The Social Theories of Georges Sorel* (Carbondale: Southern Illinois University Press, 1961), p. xiii.

24. See Rostow's long interview with *The New York Times*, January 5, 1969.

25. Eugene McCarthy, *The Year of the People* (Garden City, N.Y.: Doubleday & Company, 1969), p. 260.

26. Lionel Trilling, *The Liberal Imagination* (London: Secker and Warburg, 1951), pp. ix–x.

27. New York *Herald Tribune*, January 28, 1969.

28. *The New York Times,* October 20, 1972.

29. Recall the title of the collection of essays from *Studies on the Left* assembled by James Weinstein and David W. Eakins, eds., *For a New America* (New York: Random House, 1970).

30. Norman Mailer, "The Great Society?" *We Accuse,* James Petras, ed. (Berkeley, Calif.: Diablo Press, 1965), p. 17.

31. Sontag, *Styles of Radical Will,* p. 267.

32. Mailer, *The Armies of the Night,* p. 131.

Bibliography

The following is a selected and selectively annotated list of books used for background or direct citation in *The Long Dark Night of the Soul*. Space limitations preclude listing the articles read and used in newspapers and periodicals. Those of most significance are footnoted in the text.

On and by Intellectuals

Aaron, Daniel. *Writers on the Left*. New York: Avon Books, 1965. Invaluable treatment of the impact of the idea of Communism on the American Literary Left by a respected professor of English. See also: *The Unwritten War: American Writers and the Civil War*. New York: Alfred A. Knopf, 1973. It is a disquieting revelation of the relation of the intellectual to his government and society. It seems informed by and suggestive for a reading of literary response to the Vietnam experience.

Aron, Raymond. *The Opium of the Intellectuals*. Garden City, N.Y.: Doubleday & Company, 1957. Superb analysis of left-wing ideologies and their acceptance by intellectuals, especially in France. Aron provoked comparable controversy with this book and *The Elusive Revolution*, his critical dissection of the French student revolt in 1968.

Baumer, Franklin L. *Intellectual Movements in Modern European History*. New York: The Macmillan Company, 1965. Ten essays on intellectual "revolutions" from the Renaissance to existentialism.

Benda, Julien. *The Treason of the Intellectuals (La Trahison des clercs)*. Translated by Richard Aldington. New York: William Morrow and Company, 1928. Important in its own right and for its influence on the American Intellectual Left.

215

Bibliography

Berman, Ronald. *America in the Sixties: An Intellectual History*. New York: The Free Press, 1968. Lively treatment of contemporary intellectual trends by professor of literature.

Black, Max, ed. *The Morality of Scholarship*. Ithaca, N.Y.: Cornell University Press, 1967. Most important for the essay entitled "Politics and the Morality of Scholarship," by Conor Cruise O'Brien.

Bottomore, T. B. *Critics of Society: Radical Thought in North America*. New York: Pantheon Books, 1968.

Bourne, Randolph S. *War and the Intellectuals: Collected Essays, 1915–1919*. Edited and with an Introduction by Carl Resek. New York: Harper & Row, 1964. Bourne was a precocious contributor to the early *New Republic*. Critical of U.S. entry into World War I and the effect of the experience on intellectuals, he created a legend that has become an essential part of American intellectual history. Witness the invocation of Bourne by Dwight Macdonald and Noam Chomsky.

Chomsky, Noam. *American Power and the New Mandarins*. New York: Random House, 1969. This collection by a professor of modern languages is among the most significant publications of political essays to emerge from the Vietnam experience. It includes two landmark pieces first published in *The New York Review*, "The Responsibility of Intellectuals" and "On Resistance."

Coser, Lewis A. *Men of Ideas: A Sociologist's View*. New York: The Free Press, 1965.

Cruse, Harold. *The Crisis of the Negro Intellectual*. New York: William Morrow and Company, 1967. The very title of Cruse's book constituted an important event in intellectual circles since it dispelled the American myth of a raceless intelligentsia and set up a separate "class" of black intellectuals with its own problems.

Deak, Istvan. *Weimar Germany's Left-Wing Intellectuals: A Political History of the Weltbühne and Its Circle*. Berkeley, Calif.: University of California Press, 1968. Representative of the new wave of interest in Weimar intellectuals to parallel the dilemmas of the U.S. Intellectual Left in the 1960s.

De Huszar, George B., ed. *The Intellectuals*. New York: The Free Press,

Bibliography

1960. Sixty-eight articles on the political responsibility of intellectuals in the nineteenth and twentieth centuries.

Duchêne, François, ed. *The Endless Crisis: A Confrontation on America in the Seventies.* New York: Simon and Schuster, 1970. This is a record of a meeting of well-known social thinkers under the auspices of the International Association for Cultural Freedom at Princeton, N.J., in December, 1968.

Forcey, Charles. *The Crossroads of Liberalism: Croly, Weyl, Lippmann, and the Progressive Era, 1900–1925.* New York: Oxford University Press, 1961.

Fredrickson, George M. *The Inner Civil War: Northern Intellectuals and the Crisis of the Union.* New York: Harper & Row, 1965. Precedent for the type of study of attitudes attempted in this book.

Gay, Peter. *Weimar Culture: The Outsider as Insider.* New York: Harper & Row, 1968. Another index to the revival of American scholarly interest in Weimar intellectuals.

Gilbert, James Burkhart. *Writers and Partisans: A History of Literary Radicalism in America.* New York: John Wiley and Sons, 1968. Expansion of a dissertation done at the University of Wisconsin on *Partisan Review* and its relation to the decline of literary radicalism, 1912–52.

Goodman, Paul, ed. *Seeds of Liberation.* New York: George Braziller, 1965. One of the few "over thirty" trusted by young people, he was best-known in the 1960s for *Growing Up Absurd.* He became the editor of *Liberation,* from which this collection derives, in 1960. He drew his philosophical position from Kropotkin, Gandhi, Jefferson, and Wilhelm Reich and believed that institutions alienate man from his true self. Other important books by Goodman relevant to this study include: *Communitas, People or Personnel, Like a Conquered Province,* and *The New Reformation.*

Hentoff, Nat, ed. *The Essays of A. J. Muste.* New York: Simon and Schuster, 1967. Writer married to another writer, Margot Hentoff.

Horowitz, Irving L., ed. *The Anarchists.* New York: Dell Publishing Company, 1964. One of the most prolific writers on philosophies and ideologies important in American intellectual history.

———, ed. *Power, Politics and People: The Collected Essays of*

217

Bibliography

C. Wright Mills. New York: Oxford University Press, 1962.

————. *Radicalism and the Revolt Against Reason: The Social Theories of Georges Sorel*. Carbondale: Southern Illinois University Press, 1961.

Howe, Irving. *Decline of the New*. New York: Harcourt Brace Jovanovich, 1970. Author, critic, professor of English, and editor of *Dissent*. A self-proclaimed socialist and "democratic radical" notable for his opposition to the "authoritarian Left" in intellectual circles. In addition to books noted below, see: *A World More Attractive* (1963). Among his many articles, the most important in this context are: "New Styles in Leftism" and "The New York Intellectuals."

————, ed. *The Radical Papers*. Garden City, N.Y.: Doubleday & Company, 1966.

————. *Steady Work: Essays in the Politics of Democratic Radicalism, 1953–1966*. New York: Harcourt Brace Jovanovich, 1966.

Hughes, H. Stuart. *The Obstructed Path: French Social Thought in the Years of Desperation, 1930–1960*. New York: Harper & Row, 1966. An analysis of Sartre and other French intellectuals and an excellent treatment of modern French social thought. It suggests relationships between contemporary French and American intellectual history.

Kazin, Alfred. *Starting Out in the Thirties*. Boston: Little, Brown and Company, 1962. One of America's most influential literary critics, who moved in the liberal-radical milieu of the 1930s, beginning with *The New Republic* and surrounded eventually by the founders of *Partisan Review*.

Lasch, Christopher. *The Agony of the American Left*. New York: Alfred A. Knopf, 1969. This historian is most important for his argument that modern radicalism or liberalism can best be understood as a phase in the social history of the intellectuals.

————. *The New Radicalism in America, 1889–1963*. New York: Alfred A. Knopf, 1965. See also: *The World of Nations: Reflections on American History, Politics, and Culture*. New York: Alfred A. Knopf, 1973.

Lynd, Staughton. *Intellectual Origins of American Radicalism*. New

Bibliography

York: Pantheon Books, 1968. This Quaker historian, civil rights
activist, and strong opponent of the Vietnam War also wrote:
Nonviolence in America: A Documentary History and *The Other
Side* (with Tom Hayden). His politics often seemed a tortured
mixture of Thoreau and John Brown.

Macdonald, Dwight. *Memoirs of a Revolutionist: Essays in Political
Criticism*. New York: Farrar, Straus and Giroux, 1957. This book
is important for showing the changes in the political convictions
over two decades of one of the nation's most prescient critics.
See also: *The Root Is Man* (1953) for his philosophy of "radical
humanism" and *Against the American Grain* (1962) for Macdonald's attack on "masscult" and "midcult." Renowned for a political
flexibility which reflects the political currents of the U.S. Intellectual Left, Macdonald once stated: "The speed with which I
evolved from a liberal into a radical and from a tepid Communist
sympathizer into an ardent anti-Stalinist still amazes me."

Mailer, Norman. *Advertisements for Myself*. New York: G. P. Putnam's
Sons, 1959. Written by the ofttimes existential hipster and Pulitzer Prize-winning author of *The Armies of the Night* (1968),
which is a novel-history of the March on the Pentagon in 1967. Co-
founder of *The Village Voice* and an editor of *Dissent*, 1953–63.
Other important books: *The Naked and the Dead* (1948), *The
Deer Park* (1955), *The Presidential Papers* (1963), *An American
Dream* (1965), *Cannibals and Christians* (1966), *Why Are We
in Vietnam?* (1967), and *Miami and the Siege of Chicago* (1968).

Morgenthau, Hans J. *Truth and Power: Essays of a Decade, 1960–70*.
New York: Praeger Publishers, 1970. This particular book is significant for showing the progressive radicalization and political
disillusionment of Morgenthau because of the Vietnam experience
during the 1960s. This acerbic professor of political science and
modern history may be best known for *Politics among Nations*
(1948). See also: *A New Foreign Policy for the United States*
(1967).

Niebuhr, Reinhold. *Moral Man and Immoral Society*. New York:
Charles Scribner's Sons, 1932. For a good collection of writings
by this distinguished theologian and social critic, see: *Reinhold*

Bibliography

Niebuhr on Politics: His Political Philosophy and Its Application to Our Age as Expressed in His Writings, edited by Harry R. Davis and Robert C. Good.

O'Brien, Conor Cruse. *Writers and Politics.* New York: Pantheon Books, 1965.

Phillips, William. *A Sense of the Present: Essays and Stories of Two Decades.* New York: Chilmark Press, 1968. A valuable collection by one of the founding editors of the *Partisan Review.*

Podhoretz, Norman. *Making It.* New York: Random House, 1967. Insider's view of the American intelligentsia by one who became editor in chief of *Commentary* in 1960. See also: *Doings and Undoings: The Fifties and After in American Writing.*

Rahv, Philip. *The Myth and the Powerhouse.* New York: Farrar, Straus and Giroux, 1965. By one of the founding editors of *Partisan Review.*

Raskin, Marcus G. *Being and Doing.* New York: Random House, 1971. This is a reflective book by the co-founder of the Institute for Policy Studies. A leader in antiwar resistance, he was briefly notorious as one of the defendants in the "Boston Five" draft-conspiracy case.

Rieff, Philip, ed. *On Intellectuals.* Garden City, N.Y.: Doubleday & Company, 1969. Helpful collection of theoretical and case studies.

Rogin, Michael Paul. *The Intellectuals and McCarthy: The Radical Specter.* Cambridge, Mass.: The M.I.T. Press, 1967.

Roszak, Theodore. *The Dissenting Academy.* New York: Random House, 1967. Essays criticizing the teaching of the humanities in American universities.

Shils, Edward. *The Intellectuals and the Powers and Other Essays.* Chicago: The University of Chicago Press, 1972. Most helpful in this context are two essays by the noted professor of sociology and social thought: "Intellectuals and the Center of Society in the United States" and "The Intellectuals and the Future."

Strout, Cushing, ed. *Intellectual History in America.* Vols. 1–2. New York: Harper & Row, 1968.

Trilling, Lionel. *The Liberal Imagination: Essays on Literature and Society.* London: Secker and Warburg, 1951. He and his wife,

Bibliography

Diana Trilling, proved to be influential, liberal naysayers in the 1960s.

Wolff, Robert Paul. *The Poverty of Liberalism.* Boston: The Beacon Press, 1968. This philosophy professor's book is addressed critically to liberal and radical intellectuals. See also: his contribution to *A Critique of Pure Tolerance* (1965) and *In Defense of Anarchism* (1970).

On and by the New Left

Aron, Raymond. *The Elusive Revolution: Anatomy of a Student Revolt.* New York: Praeger Publishers, 1969.

Baritz, Loren, ed. *The American Left: Radical Political Thought in the Twentieth Century.* New York: Basic Books, 1971.

Brown, Michael, ed. *The Politics and Anti-politics of the Young.* Beverly Hills, Calif.: Glencoe Press, 1969. Includes helpful essays by Mario Savio and Tom Hayden.

Buckman, Peter. *The Limits of Protest.* Indianapolis: The Bobbs-Merrill Company, 1970.

Cantor, Norman F. *The Age of Protest: Dissent and Rebellion in the Twentieth Century.* New York: Hawthorn Books, 1969.

Cleaver, Eldridge. *Soul on Ice.* New York: Dell Publishing Company, 1968. Landmark book written by young Black Panther while in California's Folsom State Prison.

Cohn-Bendit, Daniel, and Cohn-Bendit, Gabriel. *Obsolete Communism: The Left-Wing Alternative.* New York: McGraw-Hill Book Company, 1968. Speaks of student rebellion from Berkeley to Berlin.

Cranston, Maurice, ed. *The New Left, Six Critical Essays.* London: The Bodley Head, Ltd., 1970.

Dellinger, David. *Revolutionary Nonviolence.* Garden City, N.Y.: Doubleday & Company, 1971. Important because of the role of its author: founding editor of *Liberation*, co-chairman of the New Mobilization Committee to End the War in Vietnam, civil rights activist, and long-time pacifist imprisoned for three years for refusal to register for the draft in World War II.

Bibliography

Draper, Hal. *Berkeley: The New Student Revolt.* New York: Grove Press, 1965.

Fanon, Frantz. *The Wretched of the Earth.* New York: Grove Press, 1966. Fanon was a significant influence on the American Intellectual Left of the 1960s because of his bitter indictments of colonialism and racism. See also: *A Dying Colonialism.*

Farber, Jerry. *The Student as Nigger.* New York: Pocket Books, 1970. Views students in the U.S. as society's slaves.

Friedenberg, Edgar. *Coming of Age in America: Growth and Acquiescence.* New York: Random House, 1965. Interesting book by a radical professor of sociology and frequent contributor to *The New York Review.*

Gerberding, William P., and Smith, Duane E., eds. *The Radical Left: The Abuse of Discontent.* Boston: Houghton Mifflin Company, 1970.

Gerzon, Mark. *The Whole World Is Watching: A Young Man Looks at Youth's Dissent.* New York: The Viking Press, 1969. The writer was in Harvard's Class of 1970.

Goodman, Paul. *The New Reformation.* New York: Random House, 1970.

Hampden-Turner, Charles. *Radical Man: The Process of Psycho-Social Development.* Cambridge, Mass.: Schenkman Publishing Company, 1970. Expatriate Englishman's attempt to restore a moral impulse to social science.

Hayden, Tom. *Trial.* New York: Holt, Rinehart & Winston, 1970. This is an insider's story of the trial for those indicted for disrupting the Democratic convention in Chicago in 1968. It was a trial that Hayden called the "watershed experience for an entire generation of alienated white youth." This primary drafter of the SDS "Port Huron Statement" moved from the influence of writers like Michael Harrington to an increasingly radical and alienated stance in the course of his commitments to civil rights, community organizing, and the peace movement. For more by this contributing editor to *Liberation* and *Studies on the Left*, see: *Rebellion in Newark* and *The Other Side* (written with Staughton Lynd after their trip to Hanoi).

Bibliography

Hoffman, Abbie. *Revolution for the Hell of It.* New York: The Dial Press, 1968. By the founder of the Youth International Party (Yippies) and an active civil rights worker for SNCC, who claimed dedication to disrupting the American system—if one could have fun doing it.

Howe, Irving, ed. *Beyond the New Left.* New York: Saturday Review Press, 1970. Helpful collection of essays by a critic of the "authoritarian Left."

Jacobs, Paul, and Landau, Saul. *The New Radicals.* New York: Random House, 1966. One of the most useful early collections of documents on the New Left, sponsored by the Center for the Study of Democratic Institutions.

Kelman, Steven. *Push Comes to Shove: The Escalation of Student Protest.* Boston: Houghton Mifflin Company, 1970. Critical evaluation of the "movement" by then Harvard leftist.

Keniston, Kenneth. *The Uncommitted: Alienated Youth in American Society.* New York: Harcourt Brace Jovanovich, 1965. A psychology professor's look at the "generation gap" in the United States.

————. *Young Radicals: Notes on Committed Youth.* New York: Harcourt Brace Jovanovich, 1968. Psychological study of a number of young people working for Vietnam Summer (1967), an organization opposing American involvement in Southeast Asia.

Kennan, George F. *Democracy and the Student Left.* Boston: Little, Brown and Company, 1968. Critical treatment of the U.S. student movement by one of the nation's most distinguished former diplomats.

Kunen, James Simon. *The Strawberry Statement: Notes of a College Revolutionary.* New York: Random House, 1969. A politicized Dustin Hoffman, who expressed the feeling common to many of his peers in the post-World War II generation: time is running out for America.

Laing, R. D. *The Politics of Experience.* New York: Ballantine Books, 1967. By the controversial British psychiatrist who addressed the alleged basis of alienation in contemporary U.S. intellectuals.

Lichtheim, George. *The Concept of Ideology and Other Essays.* New York: Random House, 1967. Written by a respected in-

223

Bibliography

fluence on both the Old and the New Left in the United States.

Lipset, Seymour Martin, ed. *The Berkeley Student Revolt: Facts and Interpretations.* Garden City, N.Y.: Doubleday & Company, 1965. Collection of articles, statements, and documents depicting events of 1964. Assembled by the prolific political scientist.

————, ed. (with Philip G. Altbach). *Students in Revolt.* Boston: Houghton Mifflin Company, 1969.

Long, Priscilla, ed. *The New Left: A Collection of Essays.* Boston: Porter Sargent Publisher, 1969. Staughton Lynd's introduction provides a helpful synopsis of the development of the American New Left.

Lothstein, Arthur, ed. *"All We Are Saying . . ."—the Philosophy of the New Left.* New York: G. P. Putnam's Sons, 1970.

Malcolm X. *The Autobiography of Malcolm X.* New York: Grove Press, 1964.

Menashe, Louis, and Radosh, Ronald, eds. *Teach-ins: U.S.A.: Reports, Opinions, Documents.* New York: Praeger Publishers, 1967. This collection includes a broad range of views on that aspect of the antiwar movement in 1965.

Newfield, Jack. *The New Left: A Prophetic Minority.* New York: The New American Library, 1966. This self-proclaimed "radical democrat" claimed that participation in the movement against the Vietnam War did the most to affect his political viewpoint.

Reich, Charles A. *The Greening of America: How the Youth Revolution Is Trying to Make America Livable.* New York: Random House, 1970. Yale professor's declaration of "Consciousness III."

Silverman, Henry J., ed. *American Radical Thought: The Libertarian Tradition.* Lexington, Mass.: D. C. Heath & Company, 1970. Excellent collection of essays ranging from Ralph Waldo Emerson to Eldridge Cleaver.

Teodori, Massimo, ed. *The New Left: A Documentary History.* Indianapolis: The Bobbs-Merrill Company, 1969. A European perspective on the American "movement."

Weinstein, James, and Eakins, David W. *For a New America.* New York: Random House, 1970. Articles taken from *Studies on the Left*, 1959–67.

Bibliography

Young, Alfred F., ed. *Dissent: Explorations in the History of American Radicalism*. De Kalb: Northern Illinois University Press, 1968. Includes pieces by Staughton Lynd, Martin Duberman, and Howard Zinn.

U.S. Political Culture and History

Almond, Gabriel A. *The American People and Foreign Policy*. New York: Harcourt Brace Jovanovich, 1950.

Arendt, Hannah. *Crises of the Republic*. New York: Harcourt Brace Jovanovich, 1972. Draws on essays by the German-born professor of philosophy and social thought which had been published previously in *The New Yorker* and *The New York Review*.

Ashmore, Harry S. *The Man in the Middle*. Columbia: University of Missouri Press, 1966. Discusses the political climate in the United States during the Johnson Administration.

Beisner, Robert D. *Twelve against Empire—the Anti-Imperialists, 1898–1900*. New York: McGraw-Hill Book Company, 1968. This book anticipates the moral objections raised by American intellectuals opposed to U.S. involvement in Southeast Asia in the 1960s.

Bell, Daniel. *The End of Ideology: On the Exhaustion of Political Ideas in the Fifties*. New York: The Free Press, 1960. Landmark book written by the educator-sociologist, then co-editor of *Public Interest* and associate editor of *Daedalus*.

Bernstein, Barton, ed. *Towards a New Past: Dissenting Essays in American History*. New York: Pantheon Books, 1968.

Cantril, Albert H., and Roll, Charles W., Jr. *Hopes and Fears of the American People*. New York: Universe Books, 1971.

Commager, Henry Steele. *The American Mind: An Interpretation of American Thought and Character since the 1880's*. New Haven: Yale University Press, 1950.

Curti, Merle. *The Growth of American Thought*. New York: Harper & Row, 1964.

Fiedler, Leslie. *An End to Innocence: Essays on Culture and Politics*. Boston: The Beacon Press, 1952.

Bibliography

Free, Lloyd A., and Cantril, Hadley. *The Political Beliefs of Americans: A Study of Public Opinion.* New Brunswick, N.J.: Rutgers University Press, 1967.

Galbraith, John Kenneth. *The Affluent Society.* Boston: Houghton Mifflin Company, 1958. Important book by the Harvard economist, notable for his activity in the Americans for Democratic Action and opposition to the Vietnam War.

————. *Economics, Peace and Laughter.* Boston: Houghton Mifflin Company, 1971.

————. *The New Industrial State.* Boston: Houghton Mifflin Company, 1967.

Gettleman, Marvin E., and Mermelstein, David, eds. *The Great Society Reader: The Failure of American Liberalism.* New York: Vintage Books, 1967.

Goodman, Paul. *Growing Up Absurd.* New York: Random House, 1956.

————. *Like a Conquered Province.* New York: Random House, 1966.

————. *People or Personnel: Decentralizing and the Mixed System.* New York: Random House, 1963.

Gordon, Kermit, ed. *Agenda for the Nation.* Washington, D.C.: The Brookings Institution, 1968. Eighteen essays on public issues facing the United States at the end of the Johnson Administration.

Gorer, Geoffrey. *The American People: A Study in National Character.* New York: W. W. Norton & Company, 1948.

Green, Philip, and Levinson, Sanford, eds. *Power and Community: Dissenting Essays in Political Science.* New York: Vintage Books, 1970. Rejects the "myth" that the American polity is a working example of "democratic pluralism."

Harrington, Michael. *The Other America: Poverty in the United States.* New York: The Macmillan Company, 1962. Important contribution by a self-styled democratic socialist who became chairman of the board for the League for Industrial Democracy in 1964 and was a conscientious objector during the Korean War. See also: *The Accidental Century* (1965).

————. *Toward a Democratic Left: A Radical Program for a New Majority.* New York: The Macmillan Company, 1968.

Hart, Jeffrey. *The American Dissent.* Garden City, N.Y.: Double-

Bibliography

day & Company, 1966. Conservative perspective on the 1960s.

Hofstadter, Richard, and Wallace, Michael, eds. *American Violence: A Documentary History.* New York: Vintage Books, 1970. One of the remarkable number of books written by the respected professor of history at Columbia University.

————. *Anti-Intellectualism in American Life.* New York: Alfred A. Knopf, 1963.

————. *The Paranoid Style in American Politics and Other Essays.* New York: Alfred A. Knopf, 1966.

————, ed. *The Progressive Movement, 1900–1915.* Englewood Cliffs, N.J.: Prentice-Hall, 1963.

Jones, LeRoi. *Home: Social Essays.* New York: William Morrow and Company, 1966. Black separatist leader and playwright.

Kammen, Michael. *People of Paradox: An Inquiry Concerning the Origins of American Civilization.* New York: Alfred A. Knopf, 1972. Pulitzer Prize-winning book by history professor.

Kaplan, Morton. *Dissent and the State in Peace and War.* New York: Dunellen Publishing Company, 1970.

Kaufman, Arnold S. *The Radical Liberal: New Man in American Politics.* New York: Atherton Press, 1968. This professor of philosophy was one of the original organizers of the Dump Johnson movement, an active participant in the civil rights movement, and a founder of the teach-ins.

Kopkind, Andrew, and Ridgeway, James, eds. *Decade of Crisis: America in the '60's.* New York: The World Publishing Company, 1972.

Kornhauser, William. *The Politics of Mass Society.* New York: The Free Press, 1959.

Krock, Arthur. *In the Nation: 1932–1966.* New York: McGraw-Hill Book Company, 1966.

Lane, Robert E. *Political Ideology: Why the American Common Man Believes What He Does.* New York: The Free Press, 1962.

Lasswell, Harold D. *Politics: Who Gets What, When, How.* New York: The World Publishing Company, 1958.

Lipset, Seymour Martin. *Political Man.* New York: Doubleday & Company, 1960.

Lowi, Theodore J. *The End of Liberalism: Ideology, Policy, and the*

227

Bibliography

Crisis of Public Authority. New York: W. W. Norton & Company, 1969.

————. *The Politics of Disorder.* New York: Basic Books, 1971.

Luce, Robert B., ed. *The Faces of Five Decades: Selections from Fifty Years of The New Republic, 1914–1964.* New York: Simon and Schuster, 1964. Arthur Schlesinger, Jr., wrote the excellent introductory portions.

McCarthy, Eugene J. *The Year of the People.* Garden City, N.Y.: Doubleday & Company, 1969.

McGovern, George. *A Time of War—a Time of Peace.* New York: Random House, 1968.

McReynolds, David. *We Have Been Invaded by the 21st Century.* New York: Praeger Publishers, 1970.

Mailer, Norman. *Miami and the Siege of Chicago.* New York: New American Library, 1968. The novelist's coverage of the Republican and Democratic conventions in 1968.

Marcuse, Herbert. *One-Dimensional Man.* Boston: The Beacon Press, 1964. "Studies of the ideology of advanced industrial society" by the Berlin-born mentor of the American New Left and noted professor of philosophy in California. See also: *Eros and Civilization* and *A Critique of Pure Tolerance,* done with Robert Paul Wolff and Barrington Moore, Jr.

Miller, William Lee. *Piety along the Potomac: Notes on Politics and Morals in the 50's.* Boston: Houghton Mifflin Company, 1964.

Mills, C. Wright. *The Power Elite.* New York: Oxford University Press, 1956. This sociologist was considered by some to be the intellectual father of the "movement." He repudiated the "ideology of an ending" and proposed that young intellectuals become the "immediate radical agency of change." Beyond those items noted here, see: *The Sociological Imagination* and his influential essays "On the New Left" and "Listen, Yankee."

————. *Power, Politics, and People.* New York: Ballantine Books, 1963.

Mitchell, William C. *The American Polity: A Social and Cultural Interpretation.* New York: The Free Press, 1962.

Morison, Samuel Eliot; Merk, Frederick; and Freidel, Frank. *Dissent in Three American Wars.* Cambridge: Harvard University Press, 1970. This timely volume on opposition to the War of 1812, the

Bibliography

Mexican War, and the Spanish-American War helped put the Vietnam conflict into perspective.

Newfield, Jack, and Greenfield, Jeff. *A Populist Manifesto: The Making of a New Majority*. New York: Praeger Publishers, 1972.

Niebuhr, Reinhold. *The Irony of American History*. New York: Charles Scribner's Sons, 1952.

Peterson, Horace C., and Fite, G. C. *Opponents of War, 1917–1918*. Madison: University of Wisconsin Press, 1957.

Podhoretz, Norman, ed. *The Commentary Reader: Two Decades of Articles and Stories*. New York: Atheneum Publishers, 1966.

Riesman, David. *The Lonely Crowd*. New Haven: Yale University Press, 1950.

Scammon, Richard M., and Wattenberg, Ben. *The Real Majority*. New York: Coward, McCann & Geoghegan, 1970.

Schlesinger, Arthur M., Jr. *The Crisis of Confidence: Ideas, Power and Violence in America*. Boston: Houghton Mifflin Company, 1969. Writer and educator and Camelot chronicler. For his reversal on the Vietnam War, see: *The Bitter Heritage*.

———. *A Thousand Days: John F. Kennedy in the White House*. Boston: Houghton Mifflin Company, 1965.

Sorensen, Theodore C. *Kennedy*. New York: Harper & Row, 1965.

Stone, I. F. *In a Time of Torment*. New York: Random House, 1967. Independent Washington journalist, long-time editor of *I. F. Stone's Weekly* (begun in 1953), and subsequent contributing editor to *The New York Review*.

———. *Polemics and Prophecies, 1967–70*. New York: Random House, 1970. A sequel in his series of collections of essays.

Tocqueville, Alexis de. *Democracy in America*. Edited and introduced by Phillips Bradley. Foreword by Harold J. Laski. New York: Alfred A. Knopf, 1945.

Wakefield, Dan. *Supernation at Peace and War*. Boston: Little, Brown and Company, 1968. One reporter's survey of the American mood, 1967–68, published first in *The Atlantic* (March, 1968).

Waskow, Arthur I. *Running Riot: A Journey Through the Official Disasters and Creative Disorder in American Society*. New York: The Seabury Press, 1970.

Wolfe, Tom. *Radical Chic and Mau-Mauing the Flak Catchers*. New

Bibliography

York: Farrar, Straus & Giroux, 1971. Wolfe caught flak from the Left.

Wolff, Robert Paul; Moore, Barrington, Jr.; and Marcuse, Herbert. *A Critique of Pure Tolerance*. Boston: The Beacon Press, 1965.

Zinn, Howard. *The Politics of History*. Boston: The Beacon Press, 1970. The professor of government and civil rights activist advocated the role of historian as actor.

————. *SNCC: The New Abolitionists*. Boston: The Beacon Press, 1964.

U.S. Foreign Policy: General

Alperovitz, Gar. *Atomic Diplomacy*. New York: Random House, 1965. An interesting contribution by an emerging postwar revisionist historian.

————. *Cold War Essays*. Garden City, N.Y.: Doubleday & Company, 1970.

Bailey, Thomas A. *A Diplomatic History of the American People*. New York: Appleton-Century-Crofts, 1950.

Ball, George W. *The Discipline of Power*. Boston: Little, Brown and Company, 1968. By one of the in-house doves.

Barnet, Richard. *Intervention and Revolution: America's Confrontation with Insurgent Movements around the World*. New York: The World Publishing Company, 1968. Seminal study on postwar U.S. foreign policy.

Bartlett, Ruhl Jacob. *American Foreign Policy: Revolution and Crisis*. Atlanta: Oglethorpe College, 1966.

Beard, Charles A. *A Foreign Policy for America*. New York: Alfred A. Knopf, 1940. Debunker of American moralism who influenced the writing of Theodore Draper, Reinhold Niebuhr, and others.

Fulbright, J. William. *The Arrogance of Power*. New York: Alfred A. Knopf, 1966.

Galbraith, John Kenneth. *How to Control the Military*. Garden City, N.Y.: Doubleday & Company, 1969.

Haas, Ernst B. *Tangle of Hopes: American Commitments and World Order*. Englewood Cliffs, N.J.: Prentice-Hall, 1969.

Bibliography

Halle, Louis J. *The Cold War as History*. New York: Harper & Row, 1968.

Hilsman, Roger. *To Move a Nation: The Politics of Foreign Policy in the Administration of John F. Kennedy*. Garden City, N.Y.: Doubleday & Company, 1967.

Hoffmann, Stanley. *Gulliver's Troubles, or the Setting of American Foreign Policy*. New York: McGraw-Hill Book Company, 1968.

Horowitz, David, ed. *Containment and Revolution*. Boston: The Beacon Press, 1967. An anthology of writers who oppose U.S. intervention in revolutions. See also: *The Free World Colossus: A Critique of American Foreign Policy in the Cold War* (1965).

Houghton, Neal D., ed. *Struggle against History: U.S. Foreign Policy in an Age of Revolution*. New York: Washington Square Press, 1968. Mixed bag of papers presented at a seminar held in March, 1967.

Kennan, George F. *American Diplomacy, 1900–1950*. New York: Mentor Books, 1963. Landmark book in U.S. consensus historiography.

Kissinger, Henry A. *American Foreign Policy: Three Essays*. New York: W. W. Norton & Company, 1969. Note particularly the third piece on Vietnam.

Lens, Sidney. *The Futile Crusade: Anti-Communism as American Credo*. Chicago: Quadrangle/The New York Times Book Company, 1964. Might also note: *The Military-Industrial Complex* (1970).

McCarthy, Eugene J. *The Limits of Power: America's Role in the World*. New York: Dell Publishing Company, 1968. Argues, not surprisingly, that the Senate Foreign Relations Committee should help guide U.S. participation in world affairs.

Marzani, Carl. *We Can Be Friends: Origins of the Cold War*. New York: Topical Books Publishers, 1952. One of earliest ventures in American revisionist historiography.

Morgenthau, Hans J. *A New Foreign Policy for the United States*. New York: Praeger Publishers, 1969. Argues that the United States needs to undergo a change in foreign policy comparable to that of 1948.

Bibliography

Oglesby, Carl, and Shaull, Richard. *Containment and Change: Two Dissenting Views of American Foreign Policy.* New York: The Macmillan Company, 1967. New Left analysis of U.S. foreign policy.

Sorensen, Theodore C. *The Kennedy Legacy.* New York: The Macmillan Company, 1969.

Spanier, John. *American Foreign Policy since World War II.* New York: Praeger Publishers, 1967.

Steel, Ronald. *Pax Americana: The Cold-War Empire the United States Acquired by Accident—and How It Led from Isolation to Global Intervention.* New York: The Viking Press, 1968. By a frequent contributor to *The New York Review.*

Stillman, Edmund, and Pfaff, William. *Power and Impotence: The Failure of America's Foreign Policy.* New York: Harper & Row, 1967.

Tucker, Robert W. *Nation or Empire?—the Debate over American Foreign Policy.* Baltimore: The Johns Hopkins Press, 1968.

————. *The Radical Left and American Foreign Policy.* Baltimore: The Johns Hopkins Press, 1971.

Williams, William Appleman. *The Great Evasion.* New York: Quadrangle/The New York Times Book Company, 1964. The author is noteworthy as a native American radical, revisionist historian, and one of the most influential exponents of the economic interpretation of American expansionism. He was significant in the early development of the U.S. New Left—active in the civil rights movement, the teach-ins, and socialist politics.

————. *The Roots of the Modern American Empire: A Study of the Growth and Shaping of Social Consciousness in a Marketplace Society.* New York: Random House, 1969.

————. *The Tragedy of American Diplomacy.* New York: The World Publishing Company, 1959.

U.S. Foreign Policy: Vietnam

Armbruster, Frank E., et al. *Can We Win in Vietnam?* New York: Praeger Publishers, 1968. A Hudson Institute publication.

232

Bibliography

Austin, Anthony. *The President's War: The Story of the Tonkin Gulf Resolution and How the Nation Was Trapped in Vietnam*. Philadelphia: J. B. Lippincott Company, 1971.

Bator, Victor. *Vietnam: A Diplomatic Tragedy*. Dobbs Ferry, N.Y.: Oceana Publications, 1965. Focuses on U.S. policy in the 1950's.

Brandon, Henry. *Anatomy of Error: The Inside Story of the Asian War on the Potomac, 1954–1969*. Boston: Gambit, 1969.

Brown, Sam, and Ackland, Len, eds. *Why Are We Still in Vietnam?* New York: Random House, 1970.

Committee of Concerned Asian Scholars. *The Indochina Story: A Fully Documented Account*. New York: Pantheon Books, 1970.

Cooper, Chester. *The Lost Crusade: America in Vietnam*. New York: Dodd, Mead and Company, 1970.

Draper, Theodore. *The Abuse of Power*. New York: The Viking Press, 1967. Lucid rebuttal of the arguments supporting U.S. policy in the Dominican Republic and Vietnam.

Ellsberg, Daniel. *Papers on the War*. New York: Simon and Schuster, 1972.

Falk, Richard A., ed. *The Vietnam War and International Law*. Princeton: Princeton University Press, 1967.

Fall, Bernard B. *Last Reflections on a War*. Garden City, N.Y.: Doubleday & Company, 1967. This talented French-born journalist was a frequent contributor to *The New Republic* and *The New York Review*. See also: *Vietnam Witness, 1953–1966* (1966), *Street Without Joy* (1961), *The Two Vietnams* (1964), and *Hell in a Very Small Place* (1967).

Fishel, Wesley R., ed. *Vietnam: Anatomy of a Conflict*. Itasca, Ill.: F. E. Peacock Publishers, 1968.

FitzGerald, Frances. *Fire in the Lake: The Vietnamese and Americans in Vietnam*. Boston: Atlantic/Little, Brown, 1972. Award-winning study on cultural—and other—impact of the U.S. presence.

Fulbright, J. William. *The Vietnam Hearings*. New York: Vintage Books, 1966. Extensive excerpts from the testimony of Dean Rusk, James Gavin, George Kennan, and Maxwell Taylor.

Gavin, James M. *Crisis Now*. New York: Random House, 1968.

Gettleman, Marvin E., ed. *Vietnam: History, Documents and Opinions*

Bibliography

on a Major World Crisis. Greenwich, Conn.: Fawcett, 1968.

Goodwin, Richard N. *Triumph or Tragedy, Reflections on Vietnam.* New York: Random House, 1966. He was Assistant Special Counsel to President Kennedy and Special Assistant to President Johnson.

Goulden, Joseph C. *Truth Is the First Casualty: The Gulf of Tonkin Affair—Illusion and Reality.* Chicago: Rand-McNally and Company, 1969.

Halberstam, David. *The Making of a Quagmire.* New York: Random House, 1964. By the Pulitzer Prize-winning journalist and onetime *New York Times* correspondent in Vietnam. See also: *One Very Hot Day* (1968).

Hammer, Richard. *One Morning in the War: The Tragedy at Son My.* New York: Coward, McCann & Geoghegan, 1970.

Hersh, Seymour M. *My Lai Four.* New York: Random House, 1970.

Hoopes, Townsend. *The Limits of Intervention.* New York: David McKay Company, 1969. Important insider's account.

Just, Ward S. *To What End: A Report from Vietnam.* Boston: Houghton Mifflin, 1968. Correspondent for the Washington *Post* in Vietnam, 1965–67.

Kahin, George McT., and Lewis, John W. *The United States in Vietnam.* New York: Dell Publishing Company, 1969. Revised edition of one of the best in-depth analyses of America's involvement in Vietnam.

Knoll, Erwin, and McFadden, Judith Nies, eds. *War Crimes and the American Conscience.* New York: Holt, Rinehart & Winston, 1970.

Kraslow, David, and Loory, Stuart H. *The Secret Search for Peace in Vietnam.* New York: Random House, 1968.

Lacouture, Jean. *Vietnam: Between Two Truces.* New York: Random House, 1966. Superb French-born reporter on Indochina. Frequent contributor to *The New York Review.*

Lifton, Robert Jay. *America and the Asian Revolutions.* Chicago: Aldine Publishing Company, 1970.

Liska, George. *War and Order: Reflections on Vietnam and History.* Baltimore: The Johns Hopkins Press, 1968.

Manning, Robert, and Janeway, Michael, eds. *Who We Are: An Atlan-*

Bibliography

tic Chronicle of the United States and Vietnam. Boston: Little, Brown and Company, 1969. Excellent collection of articles from *The Atlantic*, 1966–69.

Mecklin, John. *Mission in Torment.* New York: Doubleday & Company, 1965. Former *Time* reporter and USIA officer in Saigon.

Morgenthau, Hans J. *Vietnam and the United States.* Washington, D.C.: Public Affairs Press, 1965.

Pfeffer, Richard M., ed. *No More Vietnams? The War and the Future of American Foreign Policy.* New York: Harper & Row, 1968. Taken from the proceedings of the conference at the Stevenson Institute of International Affairs, June, 1968. First published in *The Atlantic*, November–December, 1968.

Pike, Douglas. *Viet Cong.* Cambridge: The M.I.T. Press, 1966. See also: *War, Peace, and the Viet Cong: A Study of Current Communist Strategy in Vietnam* (1969).

Raskin, Marcus G., and Fall, Bernard B. *The Vietnam Reader: Articles and Documents on American Foreign Policy and the Vietnam Crisis.* New York: Random House, 1965. Well-edited selection of articles ranging from Walt Rostow to Mao Tse-tung. It was a bible for the teach-in movement.

Reischauer, Edwin O. *Beyond Vietnam: The United States and Asia.* New York: Alfred A. Knopf, 1967.

Rovere, Richard H. *Waist Deep in the Big Muddy: Personal Reflections on 1968.* Boston: Little, Brown and Company, 1967.

Salisbury, Harrison E. *Behind the Lines—Hanoi: December 23– January 7.* New York: Harper & Row, 1967. An account of a visit to North Vietnam by the respected *New York Times*man.

Schlesinger, Arthur M., Jr. *The Bitter Heritage: Vietnam and American Democracy, 1941–1966.* Boston: Houghton Mifflin Company, 1967.

Schurmann, Franz; Scott, Peter Dale; and Zelnik, Reginald. *The Politics of Escalation in Vietnam.* Boston: The Beacon Press, 1966. A citizens' "White Paper" indicting the Administration's approach to negotiations.

Shaplen, Robert. *The Lost Revolution: The Story of Twenty Years of Neglected Opportunities in Vietnam and of America's Failure to*

Bibliography

Foster Democracy There. New York: Harper & Row, 1965. See also: *The Road from War, 1965–1970* (1970); *Time Out of Hand, Revolution and Reaction in Southeast Asia* (1969).

Sheehan, Neil; Smith, Hedrick; Kenworthy, E. W.; and Butterfield, Fox. *The Pentagon Papers.* New York: Quadrangle/New York Times Book Company, 1971.

Sweezy, Paul M.; Huberman, Leo; and Magdoff, Harry. *Vietnam: The Endless War.* New York: Monthly Review Press, 1970.

Taylor, Maxwell D. *Responsibility and Response.* New York: Harper & Row, 1967.

Thompson, Robert. *No Exit from Vietnam.* New York: David McKay, 1970.

Trager, Frank N. *Why Vietnam?* New York: Praeger Publishers, 1966. A statement supporting the Administration's position.

United States Senate, Committee on Foreign Relations. *Background Information Relating to Southeast Asia and Vietnam.* Washington, D.C.: U.S. Government Printing Office, 1969. Its chronology is especially helpful.

Zagoria, Donald S. *Vietnam Triangle: Moscow, Peking, Hanoi.* Indianapolis: Pegasus, 1967.

Zinn, Howard. *Vietnam: The Logic of Withdrawal.* Boston: The Beacon Press, 1967.

Protest Against the Vietnam War

Aptheker, Herbert. *Mission to Hanoi.* New York: International Publishers, 1966. With prefaces by Tom Hayden and Staughton Lynd, who accompanied him on the trip to North Vietnam.

Berrigan, Daniel. *The Dark Night of Resistance.* New York: Doubleday & Company, 1971. Jesuit priest and poet who was imprisoned for burning draft files in Catonsville, Maryland, in 1968.

———. *Night Flight to Hanoi: Daniel Berrigan's War Diary with Eleven Poems.* New York: The Macmillan Company, 1968. See also: *Prison Journals of a Priest Revolutionary*, by his brother, Philip Berrigan.

———. *The Trial of the Catonsville Nine.* Boston: The Beacon Press, 1970.

Bibliography

Bly, Robert, and Ray, David, eds. *Poetry Reading Against the Vietnam War*. New York: H. Gantt, 1966.

Brown, Robert McAfee; Heschel, Abraham J.; and Novak, Michael. *Vietnam: Crisis of Conscience*. New York: Association Press, 1967.

Chomsky, Noam. *At War with Asia: Essays on Indochina*. New York: Vintage Books, 1970. A political brief against U.S. involvement in Southeast Asia, based in part on his visit to North Vietnam and Laos. See also: *For Reasons of State* (1973).

Dellinger, David. *In the Teeth of War*. New York: OAK Publications, 1967. Primarily a photographic essay on a peace march of the 1960s, with comments by Norman Mailer and others.

Duffet, John. *Against the Crime of Silence: Proceedings of the Russell International War Crimes Tribunal*. Flanders, N.J.: O'Hare Books, 1968. Excellent primary data, from Sartre to Oglesby, from the conference held in Stockholm.

Epstein, Jason. *The Great Conspiracy Trial: An Essay on Law, Liberty and the Constitution*. New York: Random House, 1970.

Finn, James, ed. *Protest: Pacifism and Politics*. New York: Vintage Books, 1968.

Galbraith, John Kenneth. *How to Get Out of Vietnam*. New York: New American Library, 1967.

Horowitz, Irving Louis. *The Struggle Is the Message: The Organization and Ideology of the Anti-War Movement*. Berkeley, Calif.: The Glendessary Press, 1970.

Howe, Irving, and Coser, Lewis, eds. *A Dissenter's Guide to Foreign Policy*. New York: Praeger Publishers, 1968. Emphasis on the writing of democratic radicals associated with *Dissent*.

Kempton, Murray, Intro. *Trials of the Resistance*. New York: Vintage Books, 1970. Essays on political trials of the 1960s, originally published in *The New York Review*.

Klein, Alexander, ed. *Dissent, Power, and Confrontation*. New York: McGraw-Hill Book Company, 1971.

Lowenfels, Walter, ed. *Where Is Vietnam? American Poets Respond*. Garden City, N.Y.: Doubleday & Company, 1967.

Lynd, Staughton, and Hayden, Thomas. *The Other Side*. New York: New American Library, 1966.

McCarthy, Mary. *Hanoi*. New York: Harcourt Brace Jovanovich, 1968.

Bibliography

An exchange of shots with Diana Trilling and four reflective reports on her visit to North Vietnam.

————. *Vietnam.* New York: Harcourt Brace Jovanovich, 1967. Product of her trip to South Vietnam in February, 1967. First published in *The New York Review,* it was admittedly biased: "I confess that when I went to Vietnam early last February I was looking for material damaging to the American interest and that I found it. . . ." See also: *Medina.*

Mailer, Norman. *The Armies of the Night.* New York: New American Library, 1968. Mailer marches on the Pentagon, October, 1967.

Mitford, Jessica. *The Trial of Dr. Spock.* New York: Alfred A. Knopf, 1969. Highly critical of the Johnson Administration.

Petras, James, ed. *We Accuse.* Berkeley, Calif.: Diablo Press, 1965. Fiery record of Berkeley anti-Vietnam teach-in, 1965.

Pickus, Robert, and Woito, Robert. *To End War,* Berkeley, Calif.: World Without War Council, 1970. A bibliographic essay with a purpose and bias.

Rosenberg, Milton J.; Verba, Sidney; and Converse, Philip E. *Vietnam and the Silent Majority: The Dove's Guide.* New York: Harper & Row, 1970. Specialists in public opinion provide guidelines to help turn voters against the Vietnam War.

Sontag, Susan. *Styles of Radical Will.* New York: Farrar, Straus & Giroux, 1969. This book is most relevant here for Miss Sontag's concluding essay on her trip to Hanoi, April–May, 1968. A frequent contributor to the "family's" journals and critic of the arts, she was concerned with being fashionably *avant-garde* and trying to relocate the center of sensibility.

Spock, Dr. Benjamin. *Dr. Spock on Vietnam.* New York: Simon and Schuster, 1967. The baby doctor and former co-chairman of SANE was indicted for "conspiracy" in aiding draft resisters.

Thomas, Norman. *The Choices.* New York: Ives Washburn, 1969. By the respected elder statesman of American socialism.

Woolf, Cecil, and Bagguley, John. *Authors Take Sides on Vietnam.* London: Peter Owen, 1967. Devastating sequel to a comparable book entitled *Authors Take Sides on the Spanish War.*

Bibliography

Johnson Administration

Anderson, Patrick. *The Presidents' Men: White House Assistants of Franklin D. Roosevelt, Harry S. Truman, Dwight D. Eisenhower, John F. Kennedy and Lyndon B. Johnson.* Garden City, N.Y.: Doubleday & Company, 1968.

Burns, James MacGregor. *To Heal and to Build: The Programs of President Lyndon B. Johnson.* New York: McGraw-Hill Book Company, 1968.

Christian, George. *The President Steps Down: A Personal Memoir of the Transfer of Power.* New York: The Macmillan Company, 1970.

Evans, Rowland, and Novak, Robert. *Lyndon B. Johnson: The Exercise of Power.* New York: New American Library, 1966.

Geyelin, Philip. *Lyndon B. Johnson and the World.* New York: Praeger Publishers, 1966. One of the best treatments of Johnson's foreign policy.

Goldman, Eric F. *The Tragedy of Lyndon Johnson.* New York: Alfred A. Knopf, 1969. Some thought it more appropriate to speak of "the tragedy of Eric Goldman" because of his ill-fated tenure as Johnson's "intellectual-in-residence."

Graff, Henry F. *The Tuesday Cabinet: Deliberation and Decision on Peace and War under Lyndon B. Johnson.* Englewood Cliffs, N.J.: Prentice-Hall, 1970. Draws on interviews with the President and his closest advisers.

Halberstam, David. *The Best and the Brightest.* New York: Random House, 1972. An appropriate sequel to his earlier work on Vietnam.

Heren, Louis. *No Hail, No Farewell.* New York: Harper & Row, 1970.

Johnson, Claudia Alta (Ladybird). *A White House Diary.* New York: Holt, Rinehart & Winston, 1970.

Johnson, Lyndon B. *My Hope for America.* New York: Random House, 1964.

———. *The Vantage Point: Perspectives on the Presidency, 1963–1969.* New York: Holt, Rinehart & Winston, 1971.

Kraft, Joseph. *Profiles in Power: A Washington Insight.* New York: New American Library, 1966.

Bibliography

Roberts, Charles. *L.B.J.'s Inner Circle.* New York: Delacorte Press, 1965.

Rostow, W. W. *The Diffusion of Power.* New York: The Macmillan Company, 1972. Self-revelation of a confessed superhawk.

Sidey, Hugh. *A Very Personal Presidency: Lyndon Johnson in the White House.* New York: Atheneum Publishers, 1968.

White, Theodore H. *The Making of the President—1964.* New York: Atheneum Publishers, 1965. See also its 1968 counterpart.

White, William S. *The Professional: Lyndon B. Johnson.* Boston: Houghton Mifflin Company, 1964.

Wicker, Tom. *JFK and LBJ: The Influence of Personality upon Politics.* New York: William Morrow and Company, 1968.

Index

Index

242

Index

243

Index

Index

Index

Index

Index

74 75 76 77 78 10 9 8 7 6 5 4 3 2 1